Designing YOUR OWN *Quilts*

Willo

Chilton Book Company
Radnor, Pennsylvania

Published in Radnor, Pennsylvania 19089, by Chilton Book Company

Designed by Anthony Jacobson
Manufactured in the United States of America

Library of Congress Cataloging in Publication Data
Soltow, Willow Ann.
Designing your own quilts / by Willow Ann Soltow.
p. cm.
Includes bibliographical references and index.
ISBN 0-8019-8244-8
1. Quilting. 2. Quilting—Patterns. I. Title.
TT835.S623 1993
746.46—dc20 92-32290
CIP

1 2 3 4 5 6 7 8 9 0 2 1 0 9 8 7 6 5 4 3

Designing YOUR OWN Quilts

Contents

To Ralph Pettie
—a rare individual and extraordinary teacher

I'm convinced by all I've seen
that every one of us is indeed an artist,
if we only have the tools.

—Molly Bang

—from the Preface to her book
Picture This: Perception & Composition
(Boston: Little, Brown and Company, 1991).

Acknowledgments

Who can count the many people who help make a book happen? As I look over my manuscript once again, I am reminded of many faces and many helpful ideas—more than I can name. To start, I'd like to thank my parents Bill and Shirley Soltow, and my grandmother Helen Winona Martin, without whom I would quite possibly never have developed my strong love of quilting.

Special thanks are due to the Shoreline Quilter's Guild of my home state of Connecticut for its support and to these members for their tireless efforts in helping me track down quilters and photographs of their work: Nancy Barnes, Judy Shea, and Terry Festa. I'd like also to thank the American Quilter's Society for its kind assistance in a similar vein.

I am particularly grateful to the following quilters who allowed me to include photographs of their work in this book: Elizabeth Akana, Dorothy Bosselman, Sally Brown, Judy B. Dales, Jo Diggs, Shirley Halstead, Debora Konchinsky of Critter Pattern Works, Diana Leone of Leone Publications, Judy Mathieson, Jane Nettleton, Kitty Pippen, Char Russell and Billie Gunderson of Tabitha Quilts, Judy Shea, Sandra Smith, Sue Tiffany, Laura Walsh, Linda Worland, Louise Young, and Edith Zimmer.

Thank you to Buzzard Studios for its excellent photography; to Bert Porreca and *The Islander* for allowing me to include a little of Sanibel in my book; and to Sandra Olenik for her wonderful stencils.

I owe a special debt to the following people who gave so generously of their time and ideas: To Emily Jayne, art historian, for her warm support and for her review of several of the chapters; To Diana Leone, author of *Attic Windows* and owner of Leone Publications for her advice and support; to Lee S. Wild of the Mission Houses Museum for kindly putting me in touch with Hawaiian quilters; to Sheila Nayor and the quilters of Amish Goods for quilting several of the projects photographed in this book; to Bob Kleinberg for taking me back to Muir Woods; and to Ellen Cohn, editor and musician, for her observation on the relationship between music, harmony, and color.

Basic Principles of Design

Introduction

What impels people to build bridges? It is more, I suspect, than a desire to get from one place to another. We cross many bridges in our lives—both real and symbolic. We have an inherent need to connect—with other people, other cultures, and other ways of thinking. With improved communication, our "bridges" are growing faster than ever. It is an exciting time to be a quilter. We have connections all over the world. Thanks to shows, books, and magazines with an international focus, we can appreciate quilts from half a world away—as well as those from across the street.

Designing Your Own Quilts was conceived as a kind of bridge. It is for the quilter who wants to explore new design options, yet is unsure of how to get started. It is for anyone who has had little success with design, yet who longs to make a personal statement.

The book is divided into two main sections. The first outlines basic principles of design. The second offers practical suggestions on ways to apply many of these principles through a series of projects."Where do you get your ideas?" is a question quilters often ask me. The project section of this book offers many ways to get started seeing and producing your own designs.

To include step-by-step projects in a book designed to help one develop *original* designs might seem contradictory. There is a rationale, however, behind the inclusion of the projects. As a student taking art courses in Europe, I was surprised to find that the main course of study consisted of copying the works of the "great masters." To an impetuous young American, this seemed like an act of denying, rather than fostering, creativity. I learned that it too had a purpose. I found that by emulating art that "worked" it was possible to gain a feeling for techniques that could later be employed in one's own designs. The same is true of the projects included here. Each contains something that "works," a practical design approach that may be mastered and used again in a more original context.

On the other hand, the projects included here do not pretend to represent masterpieces. They are offered in a more modest vein, as exercises in creative thinking. Each represents one possible approach to design. There are, of course, many more approaches to designing quilts than could possibly be covered in one book. Most of the projects included here are fairly easy. Each begins with an assessment of difficulty level so that you will know right from the start if you might be getting in over your head. More in-depth reading is suggested for those readers who are intrigued by any one approach. The projects are intended not as a regimen, but as a springboard for creativity. Feel free to adapt them to reflect your personal taste.

Good design does not manifest itself overnight. It is a process that happens a little at a time—like bridge building. Many people and experiences influence that process. This book is a tool to help you get from where you are to wherever you want to be—as a designer of your own quilts. May you enjoy the journey.

1

Quilts and Creativity

A pioneer woman sits piecing a quilt top by candlelight. Her thoughts, as she sews, are of family and community. The fabric scraps in her hand bring to mind those she loves. Here is a triangle cut from her husband's old work shirt, and there a diamond-shaped bit from her daughter's outgrown dress. Perhaps she looks ahead to when she will host a quilting bee and her neighbors will help get her tops quilted.

Such a quilter may well have enjoyed thoughts like these as she sewed. It is almost certain, however, that she did not concern herself with whether she was making a work of art. A valued creation, yes. Maybe even a creation that told something about her. But art?

Years ago, a work of art was a framed canvas in a museum. The twentieth century removed such comfortable definitions. Today art is not just a picture on the wall. It can be a free-moving sculpture, a display of colored lights, a yellow square on a black canvas, or a collection of Campbell's soup cans.

QUILTS AND QUILT ART

Fabric art has a magic all its own. There is, to begin with, a kind of magic involved in any art form that can take a three-dimensional image from real life and reproduce it on a two-dimensional plane. Unlike paintings or prints, however, quilts are extremely approachable. We may be moved by a painting, but not necessarily to the point of wanting to touch it. Quilts are rich in accessible human qualities. They hint at the momentous things that happen in bed—birth, death, and love. They invite observation and touch.

Generations of women have regarded their quilts as being aesthetically unworthy because of—what? Those accessible human qualities? Even today, many quilters have an aesthetic inferiority complex. We tend to value traditionally masculine art forms like painting above traditionally feminine ones like fiber arts. That is slowly changing. Ironically, one of the events that sparked the change was an exhibit organized in part by a man. In 1971, Jonathan Holstein and Gail van der Hoof put together an exhibit at the Whitney Museum of Art titled "Abstract Design in American Quilts." By showing quilts in a museum setting, the exhibit broke new ground, giving quilts an aesthetic recognition long overdue. In addition, Holstein pointed out the many ways in which traditional quilts were similar to contemporary painting:

> *The often startling resemblances between the total visual effects of some pieced quilts and certain examples of modern painting are intriguing. Some of the more obvious areas of comparison would include:*
>
> *—That manipulation of geometric form which has characterized the work of many painters since the advent of Abstractionism.*
>
> *—The optical effects of such quilts as Baby Blocks . . . and the work of Vasarely and others who have explored the possibilities of various modes of retinal stimulation through color and form relationships, optical illusion, manipulations of linear effects.*
>
> *—The use of repeated images drawn from the environment . . . and the sequential use of images in the work of such artists as Andy Warhol.*

White Line Square I, c. 1966, by Josef Albers. Photograph courtesy of the National Gallery of Art, Washington, gift of Gemini G. E. L.

—The repetitive use of highly reduced geometric forms . . . and the work of the systemic painters.

—The color variations on a single format, as in the Amish quilts, and such paintings as Albers' Homage to the Square *series.*

—The manipulation for visual effect of chromatic possibilities in a geometric framework as in . . . the work of such painters as Kenneth Noland.[1]

All quilts are not art just as all watercolors or all oil paintings are not art. All of us are not professional quilters. However, we can all express ourselves in an artistic manner to the best of our ability. One purpose of this book is to explain fundamental art principles as they relate to quilting. Often today's quilter finds herself dancing around the boundaries of art. Maybe she produces a design a certain way just because it "looks nice." Or, maybe she is aware that a form or color produces a certain emotion in her without sensing why that might be the case.

Naive design is fine—as long as one accepts it for what it is. Sometimes it works; sometimes it doesn't. How often have you gotten halfway through a quilt project only to lament, "Oh, if only I'd done it *that* way!" Understanding the principles of design can help any quilter become a better designer. Learning how the elements of design work helps assure more consistent results. It can help us visualize many possibilities at once—before they are anchored in stitches. On the other hand, a great quilt design cannot be produced by a recipe, like a tea cake. Art is not an exercise. Learning what constitutes good design is not enough. You also have to feel it.

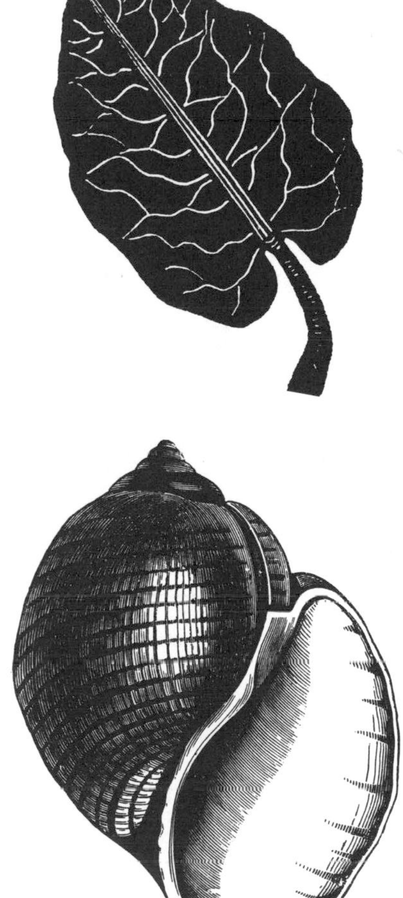

DISCOVERING DESIGN

Design is all around us. There is design in the shape of a leaf, in the spiral of a shell, in the lines of a picket fence. There are elements of design, such as symmetry and contrast, in the furniture we live with and in the landscape we look out upon. Design is there, but we do not always see it. We need to learn to see, not merely look, if we are to capture the essence of good design in our fabric art.

A successful design is like a good friend—alike, yet different. We select our friends because they share with us common interests, values, and qualities. Yet how dull is a mirror-image of oneself! We have need for unity and variety in the people with whom we associate. It is the same with design. A good design has balance. It contains recognizable elements that speak directly to our experience. We look at it and say, "Yes, I have seen or felt that also."

A good design, however, also contains a certain amount of tension. It offers a manageable amount of new information. It gives us something fresh and different to think about. In a landscape we might say, "What an interesting contrast between land and sky," or "The color of the sand is different from any I have ever seen."

Beauty is an important element of design. Often a design can be beautiful although it is not pretty. How can this be? A traditional Sunbonnet Sue quilt may be pretty. It may feature appealing calicoes that are also pretty. A quilt depicting an urban scene may not be pretty; it may feature harsh colors, sharp contrasts, jagged edges. Yet it may be quite beautiful for having been created with attention to basic principles of design.

Some quilters think all quilts are beautiful. In that pristine moment when one first walks into a quilt show, indeed, all quilts seem beautiful. The mere quantity of creative effort in evidence at a quilt show is thrilling. Beauty, however, is not so easy to come by. At any quilt show, a second glance can reveal works that are quite dreadful—revolting color combinations, overly cute motifs, quilts made prissy with ruffles and flounces.

Some of us dismiss the atrocities with the adage that "beauty is in the eye of the beholder." But it is not the viewer who brings beauty to a quilt; it is the maker. And, just as every quilter can improve the ability to make tiny, even stitches, so every quilter can improve the ability to produce successful designs.

SEEING WITH NEW EYES

Just what constitutes a successful design? Kenneth Bates tells us that "a good design is one to which no more can be added, and at the same time, one from which nothing can be subtracted without causing an emptiness or feeling of incompletion."[2] What makes up a design? It depends on how you define your terms—and each source defines them a little differently. In this book we will talk about the visual elements of a design in terms of *line, form*, and *space*. We will also talk about the principles of design—*balance, proportion, movement, mood, contrast,* and *rhythm*—which guide us in deciding how to manipulate line, form, and space.

Most people are somewhat lazy when it comes to seeing. We would rather glance at something than look at it carefully. All too often when we *do* glance, a funny thing happens. Memories and preconceptions replace the thing that is seen. For a design to be understood quickly, it has to fit our preconception of what it is supposed to do. Even Lord Byron once observed, "You must recollect . . . that I know nothing of painting; and that I detest it, unless it reminds me of something I have seen, or think it possible to see. . . ."[3]

Let us say that we were to look at a pictorial quilt—an ocean scene, for instance. In order to size it up quickly, it would have to fit our preconceptions of what an ocean scene was supposed to have in it: a horizon line, a sailboat, a sandy beach, or frothy waves. If it did not have at least one or two of these things in it, we might not recognize it as an ocean scene at all.

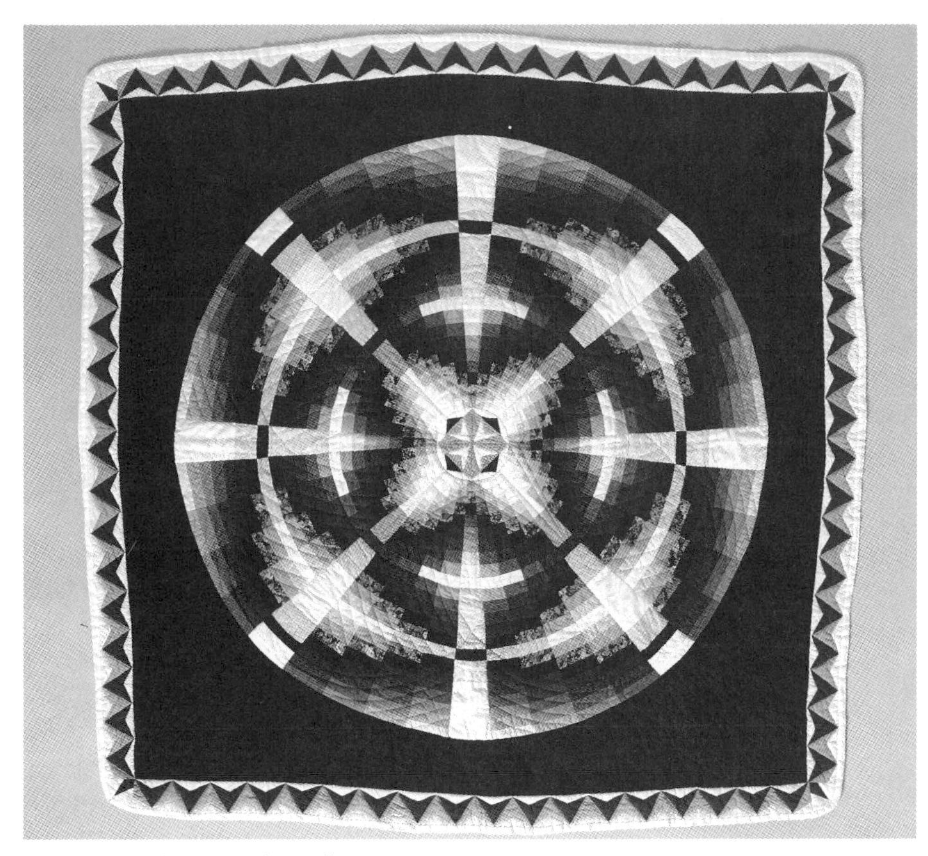

Fabric Incandescence, by Sally Brown.

Let us say that we were to design an ocean scene. We might be inclined to design the scene so as to fit our preconceptions. That is, we might design it so that it had in it a horizon line, a sailboat, a sandy beach, and frothy waves. But what if we discard our preconceptions about ocean scenes altogether? Then the design could take on untold possibilities: mood, metaphor, or abstraction. The scene that we designed might have in it a horizon line, but no sailboat; a sandy beach but no waves. It might not even end up as an ocean scene at all by the time we were done with it. That would be OK—because we would have learned from our experience designing it. By discarding our preconceptions, we can begin to see and to create in new, exciting ways rather than merely expressing the familiar.

Artists are inventors. Deliberately or instinctively, they have discarded old habits of seeing and doing. Instead of relying on a glance and a memory of a similar item, they see everything with fresh eyes. With the help of this talent, they impart new ways of seeing familiar objects to others. Seeing creatively is the first step in expressive design. Before proceeding to a focus on design principles, let's consider creativity and ways to keep one's creative vision fresh and alive.

THE JOY OF CREATIVITY

In today's world we are constantly bombarded by visual impressions. They assail us from every direction—from television, junk mail, traffic signs, billboards, posters, and more. Our designs must be carefully thought out if they are to compete successfully for attention. To some people, careful planning and creativity do not seem to go together. Successful design is like a ballet dancer. When she goes on stage, her dance appears fluid and effortless. But, in fact, years of training have gone into her performance of the moment. The key to successful design is to create that which appears spontaneous and therefore effortless. But even though a great design may appear simple, it reflects the sum of a designer's creative endeavor up to that point—a significant effort indeed.

There are methods for keeping one's creative vision alive. Creative people are not necessarily more inspired than the rest of us. But they may be more disciplined. They integrate creativity into their entire life-style. They never let an idea escape without recording it in some fashion. They practice seeing and thinking creatively. Whether they do so consciously or unconsciously, the effect is the same. They are open to new ideas, new ways of doing. They also have a certain self-confidence. They believe that what they have to say is worth saying.

Creativity always involves a personal statement. A work of art reveals something about its creator. Creativity and self-esteem are intertwined. Creative people accept that what they have to say is important—just because they are saying it.

Creativity means trying new ideas—even "crazy" ones. It means not being stopped by convention. If convention says you cannot put one color or fabric with another, try it and see what happens. Often when you experiment with one idea, you are led to new and exciting results.

Traditional quilts are wonderful, but there is nothing more satisfying than producing your own design. It says something about you, about your culture, about the age in which you live. As quilter Judi Warren has said:

> *If we're going to make quilts . . . we are duty bound to add to the heritage, not just keep repeating the same images. They were beautiful and wonderful, but we have our own images, and these should be added to that store of the design heritage. We take designs from the traditional, we shuffle them, we divide the square up in new ways. And then we begin to notice potential quilt designs everywhere. I think that's how it becomes current, vital, and more than just a return to nostalgia.*[4]

METHODS FOR MOTIVATION

You can assist your own natural creativity in a number of ways. Keep a record of your ideas. It can be a formal journal or a box of loose sheets. Save ripped-out pictures from magazines, bits of fabric, sketches, photographs—anything that strikes you as unique for its design characteristics. Turn to your creativity box when you need a new idea. If you cannot go to work at once when a creative idea hits, keep track of it. This sounds easy, but it takes discipline. Great ideas strike when you least expect them. It is all too easy to say, "I'll remember that." And, of course, we seldom do. The answer? Sketch it, write it down in words, record an impression on a mini tape recorder—but don't let that idea escape!

Take stock of your fabric often. It is your palette, your raw material. You might want to keep a tiny swatch of each fabric on a set of cards to keep with you so that you will have them when new ideas appear.

Pay attention to the quilts you really like. Ask yourself why you are drawn to them. Analyze what design elements are at work and why they function the way they do. Then see if one or more aspects of the design can be reworked in an entirely new pattern of your own.

Attend as many quilt shows as possible. Take a camera. Always ask before shooting if photos are permitted. Sometimes the use of a flash is prohibited, but otherwise photos are often OK. If so, you can review what you have seen and translate it into new designs that are uniquely your own.

Become a regular (if you are not already) at your library. Search for inspiration in books about the art of other cultures as well as our own. Don't miss the "oversize" section where all the great coffee-table books are with their brilliant photos of plants, flowers, animals, insects, stars, and more.

Most of all, be honest with yourself. Never copy another's design in whole or in part. If you can recognize it as someone else's, it is not your own. Go back to work on it. Believe in yourself. Believe that what you have to say is worth saying—just because it comes from you.

Notes

1. Jonathan Holstein, *The Pieced Quilt: An American Design Tradition* (Boston: Little, Brown and Company, 1973), p. 113.

2. Kenneth F. Bates, *Basic Design* (New York: Funk & Wagnalls, 1975), p. 17.

3. Frank Muir, *An Irreverent and Thoroughly Incomplete Social History of Almost Everything* (New York: Stein and Day, 1976), p. 253.

4. Judi Warren, quoted in *Quilter's Newsletter Magazine* (May 1986), p. 39.

2 Style and Structure

How do you go about designing your quilts? Everyone is different. Perhaps sometimes you see a special fabric that sparks an idea. Another time you may see an object that instills a certain feeling and decide to reproduce the object or the feeling connected with it using your design skills. Yet another time you may be moved to create by a memory or a dream. Sometimes the idea for a quilt presents itself in combination with a clear impression of how it should be reproduced. Other times, the actual making of the idea into a quilt requires some exploration.

Quilts may be *pictorial, abstract,* or *figurative.* A pictorial quilt is exactly what it suggests—it is a picture. Often pictorial quilts are appliquéd and feature realistic curves and shadows. An abstract design is usually, but not always, pieced and geometric. An abstract design is not realistic. That is, it does not offer a picture image of reality. A figurative quilt generally has both pictorial and abstract design elements. It contains recognizable images, yet leaves much to the viewer's imagination; it is not a clear-cut rendition of something the designer has observed.

CHOOSING A STYLE

The choice of style has a lot to do with subject matter. Suppose you want to portray a childhood memory, a kind of snapshot from your past. Then you might opt for the pictorial style—the most realistic portrayal possible to mimic what you remember. Are you interested in conveying a strong emotion that you have felt? Perhaps abstraction is called for. Let's say you want to portray a dream you had. The figurative style combining simple, semi-realistic images may be what you want to work in. Sometimes the style in which a design is to be produced suggests itself right from the outset. Even when this is the case, you may want to experiment with different style options before settling on a design format.

As an exercise in different styles, try setting up and drawing an uncomplicated still life. It should consist of no more than two or three objects. Use colored pencils on graph paper to portray the still life in each different style: pictorial, abstract, and figurative. Remember, the quality of your drawing is less important than your experience of seeing. Concentrate on exercising your observation skill, rather than your drawing skill.

For the pictorial representation, pay attention to light and dark. Indicate where the shadows fall on your objects by shading them in with the side of your pencil.

For the abstract representation, focus on the still life as a collection of shapes, rather than specific objects. Try to see them as a triangle and a collection of circles, for instance, rather than a pear and a bunch of grapes. Select one part that especially interests you and try repeating it in one corner or in a diagonal line across the page.

For the figurative representation, reduce the objects to their simplest values. Make flat, simple two-dimensional drawings. Then experiment with ways to add interest, perhaps by adding different geometric shapes suggested by your still life objects. A simple exercise such as this gives you practice in observing and enhances your ability to produce interesting designs.

In order to turn an idea into a quilt, the designer needs to decide which style best complements the idea to be portrayed. All too often, of course, many of us choose the style with which we are most familiar. A lot can be gained, however, by venturing into unexplored realms.

PICTORIAL STYLE

A pictorial quilt is a visual representation of a real scene or objects. It speaks clearly of what is seen, though not necessarily of what is felt. A specific scene may evoke an emotion for the designer. For instance, the image of a stream may be connected in the quilter's mind with a feeling of calm. In that case, our mind processes the image as a picture (of a stream) first and a feeling (calm) second. This means the artist gives up a certain amount of directness if what she or he is mostly interested in is portraying the feeling of calm. For some artists, however, the value of working with a familiar image is more important than speaking directly to the viewer's emotions.

If you have concentrated on sewing traditional geometric patterns, you may wonder how to go about making an original quilt "picture." The best way is to start small. Many traditional-style quilters say they would love to design a pictorial quilt but feel that their drawing skills are not good enough. Practice is the only way around that problem, of course, but where can you begin on your own? You might want to start a drawing journal. It is like a diary, but instead of writing a few lines every day, you make a simple drawing. Even if all you have time for is a quick, five-minute sketch, the value of drawing a little bit every day is tremendous. To get yourself started, try this brief exercise.

In her workshop on drawing from nature, artist Clare Walker Leslie has participants complete a "blind" drawing. She asks them to select a

Detail, *All Things Bright and Beautiful,* a pictorial quilt by Sandra Smith. Photograph by Buzzard Studios.

single item—a flower, for instance. She then asks them to trace the lines of the flower onto their paper *without looking down at the paper*! Sounds funny? It works! The pencil becomes a tool to sense and appreciate the flower's shape. Such "blind" drawings are often surprisingly accurate. But that is a side benefit. The activity is valuable, not because it provides an accurate rendering, but because it leads to the experience of nature. As the artist herself puts it, "I draw in my journal to make contact with nature. How I draw and what it looks like are irrelevant to the process and experience of being with nature."[1] If your drawing skills could benefit from some practice, you will be sure to draw inspiration from Clare Walker Leslie's *Nature Drawing: A Tool for Learning*, as well as her other books on drawing (see Recommended Reading).

ABSTRACT STYLE

To some, abstract art appears removed from human experience. There is little or nothing pictorial about it. It represents reality not as it is seen, but as it is felt or experienced. Some people are uncomfortable with abstract designs. They may find them disturbing—even alienating.

Dangling Participles, an abstract quilt by Judy B. Dales, constructed from a unique variety of unfinished projects.

Cartoonist Al Capp once humorously criticized abstract art as "a product of the untalented sold by the unprincipled to the utterly bewildered."[2] Quilters know better. Abstract quilts are among some of the most exciting fabric art being created today. Indeed, the medium of fabric has special attraction for many contemporary artists because it provides a human softness to what might otherwise appear stark designs. Abstract designs can indeed be intimidating to those who have not learned how to look at them. Everyone understands a quilt on at least some personal level—even if the intricacies of the design escape them.

What is the point, some might say, of representing something using an abstract approach instead of simply making a picture of it that everyone can understand? It is a little like asking why make a quilt to portray something, instead of just telling others how you feel or what you saw. Quilting is your medium. It is how you express yourself. For some artists, abstraction is the main mode of self-expression.

Not everything can be understood in concrete terms. How do you portray a feeling? You can portray someone experiencing the feeling, but that is not the same as portraying the feeling itself. How do you depict joy? Not someone experiencing joy, but joy itself? To one artist, joy might be portrayed as a color. To another, it might be best represented by vibrant, wavy lines. To yet another, joy might be a lively series of shapes.

Sometimes abstract images convey a message directly to the emotions where a pictorial image speaks only to the intellect. Artist Paul Cézanne once observed, "Literature expresses itself by abstractions, whereas painting by means of drawing and color gives concrete shape to sensations and perceptions." [3] That is, literature is made up of words or symbols for actions and feelings. Visual images need not rely on symbols to convey meaning; they speak directly to the heart.

If you have never created an abstract design, where do you begin? You might get started by thinking about a certain fabric that especially pleases you. Give thought to its texture, print, and color. Consider what feelings these evoke in you. Is the fabric a calico print? Then perhaps it suggests warmth and a home-like quality. Or you may find the pattern of the print calls to mind tension or confusion. Concentrate on the qualities of the pure fabric.

Consider ways in which the fabric may be cut apart and resewn to enhance the feelings it evokes in you. Warmth may best be suggested by rounded abstract elements; tension by juxtaposing angles of squares or triangles. These are just two options. The possibilities are endless in terms of both the feelings to be expressed and the means of expressing them. In subsequent chapters, the relationships of visual elements of a design will be explored in greater depth.

FIGURATIVE STYLE

Sometimes a design has elements of realism, yet it is not what we would describe as a strictly realistic picture. It may combine abstract elements with images we recognize. It may reduce familiar images to their simplest terms. It may be wildly imaginative, juxtaposing images we would seldom see combined in reality. Such a style can be described as figurative because it represents elements from nature without attempting to portray them as they would actually be seen. (It should be noted that *figurative* is generally used in art texts to refer to the human figure.)

For some people, the figurative style can be a good bridge to creativity. It allows the suggestion of a realistic image, without the confinement of copying reality. A figurative design is often simplicity itself—a basic, unadorned image with little or no detail.

A good way to tackle a figurative design for the first time is to select a simple image, then write down all of the thoughts connected in your mind with that image. You may decide to draw what comes to mind instead of using words. When you feel your list is complete, think about ways to combine the related impressions into a single visual image. You may find that you can use a different block for each impression you wish to portray. Or you can separate the different impressions through the creative use of space and form.

STRUCTURE

Structure is another consideration that plays an important part in initial design. (What we call *structure* here may be seen by some artists as part of composition. Composition has to do with how an entire design is put together—its outer shape and its surface design. For clarity, we will use the word *structure* to mean the outer shape of a quilt and/or its main sections.) A quilt can be structured in a number of ways. It can be flat or

Mosaic-style pieced house, a figurative quilt. Photograph courtesy of the Board of Trustees of the Victoria & Albert Museum, London.

three-dimensional. It can be square, circular, hexagonal, or any other shape. It can be a single-unit design with one main subject, or it can be a multiple-unit design with many subjects.

Structure is one of the most basic design considerations. Before you can begin designing, you will have to decide, for example, if your quilt is going to be flat—to hang on a wall or lie upon a bed. Or is it going to be spherical—and be suspended from the ceiling? To some of us, questions like these answer themselves. Before you begin designing, however, it is important to consider *all* of the options.

You will also have to decide on the basic shape of your quilt. Will it be four-sided? Will its shape be determined by how you put parts of it together as you go along? Sometimes the overall shape of a quilt can change as you go, but usually it helps to have a sense of where you are going.

Four-sided quilts are generally horizontal rectangles, vertical rectangles, or squares. Each shape sends the eye in a different direction. Each structural option has its own thrust. In a horizontal rectangle the eye is led across the design surface. In a vertical rectangle, the eye is encouraged to move up and down. In a square, the thrust is equal. The eye is not strongly impelled to move up and down, or right to left. The square format is a static composition—and restful to the eye.

You will want to choose a structural format that matches what you are trying to portray in your design. A horizontal format might work best for an image of a long city street. A vertical rectangle might be most effective if you want to emphasize the height of a towering skyscraper. You might choose a square format if your subject were a quiet pond in the local park.

Before proceeding with the design, you must also consider whether you want to make a quilt that is based on one unit or more. It may not be necessary to decide at the outset how many more. But you need to know whether your design will focus on a single overall unit or multiple units. In other words, will it be a single, large scene or different blocks featuring different images? If it is made up of blocks, will the blocks be the same size or different sizes? Will they be the same shape or different shapes? The actual arrangement of the units within your quilt *does* have to do with composition and will be discussed later.

How will your finished quilt be displayed? The environment in which your quilt will eventually reside can play a part in your decisions about its structure. Consider the available light, the shape of the wall, and the color of the room. Remember, however, that the setting in which your quilt is to be displayed should not dictate your design. Your creative message should always come first. A reliance on a particular color scheme, for example, simply because it matches the room decor, would be too limiting. Do painters limit themselves to such a palette? Seldom, if ever. Keep in mind the environment in which your quilt is to be displayed, but if the setting begins to play too important a part in your decisions, follow your creative instincts and plan to put the quilt someplace else.

Border "A" is weak and border "B" is overpowering. Only border "C" balances well with its subject.

A

B

C

BORDERS

Borders (or the lack of them) are part of a quilt's structure. In the classic *The Standard Book of Quilt Making and Collecting*, Marguerite Ickis has quilters add a border a few inches wider than a standard block. Of course, she focused her entire book on block quilts. But her point is well taken. The size of a border is partly determined by the size of different shapes within a quilt design. If the design is made up of blocks, those blocks may well dictate whether a border appears strong and appropriate. Her rule that a "border is well proportioned when it is a little wider than each of the center blocks" is a safe option.[4] However, this does not mean that you cannot experiment with different-sized borders. You will find that some work and others do not. Avoid borders that fight for attention with the design's main subject. On the other hand, a thin, weak border generally does little to enhance a design. It too should be avoided.

This busy border is not clearly separated from the central theme and consequently competes with it.

A border should support the central image. It cannot do this if it is narrower than most of the visual elements in the quilt. That is, if your design is made up largely of 6″ shapes, a border that is much narrower than 6″ wide may not be strong enough to support such large design motifs. An overly narrow border may appear weak and unnecessary.

On the other hand, a border also fails in its supportive role if it is too wide or too busy. A border should not dwarf the rest of the quilt or it can cause the central design image to collapse. Neither should it feature such large motifs of its own that it draws attention away from the main part of the design. The result of an overly busy border is confusion on the part of the viewer who does not know where to look consequently losing the visual impact of the design.

The double border holds interest, yet is not overpowering.

Avoiding busyness is one thing. Do not let this keep you from using bold fabrics in the border. Indeed, some of the most exciting quilts being made today feature strong, vibrant print or pieced borders. One trick for using a flamboyant print or pieced fabric in the border is to make a double border. A narrow solid fabric border may be used around the main part of the design. On a crib quilt, it may be no more than 2″ wide. It provides a simple, stabilizing frame for the central image. Around this may be used a much wider patterned or pieced fabric border. The result can be very dynamic, especially where colors and motifs from the main part of the design are repeated, sending the viewer back to the central theme.

BACK FOR MORE

A final structural consideration is how you will design the back of your quilt. For many quilters, this is a non-question. At its most basic, the backing is simply a single length of fabric, with or without a seam. Even the choice of fabric may be dictated by what is readily available. Other quilters deliberately choose the fabric with which to finish the back of their quilts. And still others see the quilt back as a further arena for exercising their creativity. As Danita Rafalovich and Kathryn Alison Pellman observe in their book *Backart*: "For quiltmakers, backart encourages freedom of expression going beyond the structured rules often confronting them when designing the front. Backart provides an opportunity to take chances and experiment with new ideas, allowing room for creativity and growth."[5]

For a long time, quilters have been using the backs of their quilts to make an additional design statement, as documented by Rafalovich and Pellman. Many of today's quilters feel that the back is integral to an overall quilt design. They create backart that stands on its own or that echoes the main design on the quilt front. (For further ideas for your own backart, be sure to see *Backart: On the Flip Side* listed in Recommended Reading.)

Style and structure are the initial considerations a quilter must deal with when beginning a design. Try broadening your usual approach by using a style (pictorial, abstract, or figurative) that you have never worked with before. Consider making a wall quilt that is not square or rectangular. Include a border treatment you have not yet used such as a double border with the wide outer border in a bold, vibrant print. Or try your hand at creating your own backart. By experimenting with approaches that are new to you, you will find that you can not only broaden your creative abilities but also appreciate more the innovative work of others.

Notes

1. Clare Walker Leslie, *A Naturalist's Sketchbook: Pages from the Seasons of a Year* (New York: Dodd, Mead & Co., 1987).

2. Al Capp, quoted in *An Irreverent and Thoroughly Incomplete Social History of Almost Everything* by Frank Muir (New York: Stein and Day, 1976), p. 272.

3. Paul Cezanne, quoted in a letter to Émile Bernard excerpted by Herschel B. Chipp in *Theories of Modern Art* (Berkeley: University of California Press, 1968), p. 18.

4. Marguerite Ickis, *The Standard Book of Quilt Making and Collecting* (New York: Dover Publications, 1959), p. 155.

5. Danita Rafalovich and Kathryn Alison Pellman, *Backart: On the Flip Side* (Mountain View, CA: Leone Publications, 1991).

Visual Elements

3

Humans are analytical creatures. We scarcely know how to think about something without breaking it down into little parts. This holds true for design as well as for many things.

The visual elements of a design are the basic parts into which a design may logically be broken down for discussion. To create, an artist makes use of the visual elements of line, form, and space, which are in turn modified by such things as color, light, and texture. Yet, while we may talk about visual elements as though they were separate items, they are, of course, interdependent. Forms exist in space, in relation to other forms—not in a vacuum. (Lines do not really exist at all, being a kind of shorthand by which artists portray the outlines of forms!) We can talk about visual elements as if they were separate items. When we design, however, we must remember to treat them as part of a unified design. This is not always easy. Being analytical has its drawbacks. For now, though, let us consider the elements of design individually before discussing them in terms of how they work together.

LINE

Line plays a wide and varied role in our lives. With the help of line, humans have developed written language, allowing us to communicate with others in the present as well as in the future. Line is indispensable to our way of life. It tells us of the feelings of others. It helps us coordinate activities. It allows us a depth of experience in which we can step beyond our personal, temporal, and geographical limits.

Calligraphy is the art of beautiful lettering. The lines of calligraphy imbue a written statement with visual beauty and grace. Calligraphy serves as a bridge between lines that communicate verbally and lines that communicate nonverbally. Different kinds of lines express different characteristics. To some extent, these characteristics are fairly universal. Vertical lines give a sense of formality, strength, power, and loftiness.

Calligraphy represents a blending of line and image.

Horizontal lines give the impression of informality, calmness, gentleness, and accessibility. Diagonal lines are dynamic and lively. They defy the pull of gravity. Being neither rigidly upright, nor level and at rest, they suggest tension and interest. Deeply curving lines often suggest restlessness, while gently curving ones may imply grace and lyricism. Zigzag lines are often associated with feelings of excitement and vitality.

For the quilter, line can be expressed in a variety of ways. The outer edge of a pieced fabric shape is defined by line. Rounded shapes are created by softly curving lines; flat-edged shapes like squares and triangles are created by straight lines. When the pieces are sewn together, the linear effect can be dazzling. The lines created by the edges where the fabric pieces are joined make a patchwork not only of shapes but of lines as well. Yet in looking at a quilt, it is often only the shapes themselves we notice, not the pattern of lines created by their outlines.

This quilt shows how a linear image can be formed by patchwork shapes, seams, and quilting. Photograph courtesy of the Board of Trustees of the Victoria & Albert Museum, London.

Quilting is a form of linear expression. A line of quilting can follow and add emphasis to the surface pattern of a design. A quilting line can also run contrary to the surface design, creating a pleasing visual tension.

Lines can be introduced into the body of a design by using fabric with a linear pattern—stripes or pattern elements that repeat themselves in a line. Lines may also be painted on fabric to produce interesting visual effects.

FORM

Form is another basic visual element. Form that is flat and two-dimensional is often referred to as a *shape*. Form that has depth, or is three-dimensional, is referred to as a *solid*. Forms are based on the images we find in nature. The artist Paul Cézanne once observed, " . . . treat nature by the cylinder, the sphere, the cone. . . ,"[1] by which he meant that all images in nature could be portrayed using variations of only these three forms.

A few experimental quilts are three-dimensional. Most quilts, however, are flat. Their forms, too, are flat and two-dimensional. In a quilt as in a painting, however, forms can be manipulated to give the impression of having three dimensions. Use of light and shadow upon forms is used to establish a sense of depth.

Forms generally have significance beyond their pictorial symbolism. We are eager to attach meaning to pictorial images. It is in the realm of pictorial images that most of us feel we are on firm ground in viewing quilted works of art. We know whether we have seen or experienced a similar image; we know what it felt like. We can relate easily to pictures of scenes or objects. We are often less quick to assign meaning to abstract images. Yet abstract forms, too, have the power to evoke feelings.

What kinds of feelings are evoked by pure form? Rounded forms tend to suggest warmth and softness. Squared ones often suggest solidity and strength. The same is true of their three-dimensional counterparts. While a sphere gives the impression of freedom of movement, a cube suggests immobility. Conical forms, with their pointed ends, may be used to portray restlessness, animation, and even fear or violence. A quilt artist may employ these and other forms to suggest a feeling directly, rather than portraying objects associated with that feeling.

Fabric art gives us a means to communicate without words. Any emotional, internal experience may be expressed using the symbolic imagery of interacting forms. Form itself may be used to express a series of emotions for which no words exist. Quilters who use interacting forms to represent an emotional state often find that they relate strongly to the works of Expressionist painters like Henri Matisse and Wassily Kandinsky.

Other quilt artists are interested in the intrinsic qualities of forms apart from any feelings they may suggest. They do not see form as having any kind of narrative or expressive characteristics. Instead, they see combinations of forms as being aesthetically interesting in themselves. The interest may be stimulated by creative use of light, texture, and color. These fabric artists are often drawn to the works of painters like Piet Mondrian and Josef Albers.

SPACE

The creative use of space is every bit as important as that of line and form. Hawaiian quilts provide a graphic example. In a two-color Hawaiian design, perception of the design is only possible through observation of the negative space. The negative space defines the pictorial image. In other kinds of quilts, the deliberate use of space may be less obvious at first glance, yet the power of space to define an abstract or pictorial image cannot be underestimated:

Press Gently, a traditional Hawaiian quilt. In Hawaiian quilts, the negative space defines the pictorial image. Photograph courtesy of the Honolulu Academy of Arts.

Negative spaces are not waste space. They are part of the total space which an artist professes to control. If they are themselves without interest, if they have no formal justification except the empty one that they fill out the unused areas between figures or between figures and the frame, the artist has defaulted.[2]

The word *space* can be used to mean different things. Space can be the negative area of a two-dimensional design—the image area in which line and form are not. It can also be the spatial field in a three-dimensional design.

Throughout history, artists have used a variety of optical tricks to give the impression of depth in their works. Among these are the placing of one object in front of another, the use of vanishing points to create a sense of movement into depth, and the use of objects that diminish progressively in size into the background. A sense of distance is established in other ways as well. For instance, an object whose outline appears hazy or lost in mist often appears far away. An image that appears higher on the picture plane may seem more distant. Graduated colors, from dark in the foreground to light along the horizon line, give an impression of distance as well.

Space can have characteristics of its own. Space can be personal or impersonal. It can suggest warmth or coldness. It can enclose or confine its subject or place its subject in an atmosphere of freedom and openness. Spatial areas should never compete with the main area of interest in a design. In addition, a fabric artist needs to weigh areas of space and form so that one does not overpower the other and a sense of balance is established.

SUPPORTING ELEMENTS

In addition to line, form, and space, other supportive visual elements include *color, light,* and *texture.* The complexities of color are such that they will be dealt with in a chapter of their own (see Chapter Six).

Artists and designers today are fascinated by light. Its creative use has greatly influenced not only art, but clothing, interior design, and architecture. Where this element was once thought of as something that enhanced expression of form, today it is seen almost as a raw material in itself. It is manipulated like paint, fiber, or other art materials. Dramatic use of light provides intensity in any design.

For the quilter, light expresses itself in a variety of ways. A light source may be established in a pictorial design, adding depth and drama to a picture image. Directional movement based on one or more light sources may be established through the use of a graduated color scheme, particularly in abstract designs.

Light may be introduced into a design through the use of reflective metallic fabrics. In addition, different fabrics reflect light in different ways. For instance, satin is highly reflective; velvet absorbs light.

Of special significance to the quilter, light creates shadows that help us differentiate one form from another. Light allows us to appreciate the depressions and contours created by lines of quilting. Light may also be used to intensify shadows along lines of movement in a design, enhancing appreciation of directional movement in a work.

Light has unique appeal. It is intangible. We cannot touch it, yet it points out the tactile qualities of a quilt. We cannot feel it, yet it heightens our awareness of feelings evoked by a design image. Light is mysterious. It has traditionally been used as a symbol for the divine—for that which is beyond our understanding, though we yearn to understand it. It is also a symbol for knowledge and for good. No wonder contemporary artists, as well as their predecessors, have found light worthy of attention. Quilters who are intrigued with the use of light in their designs often are attracted to the works of painters like Caravaggio, Rembrandt, El Greco, Monet, Renoir, and van Gogh. These artists found different ways to express their fascination with light.

The appreciation of texture is dependent upon light. Texture may be appreciated as both a visual element and one that appeals to our sense of touch. Even where viewers are discouraged from actually handling a quilt, they can appreciate the tactile qualities of fabric. They know from their own experience that cotton is smooth, velvet is soft, corduroy has ridges, burlap is rough and nubby. Antique quilts are pleasingly worn and indicative of the passing of time. New quilts are crisp and promising. Indeed, it is the tactile quality of quilts that makes them accessible and appealing. Because we "feel" texture not only with our hands, but with our eyes, we often appreciate fabric art on more levels than we do other art forms.

Quilters can use different fabrics to create unique textural effects. Shiny fabrics evoke a feeling of weightlessness, whereas more opaque fabrics suggest density. Printing, painting, or embroidering on fabric are other ways in which surface texture may be enhanced. Printed patterns are often combined with solid color fabrics to create tension, each fabric contrasting with the other. In addition, many contemporary quilters currently explore the qualities of texture through the use of objects both natural and manufactured. Buttons, sequins, shells, beads, bits of wood, and natural fibers are used to create a wide variety of effects.

BE SPECIFIC

In an actual design, line, form, space, color, light, and texture are interactive. A quilt artist must think of the visual elements of a design both as individual "players" and as a whole. In order for a design to have

Aquarium City, by Judy Mathieson. One way to heighten interest in a design is to pay close attention to detail.

interest, its parts must be interesting in themselves. One way to heighten the interest of individual elements of a design is to be specific.

All too often in our lives we generalize. We eat an *apple*—not a *Winesap* or a *Macoun* apple. Or we see a *plant*—not a flowering *herb* or spike of *hyssop* swaying in the sunlight. Learning to see carefully is an important step in creativity. As artist Frederick Franck observes:

> *We do a lot of looking: we look through lenses, telescopes, television tubes. . . . Our looking is perfected every day—but we see less and less. . . . We know the labels on all the bottles, but never taste the wine. Millions of people, unseeing, joyless, bluster through life in their halfsleep, hitting, kicking, and killing what they have barely perceived. They have never learned to SEE. . . .*[3]

SEEING VS. LOOKING

Take a moment right now to practice *seeing* as opposed to *looking*. Choose something easy to see, preferably an inanimate object. Choose something worth seeing—not a crumpled paper or this morning's empty coffee cup, but a lighted candle, a flower, a piece of fruit. Ask yourself to observe all of the following:

- What color(s) is it?
- How does the color change from one part to another?
- What is the texture?
- What is the shape?
- What is the size?
- What other senses besides your sight does this object engage?
- What is its scent, sound, or taste?
- What does it feel like when you touch it?
- How does the light fall on this object at this particular time and in this space?
- If you were to draw this object, what part would be shaded?
- Does the object itself make a shadow?
- What part of this object is hidden from your view? (The wick inside the candle, the veins in the flower's leaves, the inner core of the fruit.)
- What associations—good or bad—do you have with this object? (Perhaps a candlelight dinner, an argument, or a childhood memory.)
- How does this object differ from others of its kind; in other words, what makes it unique?

From observing a single inanimate object, go on to a real challenge—a person, an animal, or a place. Ask yourself the same kinds of questions. While you are at it, make up some new questions.

Many tiny details color the visual elements of a good design. These detailed visual elements together establish feeling. The details may well be too many, too fleeting for the viewer's eye to pick up consciously. Yet the overall effect is felt. The visual elements have said all they have to say.

Just what does this mean for the quilter? It means *be specific.* If the design you have in mind includes a tree, decide exactly what kind of tree

Close observation shows us the many variations found in nature. For example, leaves may be alternate, compound, palmately compound, whorled, basal, lobed or toothed—to name a few possibilities.

is to be portrayed. Decide that it is a pine, or an oak, or a willow tree. Decide that it is slender, or wide, or young, or old. Look it up in the encyclopedia and see what kinds of other trees grow near it, what kinds of animals live in it. Get to know the tree you have chosen to portray before you portray it.

If you are working from life, go back to the original scene. Observe it carefully or photograph it to study later. You need not stick to its realism. But if you are changing the elements of an actual scene that appealed to you, know why you are changing it. Decide what to take out of the design and what to leave in.

If you are creating a spontaneous abstract design, many of the above questions still apply. Be clear about what the design means to you, whether it reflects an emotion, a memory, or an impression of light, color, and movement. Only by being specific, by highlighting all that a design image has to offer, can we make line, form, and space work most effectively for us.

Notes

1. Herschel B. Chipp, *Theories of Modern Art* (Berkeley: University of California Press, 1968), p. 19.

2. John F. A. Taylor, *Design and Expression in the Visual Arts* (New York: Dover Publications, 1964), p. 33.

3. Frederick Franck, *The Zen of Seeing* (New York: Vintage Books, 1973), p. 4.

4 Relationships of Visual Elements

Having identified the visual elements of a design—line, form, and space—we now consider how they interact with one another. To see relationships between these elements is to experience design. The relationships may be subtle. (They may be so subtle as to be nonexistent for some viewers.) Yet such relationships affect how we see a design even when we are not fully aware of their influence.

"Wait a minute," you may say. "Relationships are between people—not between lines, spots, and spaces." Such is the difficulty of putting a visual experience into words. Sir Joshua Reynolds knew what he was talking about when he observed, "It has been the fate of arts to be enveloped in mysterious and incomprehensible language."[1] On the other hand, if art were totally lacking in mystery, everyone would be an artist and there would be no need for a book about design any more than for one about breathing.

Let us begin to unravel the mystery by asking exactly what happens when we look at an especially appealing design. Our eyes seldom remain fixed on a single interesting item. Instead, they move from one element of the design to another. Looking at a quilt, a painting, or a fine piece of furniture is like being invited on a journey. In a good design, that journey is largely predetermined.

As in a poem or a symphony, an excellent visual design generally has a theme, a development of that theme, and an ending. That is to say, we are attracted first to a dominant feature, yet other features beckon, causing our eyes to move back and forth from one part of the design to another. In order for a main theme to exist, it must be expressed more strongly than any others. Yet relief from the main theme is also needed if only to serve as a foil by which the importance of the main theme can be appreciated.

To encourage a "journey of vision" on the part of others, artists make the most of design. They create appeal by making visual elements relate to each other in interesting ways. Balance, proportion, movement, mood, contrast, and rhythm all have to do with the relationships of visual elements. They are the principles of design.

BALANCE

Who needs balance? We all do. Someone who is unbalanced is out of control. Balance in a design means that the design as a whole has equilibrium. The design instills in the viewer a sense that everything in the design is just the way it should be.

A balanced design is not necessarily pretty. A visual image can be disturbing from a thematic standpoint and still give the impression of balance by the way in which its visual elements relate to one another. In a good design, the relationships between the visual elements are as important as the immediate thematic message carried by the design as a whole.

SYMMETRY

Symmetry is part of balance. When two halves of a design are mirror images of each other, they demonstrate symmetry. The two halves together form a balanced, harmonious unit in which neither side is fighting too hard for attention.There is symmetry in the paired wings of a butterfly. There is symmetry in a snowflake and in a Hawaiian quilt.

Symmetry has the effect of calming the mind. It gives an impression of stability. No matter where the eye travels in a symmetrical design, it always returns to the center. Sometimes a small variation in the symmetry of one-half of a design may be balanced by a corresponding variation in the opposite half. This can make for added interest so long as the overall balance is not threatened.

There are different kinds of symmetry. In bilateral symmetry, the elements on each side of a single axis are equal and in mirror image from one another. In quadrilateral symmetry, we must imagine two axes that cross at 90-degree angles. The elements on each side of each axis are also equal and in mirror image from one another. Radial symmetry is when the elements are equal, in mirror image from one another, and are arranged in a pattern that goes from the center out like the spokes of a wagon wheel.

There is symmetry in a snowflake. Photograph courtesy of the Department of Library Sciences, American Museum of Natural History. Photo by R. E. Logan (neg. no. 2A5143).

ASYMMETRY

Symmetry is one aspect of balance, but a design can have balance and be asymmetrical. Symmetry is a balance of equal parts, but a balance of unequal parts can be just as pleasing. A small area of a design can balance with a larger area so long as the small area contains the item of greater visual importance. In such a design, the eye travels first to the smaller area and then moves to the larger part of the design, which has

The Comb of Kaiulani, traditional Hawaiian quilt. Photograph courtesy of the Honolulu Academy of Arts.

A quilt block may reflect bilateral (left), quadrilateral (center), or radial symmetry (right).

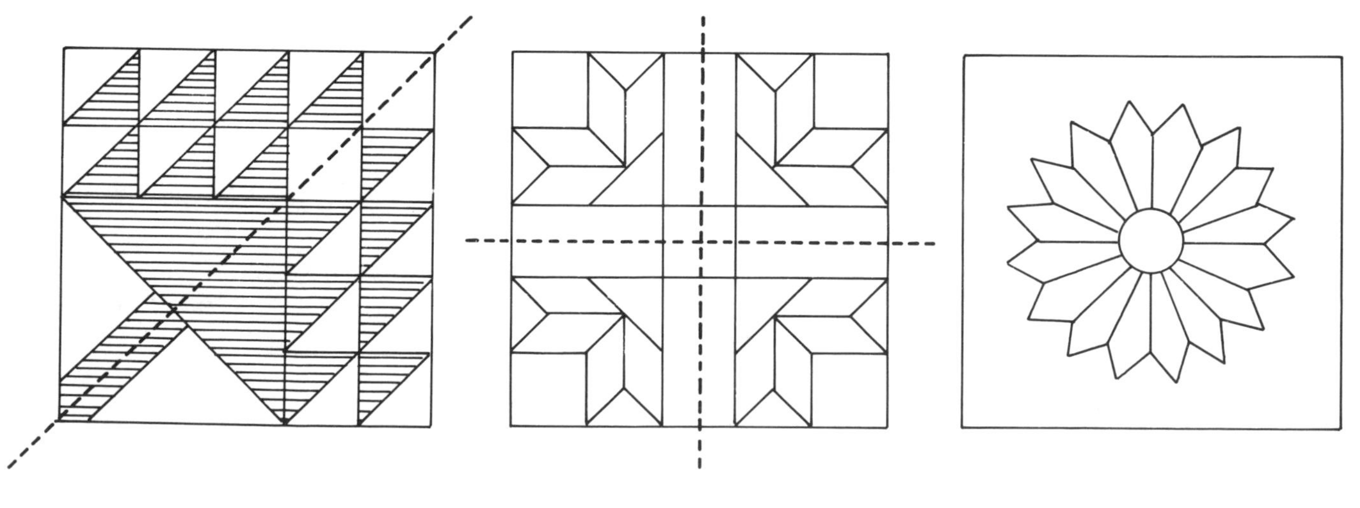

Sailor's Valentine, handmade from shells found on the beach by Bert Porreca. A balance of unequal or nearly equal parts can be as pleasing as a balance of equal parts. Photograph courtesy of *The Islander,* Sanibel Island, Florida.

less visual impact. Yet the size of this larger area makes it more or less equal in visual importance to the smaller area with its item of interest.

Would the same design be just as interesting if the item of interest were not in balance with the larger space? Probably not. Can there be such a thing as too much balance? Indeed! A design in which the item of interest is exactly centered is often less appealing; it may be too stable, too passive because it fails to invite the eye to move from one place to another. In addition, when the item of visual importance is overwhelming and out of balance with the remaining space, the result can be equally unappealing. It feels lopsided as if all the interest is in one place with no room for the eye to travel.

PROPORTION

Closely related to balance is proportion. Proportion has to do with the comparison of one part of a design with the whole design, or with other parts of it. In portraying the human body, for instance, for the head to be *in proportion* to the rest of the body, it must be about one-seventh the height of the body. If the head were to be more or less than this, we would say it was *out of proportion* to the rest of the body. Of course, if the head were out of proportion to the rest of the body, we might also say that the design was unbalanced. This gives an idea of how closely the two principles of balance and proportion are intertwined. We use the word

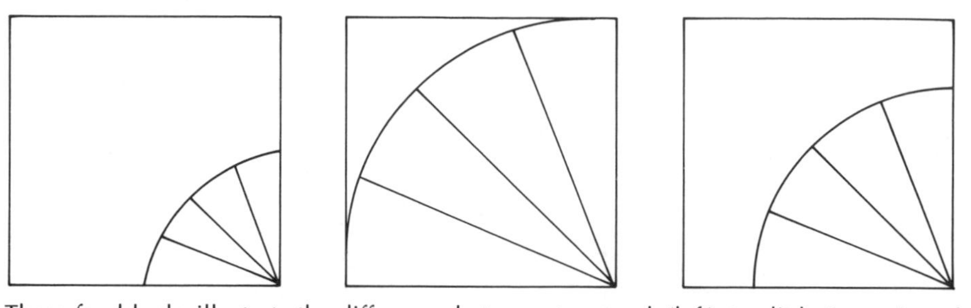

These fan blocks illustrate the difference between too much (left), too little (center), and just the right amount of space (right) in a design.

proportion, however, when referring to ratios—mathematical comparisons of amounts or sizes—within a design.

It is easy to see how we might speak of ratios in a design when talking about sizes—like the head-to-body ratio above. We can talk about other elements of a design in terms of ratios, too. We can speak of the proportion of a certain color in a design (the amount of blue, for instance, in relation to the amount of other colors). We can discuss the proportion of certain forms (the number of squares in relation to the number of triangles) or the proportion of space (the relation of a small spatial area in comparison to a larger one).

We saw that a balanced design can be symmetrical or asymmetrical. In the same way we can discuss proportions that are equal or unequal. A 1:1 proportion is perfectly equal. In a block quilt, the proportions are 1:1. The equal proportions lend the design a feeling of stability. Often, however, unequal proportions generate more interest. In a landscape design a 2:3 proportion may be more appealing. The eye has to work a little harder to take in the differences between the spatial areas. The added differences make the design of unequal proportions more satisfying than the one whose measurements are identical.

Similarly, a block quilt in which the blocks are of unequal sizes appears more challenging to view than one in which the blocks are all

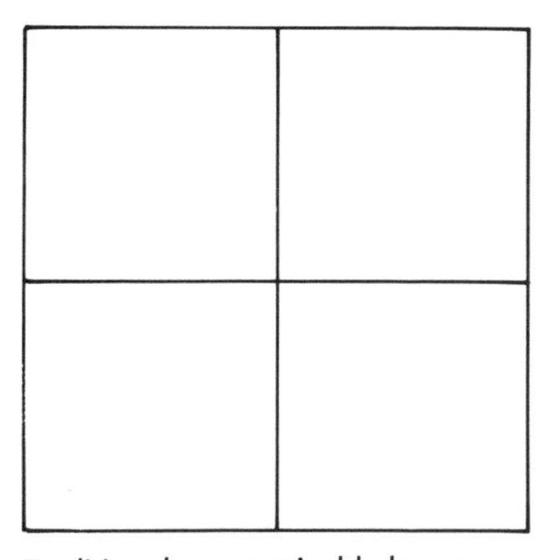

Traditional symmetrical balance

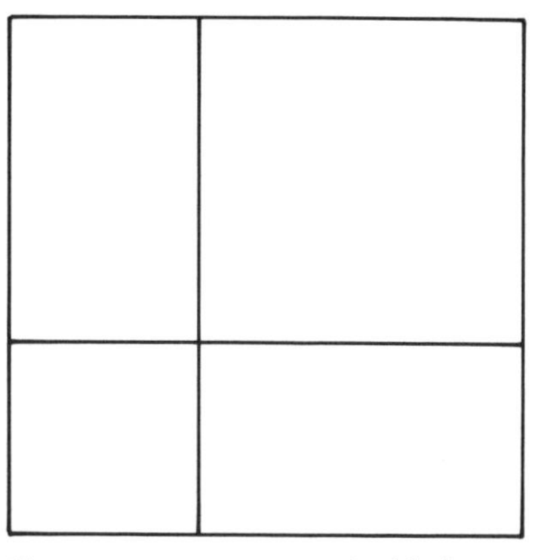

Contemporary asymmetrical balance

Examples of block division.

the same size. The viewer, however, need not always choose to be challenged and therein lies the timeless appeal of the traditional square block design. Those who enjoy classic qualities and a connection to the past enjoy a design in which the proportions are all regular and alike. There is nothing wrong with that. It suggests security, a respite in a hectic world. Others, however, might find such proportions confining. A more contemporary design, therefore, justifiably incorporates a variety of blocks and rectangles for added interest, as well as the suggestion of freedom and adventure.

MOVEMENT AND MOOD

We have talked about some ways in which people experience design. A good design invites us to follow with our eyes a suggested direction of movement from one visual element to another. In each case, the suggested direction of movement also imparts its own meaning or mood.

Direction of movement can be suggested by symmetry. In a symmetrical design, the eye returns to the center. Such regular movement suggests a mood of quiet centeredness. Direction of movement can also be suggested by balance. The eye may shift back and forth between a small design element and a large area of space that balances with it. Such constant shifting back and forth suggests mild tension and adds interest.

Movement can also be suggested by lines. A horizontal line invites

Patchwork jacket by Char Russell and Billie Gunderson of Tabitha Quilts. Tabitha Quilts designs custom-made one-of-a-kind quilted articles of clothing (see Sources).

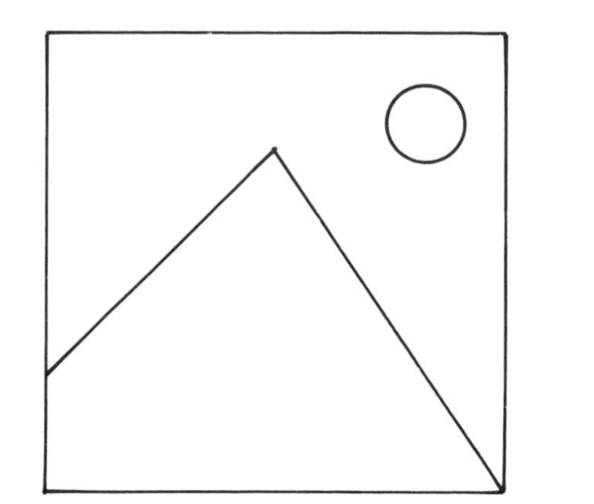

Stylized line (left) vs. realistic line (right).

the eye to follow a simple unwavering journey from right to left. It suggests a mood of calm. A horizontal line coupled with a vertical one encourages the eye to travel along one line and then the other, but always back to the meeting of the two lines. These two lines combined suggest solidity and stillness. We follow a diagonal line up or down, right off the edge of its space with no return. It suggests discovery, excitement. Our eyes cannot adequately follow a whole group of lines radiating from a center point and so these suggest unbridled activity and liveliness.

A good writer uses sentences of different lengths—perhaps a long sentence, followed by a short one, followed by one of medium length. Too many short sentences in a row and the reader does not feel challenged and grows bored. Too many long sentences and the reader tires with the effort. A similar principle holds true in visual art. Different kinds of lines, for instance, create interest. The outline of a mountain is more realistic if it is varied; it is also more interesting to look at. The image of a pine tree, for instance, may be stylized or realistic. The stylized one may be more appropriate in certain contexts. But compared by themselves and apart from any context, it is the realistic one, in which the line is more varied, that holds the viewer's interest more effectively.

Many fabric artists are inspired by nature. Quilt art, like any other art, however, is no substitute for nature. It is meaningful in itself. The natural world is three-dimensional. In any art form, the challenge is to create a synthesis of what is seen and what is felt. The designer takes those elements that are most meaningful in a personal way, and eliminates or reduces those that are less meaningful. The actual relationships between visual elements in nature are much less important than how the artist feels about those visual elements.

CONTRAST

Contrast between light and dark, between large and small, between one kind of line or form and another, all play an important part in design.

Contrast creates interest. Contrast also invites the viewer's eye on a journey from one part of a design to another.

Contrast between light and dark is what makes a simple traditional quilt pattern like Variable Star so effective that generations of quilters have turned to it over and over again. When the contrast between the background fabric and the visual elements is strong, the overall design has great appeal. It is no accident that so many quilt patterns are traditionally done in a dark solid or calico fabric on a white background. The reason is simple. It is foolproof! The good results are guaranteed because the appeal of bold, contrasting elements is built into the design.

In nontraditional designs, contrast is just as important. A visual image that does not stand out adequately from its background makes for poor design. The eye becomes confused by a lack of clear outline to follow. Direction of movement in the design is hard to perceive. However, when two or more visual elements of a design contrast successfully, each emphasizes the difference in the other. The eye naturally travels back and forth from one contrasting element to the other. Interest is maintained.

Juxtaposing large and small elements generally makes for a more interesting design. The eye travels from one focal point to another, comparing and contrasting sizes and shapes. In pictorial designs, keeping all of the visual elements at about the same size may sometimes be more realistic. In that case, realism may be less desirable than good design. In a quilted scene in which a number of objects are at the same distance from the foreground, interest is generated by portraying those objects as being of different sizes. Larger elements are often used to represent items close up, with distant objects portrayed smaller. In that case, portraying the scene with one object very close, as though shot with a camera past something in the immediate foreground, can be particularly effective. It adds interest and suggests depth.

Contrasting hard, crisp forms with soft, curved ones can make for an appealing design. In quilting, we can combine precise, geometric pieced elements with soft-edged appliqués. In that case, the fabric artist needs to determine what aspect of the image should be emphasized. Sharp rays of sunlight might lend themselves to piecing. A delicate leaf might call for

Left: Visual elements are all the same size. Right: Visual elements are different, suggesting depth and adding interest.

the gently curved edges of appliqué. When pieced and appliqué techniques are combined in the same fabric picture, each heightens the appeal of the other.

Curved piecing provides a built-in contrast of straight and curved lines and shapes. The result is an appealing contrast of hard and soft lines that stimulate directional movement. Quilters have other kinds of contrast to think about as well. Color contrasts are vital and will be discussed in more detail later. In the meantime, it should be kept in mind that colors of the same intensity should be treated as the same color. Pastels on other pastels, or bold, bright colors on other brights, are not apt to show up well. The resulting loss of contrast can create an ineffectual design.

Contrasts in printed fabrics have an effect on a design. Often, small, delicate patterns are more effective in small prints or solids. Use of a large pictorial print with a finely detailed pattern can cause visual confusion. An exception is when the pictorial pattern is so large that it becomes unrecognizable as a picture when a small shape is cut from it and appears as an abstract collection of lines and colors.

Another effective contrast is provided by combining geometric piecing with curved lines of quilting. In abstract designs especially, it can be useful to have movement in one direction provided by surface design, while lines of quilting provide opposing directional movement. The crisp, short lines created by the piecing create a pleasing visual tension with the curved, flowing lines of quilt stitches passing over them. Like the counterpoint to a melody, precise fabric edges and softly variable lines of quilting create an appealing interplay of design elements.

RHYTHM

There is rhythm in the repetition of simple objects such as a shell. Photograph courtesy of the Department of Library Sciences, American Museum of Natural History. Photo by A. Singer (neg. no. 2A12055).

Rhythm is familiar to most of us in music and dancing. Rhythm in music is the repetition of sound or beat. The regular repetition of musical rhythms plays upon our expectations. Once the rhythm of a musical work is established, we know where the beat is going to fall in it.

Rhythm in visual art involves a repetition of visual elements, which creates a regular pattern. Visual rhythms also engage our expectations. We perceive rhythm in visual arts as a sequence. Once the visual rhythm is established in a pattern, we have a feeling for where that pattern is going to lead.

In a quilt design, a rhythmical pattern may be established by the repetition of lines, forms, colors, patterns of light and dark, or spatial areas. Rhythm helps establish one or more directions of movement by which the eye perceives an overall design. The repetition in a rhythmical pattern may be linear, following a repeating line. The pattern may also be gradational, going from large elements to smaller ones, or the other way around. Either way, the eye moves steadily forward in a planned direction toward a culmination point. Colors that move in a gradual progression from light to dark across the design surface reflect another kind of gradational rhythm.

A rhythmical pattern may also be established through radiating lines or forms. In a radiating pattern, the repetition of form is outward from a central point, rather than in a straight line.

Rhythm does not always involve repetition. In painting, drawing, calligraphy, and other visual mediums, a single line may be said to embody rhythm. A rhythmical line has a lyrical quality. It may vary from thin to thick in an elegant manner. It may flow gracefully. In the same way, a line of quilting can be said to have rhythm.

THE PRINCIPLES OF DESIGN

Although we have looked separately at balance, proportion, movement, mood, contrast, and rhythm, in reality these principles work together. With each other's help, they establish interest by making visual elements in a design relate in ways that make the viewer feel rewarded. When these principles come together, the result is good design:

> *When we look deeply into the patterns of an apple blossom, a seashell, or a swinging pendulum . . . we discover a perfection, an incredible order, that awakens in us a sense of awe that we knew as children. Something reveals itself that is infinitely greater than we are and yet part of us; the limitless emerges from limits.*[2]

Good design fills us with wonder. It bridges the inner world of the human mind and the outer world of human reality. It can be felt intuitively, or it can be encouraged and developed. Once we begin to see design around us, we never see the world in quite the same way again.

Notes

1. Frank Muir, *An Irreverent and Thoroughly Incomplete Social History of Almost Everything* (New York: Stein and Day, 1976), p. 265.

2. György Doczi, quoted in *Orion* 4, 1, (Winter 1985), p. 3.

5 Composition

A carver named Robert Davidson once said that the only way you can carry on a tradition is by adding to it.[1] As quilters, we are constantly balancing the demands of tradition vs. innovation. Although most of us love traditional patterns, we want our quilts to say something about us and the times in which we live. One way we can give our quilts a contemporary focus is through innovative composition.

Composition is the way in which a design is put together or arranged as a whole. Composition is a broad term. Composition is the external shape of a design, whether the quilt is a square, a rectangle, or some other shape. Composition is also the internal part of a design—how the main elements in the design balance each other to create a unified whole. We can speak of the composition of a particular motif or element of a design and how the details of that motif relate to the design as a whole.

We have considered the visual elements of design—line, form, and space—and have seen how they relate to one another individually. In focusing on composition, we are striving to see design elements as a unified whole, rather than as individual fragments. This is the goal of effective composition—to bring a design into equilibrium, to establish it as a balanced, unified entity.

Twiga, by Jane Nettleton. In discussing composition, we try to see the design elements as a unified whole. Photograph courtesy of Buzzard Studios.

MULTIPLE-UNIT COMPOSITION

Traditionally, many quilters used a simple, foolproof method of composition. They chose repeating block patterns. The effect was consistently bold, striking, and simple. The way in which the elements of these designs worked together was clear and easy to grasp. Today's quilters often feel challenged to stretch the limits of composition. An understanding of basic compositional techniques can help us in this endeavor.

The space in a design can be divided up into a number of different ways. It can be an allover design, in which case, the design can be seen as one single unit. Or a quilt design may be divided into many blocks or units. These may be all the same size and shape, or they may be different sizes and different shapes. The composition, that is, the arrangement of the shapes, must be balanced in order for the quilt to appear as a complete and unified statement.

In a traditional quilt, the blocks are often identical. This makes it easy to create a unified composition. In relation to each other, the blocks provide strong symmetry because they are all exactly alike. The shapes that make up the individual blocks need not be symmetrical themselves for this symmetry of placement to make itself strongly felt.

In a contemporary quilt, the units may be of all different sizes. They may include squares combined with rectangles, or other shapes grouped in a pleasing manner. The blocks themselves may portray different subjects. The composition of this kind of quilt is not uniform as in traditional repeating block quilts. It is balanced in a different way. A large block on one side may be balanced by two small ones opposite it. Or the sense of balance may rely on the colors used—a warm color area may balance with another warm color area across from it.

THE MONDRIAN LAYOUT

To produce a balanced multiunit design, quilters often work in what is known to graphic designers as a *Mondrian layout*.

The Mondrian layout is named for Dutch artist Piet Mondrian, whose painted works are based on a rectangular grid structure. His paintings feature a strong sense of balance between vertical and horizontal elements. The works of Piet Mondrian have inspired many quilters. His art is known for its symmetry but not the kind of mirror-image symmetry we find in folk art. Yet the design elements balance each other.

As an experiment in composition, design your own Mondrian layout. Begin by seeing how many different ways a square can be divided using a single line. With the dividing line in the center running from left to right, a horizon line is suggested. Yet if you were to create a landscape with such a horizon line, it would appear too static, too dull. Dividing the two halves equally makes for a boring composition. With the dividing line too near the top of the square, the image becomes bottom-heavy. It features more interest than the first square, but it is still not a good composition. With the dividing line too near the bottom, the image appears top-heavy, as if it may fall over on itself. Again, not a good composition, unless you are deliberately trying to create a design that appears top-heavy. A horizontal line not too near the top or bottom generates a certain amount of interest, yet there is also a quality of restfulness about it. This might be the best composition for a design that was intended to suggest a quality of peacefulness or quiet appeal.

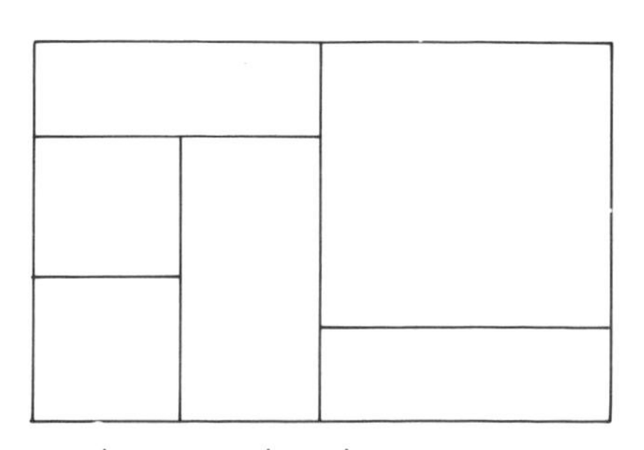
A quilter's Mondrian layout.

A square divided on the diagonal is more vibrant than one split horizontally. The triangles add interest. Each of the triangles is symmetri-

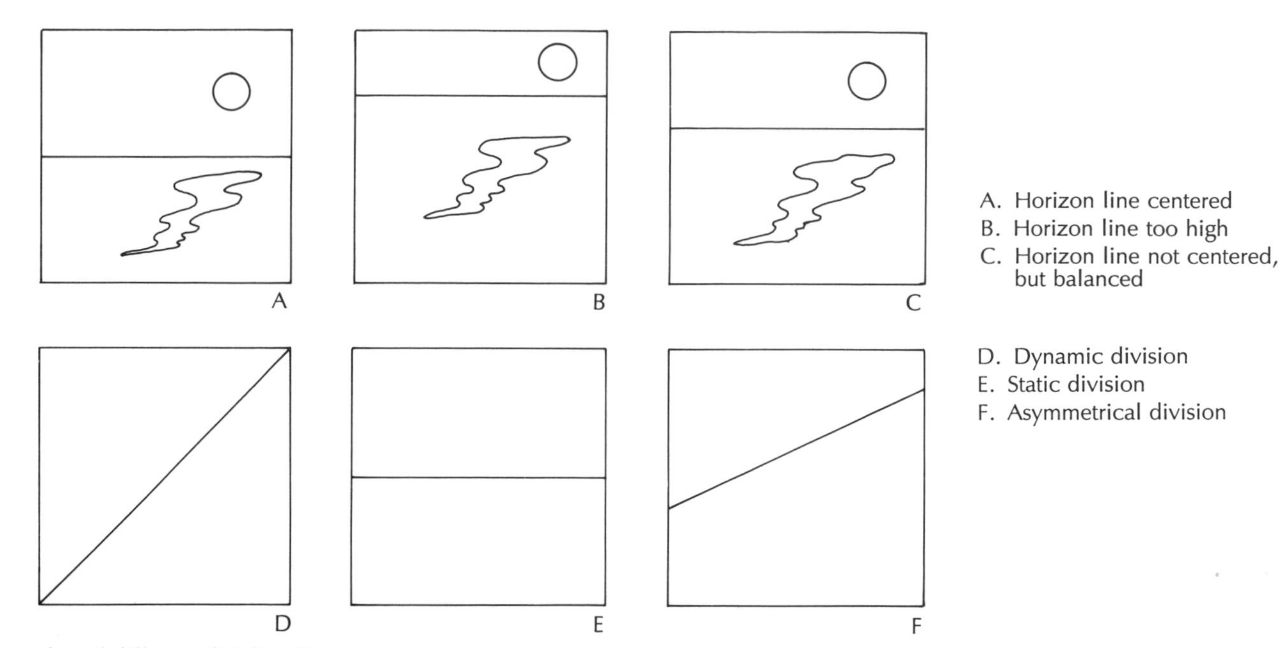

Examples of different dividing lines.

cally balanced within itself. The square may also be divided so as to create two unequal shapes. Such an asymmetrial composition could be successful if an item of strong interest were placed in the smaller section, balancing out an item of lesser importance within the larger section. Experiment further to see what other options are possible. Then try dividing a rectangle into three, four, or five units—some squares, some rectangles. Be sure that the smaller units balance with the larger ones. It may take a combination of small units to balance with one larger one. Remember, for now you are just practicing unit shape and arrangement. In an actual design, you would have many other compositional considerations to consider as well—color, design elements within the units, and more.

SINGLE-UNIT DESIGNS

What about compositions that are not divided into blocks or sections? These designs usually have a single main theme or subject. They may have secondary subjects as well, but our first concern is the main subject. We can use composition to enhance the main idea. To see how, let's consider different means of arranging simple motifs on a plain field or background.

We know that certain colors often evoke certain feelings in people. Most people see the color red as a warm color. Red may be inviting for its warmth on a cold day. It may suggest anger. Research indicates that people are more likely to fight in bright red rooms. The color blue is a cool color. To many people it suggests calm. In the same way, certain kinds of compositions evoke feelings in people. It is possible to talk of the psychology of composition. Let's take a look at some examples:

A. This composition has no movement. The square rests on the bottom of the field. It is not going anywhere. It lacks tension and is not especially interesting.

B. In this composition, the square is near the bottom of the field but does not rest on it. The square appears to be falling. It *does* appear interesting. It has movement.

C. In this composition, the square is directly in the middle. It suggests balance—a little too much balance. It might be effective in a design that was intended to suggest stability or a state of "centeredness" much as an object of meditation suggests centering the mind.

D. This square is placed near the top of the field but, again, not directly upon it. This square has upward movement. It appears interesting because it is floating away.

E. Composition can be manipulated to suggest feelings. This composition suggests loneliness and vulnerability. This tiny square is surrounded by a great deal of space.

F. In this composition the large square takes up nearly all of the available space. It is not a warm, pleasant arrangement. It is somewhat repulsive. It might be effective if the designer wanted to suggest the feeling of crowdedness in a modern world.

G. This arrangement of same-size squares is restful, though rather dull.

H. This arrangement of squares in different sizes and different distances from each other is more dynamic.

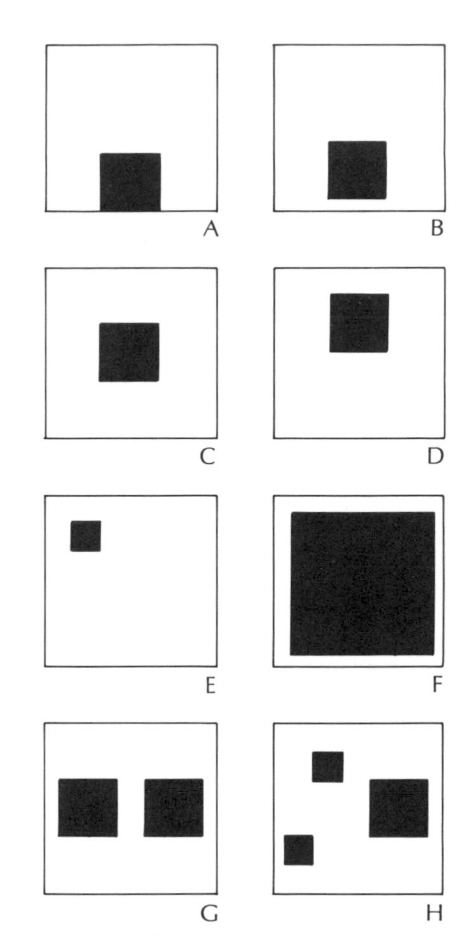

The psychology of composition.

The preceding offers just a taste of how composition can be used to enhance the suggestion of feeling in a design. To learn more, see the book *Picture This: Perception & Composition* by children's book illustrator Molly Bang. Her book (listed in Recommended Reading) provides many valuable lessons on the use of composition in a manner that is fun and direct.

Meanwhile, how can a quilt designer put what we have just illustrated to use? Your main subject might not be a square on a plain field. Suppose it was a mountain. You would need to decide whether that mountain should have jagged edges or softly curved edges. In doing so, you would want to keep in mind what kind of feeling you wanted your picture of a mountain to suggest. The jagged edges might be more interesting. They might also be more scary. The softly curved edges would be calmer, more welcoming.

Suppose your main subject was a person in a room. You could make the person tiny, engulfed by the room. That would make the person seem more alone, more vulnerable. You could make the person take up most of the space in the room. That might make the room seem too

Fibonacci Swing, by Sally Brown. The movement and rhythm of this composition generate strong interest.

small, too confining. You could make the person and the room seem more balanced in size in relation to each other. That might appear most calming and comfortable. The choice you made would depend on the feeling you wanted to portray through your picture.

SOME DO'S AND DON'TS

In art, rules are usually made to be broken—or at least tested. But the following general rules can help serve as guidelines as you design your own successful compositions.

- Be clear about the nature of your subject so that you have one main subject and perhaps one or two smaller areas of interest.
- Unless you are going for a special effect (the small, lonely person in the large room) do not make your main subject too small; it may get lost in the shuffle and go unnoticed.
- Do not make your main subject too large so that it dwarfs all other tension and movement in the design.
- Place your main subject so that some movement is suggested either by the subject itself or by other items in the composition.
- Do not arrange the elements of your design so as to appear squashed

together or isolated, unless you are striving for a special effect that incorporates these feelings into the meaning of your work.

- Avoid distributing the elements of your design in a perfectly symmetrical manner. Variety makes for interest.
- Avoid placing your subject so that it appears to be flying out of or falling off the field of vision, unless that kind of movement is important to the meaning of the work. Otherwise it will simply look like the design was not well planned and that not enough room was left to make the whole image fit.

STYLES OF COMPOSITION

A composition may be symmetrically balanced or asymmetrically balanced. In a symmetrically balanced composition, the main figure is at the center. The result is an extremely static, stable design. In an asymmetrically balanced composition, the main subject is placed slightly off-center. In that case, the main subject may be made to balance effectively with the spatial areas of the design.

Another kind of composition is based on the shape of a triangle. The elements of a single subject or a group of three subjects form a kind of pyramid. Triangular composition gives strength and solidity to a design. It implies perfect stability.

Some designs appear to have no main subject, and no outstanding group of objects on which to focus attention. Yet they convey a feeling of balance and composition. Their composition is said to be circular because the viewer's eye is carried around, from one small area of interest to another, all over the entire design. Circular composition is difficult to achieve, yet the reward, when it works, is a design full of movement and vitality.

As you look at the work of other quilters, consider the feelings that are evoked in you not just by subject matter and colors, but by shapes and their placement. Think about why you feel the way you do. Composition is an important tool in design. Composition lets us use the arrangement of forms to suggest a wide variety of feelings and emotions. Only by analyzing our visual perceptions can we practice and improve our ability to create effective compositions.

Note

1. Reported by Michael James, quoted in *Quilting II with Penny McMorris,* a guide to accompany the television series produced by WBGU-TV, Bowling Green State University, Bowling Green, OH, 1982, p. 69.

6 Color

The power of color is strong. Color in packaging can make us buy things we may not need. Colorful clothing makes people more attractive. Bright colors are used in schools to facilitate learning. Muted colors are used in hospitals to soothe pain. Color affects us in many ways. It has been observed that color-dominant people tend to be shy, sensitive, individualistic, and somewhat impractical, while form-dominant people tend to be more practical and conforming.

Most quilters relate strongly to color, yet many of us are ignorant of even basic color theory. We rely instead on an intuitive approach to color in our quilts. Some quilters even adhere to the safe rule of choosing a calico and adding two solid colors drawn from the calico print. We cannot, however, expand our creative horizon by playing it safe. The more knowledge we have about how color enriches our world, the more effectively we can exploit all that color has to offer in our design efforts. Although it is hardly within the scope of a single chapter to fully explore the properties of color, we can touch upon the basics of color theory. The resources listed in Recommended Reading will provide further direction.

COLOR AND LIGHT

Color is linked to light. We sense this as quilters. Which of us has not at some time purchased a length of fabric only to see that in the daylight, it was an entirely different color than the one we supposed? In nature, scenes change drastically as the sunlight changes. A landscape appears different as the sun moves across the sky in the course of a day. Tree shadows are altered when the sky suddenly clouds over. Mist or muted light changes a scene. Even indoor colors are affected by changes in sunlight. A good interior decorator views a client's space in both daylight and by evening in incandescent light before proceeding.

Color is light broken down into electromagnetic vibrations of varying lengths. Our minds process these differences in wavelength as color differences, although it is not yet fully understood how. We do know, however, that violet has the shortest wavelength; red has the longest. Some colors (such as violet) appear to recede. These colors have shorter wavelengths. Some colors (such as red) appear to come forward or reach out toward us. These colors have longer wavelengths.

In 1660, Sir Isaac Newton experimented with prisms to prove that color is a quality perceived by the eye and not a property of objects themselves. A prism breaks up a ray of light into the colors of the spectrum—red, orange, yellow, green, blue, and violet.

Light is reflected from surfaces. The composition of those surfaces and the amount of light available to them determines color. When we see an object as white, what is happening? It means light has come into contact with a surface that reflects all of the wavelengths equally. We see that surface as white. When a surface reflects none of the wavelengths but absorbs them all, we see the surface as black. A surface that does not absorb the blue rays of light but absorbs all the others is blue.

THE LANGUAGE OF COLOR

Artists and designers speak of the dimensions of color—*hue, value*, and *intensity*. These are useful terms in communicating about color. *Hue* is a synonym for color. *Value* describes the lightness or darkness of a color. Values range from *tints* that are light or high in value to *shades* that are dark or low in value. For example, lime green—a light green—is a tint of green. Forest green—a dark green—is a shade of green. Where we would describe green itself as medium in value, lime green would be high in value, forest green low in value.

Color values can be manipulated to obtain exciting color combinations. For instance, we know that complementary colors provide high contrast—that is a big part of their appeal. You might find the combination of yellow and violet extremely unappealing. But what happens when we manipulate these colors in terms of their value? A medium violet with a good deal of blue in it combines very well with pale yellow. Try a similar approach with other colors that contrast strongly. Being sensitive to color values can allow you to develop color combinations that are lively without being strident.

Intensity describes the brightness or dullness of a color. A color is said to be bright if it has not been grayed. Pink is therefore high in intensity, while dusty rose is low in intensity. Dusty rose is pink to which gray has been added, causing it to appear dull or less intense. When talking about color, *dull* means less bright, not necessarily less interesting.

Pink is high in intensity because it has not been grayed. Pink is also high in value because it is light. By comparison, red is not high in value.

Red is medium in value because it is not light. Yet red is also high in intensity because it has not been grayed. Maroon, a grayed red, is low in intensity. Maroon is also low in value because it is a dark red. To sum up we can say:

- Hue = color.
- Value = lightness or darkness of color. (Tints are light hues, shades are dark hues.)
- Intensity = brightness (absence of gray) or dullness of color (addition of gray).

THE COLOR WHEEL

Sir Isaac Newton also invented the color wheel, a device by which we can better understand the relationships between different colors. It may come as a surprise to some to learn that there is no definitive color wheel. Since Newton's time, many variations on the color wheel have been devised by different color theorists and artists. The color wheel in the color section of this book features the twelve basic colors. These pure, intense colors are the ones we will be discussing for the most part.

In discussing the color wheel, we talk about colors as if they were paint. This can be confusing for fabric artists because, unless we dye our

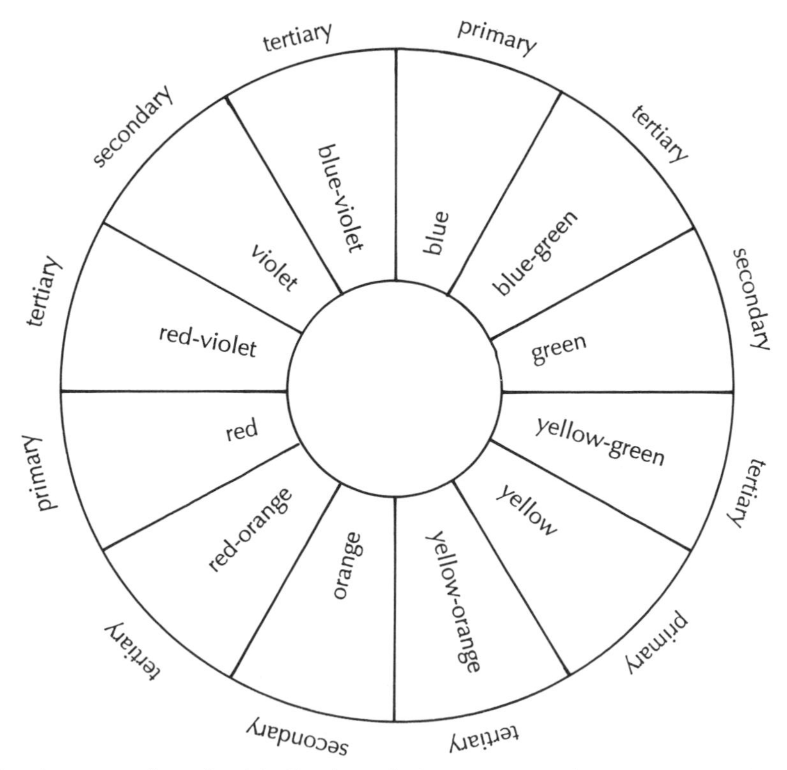

Quick-reference color wheel indicating relative positions of primary, secondary, and tertiary colors. For more in-depth understanding, be sure to see the color wheel in the color section.

own fabrics, a color is a color. It cannot be changed by mixing. And yet, for the purpose of discussion, it is useful to be able to speak of the colored fabric in the quilter's palette as if it were made up of mixable colors. It is helpful, for instance, to be able to say that we need a blue with "more gray in it" or a green that has "more yellow."

On the color wheel, red, yellow, and blue are known as the *primary* colors. They are called primary because they cannot be obtained by mixing other colors. (All of the other colors on the color wheel are obtained by mixing primary colors in different amounts.) Red, yellow, and blue form a kind of triangle on the color wheel.

Orange, green, and violet are called the *secondary* colors. When two adjacent primary colors are mixed in equal amounts, the result is a secondary color. Orange is made by mixing red and yellow; green by mixing yellow and blue; and violet by mixing blue and red. The secondary colors also form their own triangle.

What of the remaining colors on the color wheel? These are the *tertiary* colors obtained by mixing equal amounts of one primary color and one of its adjacent secondary colors. For example yellow (primary) when mixed with orange (secondary) yields yellow-orange (tertiary). The tertiary colors are always named by placing the primary color from which they are derived first in the name—yellow-orange—not the other way around.

Analogous colors are those located next to each other on the color wheel. Orange, yellow-orange, and yellow are analogous. Colors that are opposite each other on the color wheel, red and green, for instance, are called *complementary* colors. Complementary colors are any two colors that, when mixed, involve a mixture of three primaries. For instance, orange is made by mixing the two primary colors red and yellow. Orange and blue, the remaining primary color, are complementary colors. If we were to mix blue and orange, we would obtain muddy gray because we would, in a sense, be mixing blue, red, and yellow.

Complementary colors are opposites on the color wheel and visual opposites as well. As such they contrast sharply. Complementary colors are often found in nature: a pink dogwood blossom against green leaves, a purple iris with a yellow center, green sage against rust-colored desert sands. Complements can be used successfully to create dynamic color combinations. It can be most effective to combine complements of different intensities. Some of the most striking designs use subtle combinations of complementary colors—blue and peach, rather than blue and orange.

WARM AND COOL COLORS

Warm colors are those associated with fire and sunlight—yellow, red, orange. They fall near one another on one side of the color wheel. On another side of the wheel are blue, green, and violet. We speak of these as cool colors. A bit of warm color introduced into a cool one can raise the "temperature" of the cool color. For instance, a violet that is rich with red suggests warmth, as does a blue-green with lots of yellow in it. Warm colors are powerful. They grasp our attention. Cool colors are more soothing and relaxing.

When warm and cool colors are combined, the result can be delightful. A small amount of a warm color can add appeal to a quilt made up mostly of cool colors. A thin maroon accent in a design made up mostly of blues and grays adds sparkle, for example.

Research suggests that colors are conducive to specific moods or emotions. Warm colors like red and red-orange tend to raise the blood pressure, pulse rate, and respiration slightly, producing a feeling of restlessness or stimulation. Cool colors like blue and gray-blue tend to slow down these body functions. They may have a relaxing or even a depressing effect.

Light colors appear more cheerful to us than dark colors. Dark colors, though restful, may appear heavy and somber. Intense colors like magenta or brilliant turquoise are sometimes referred to as healing colors.

Colors close in value are relaxing, while those of different values are dynamic and visually exciting, even exhausting. Combining colors with the same powerful level of intensity can also be visually fatiguing. More

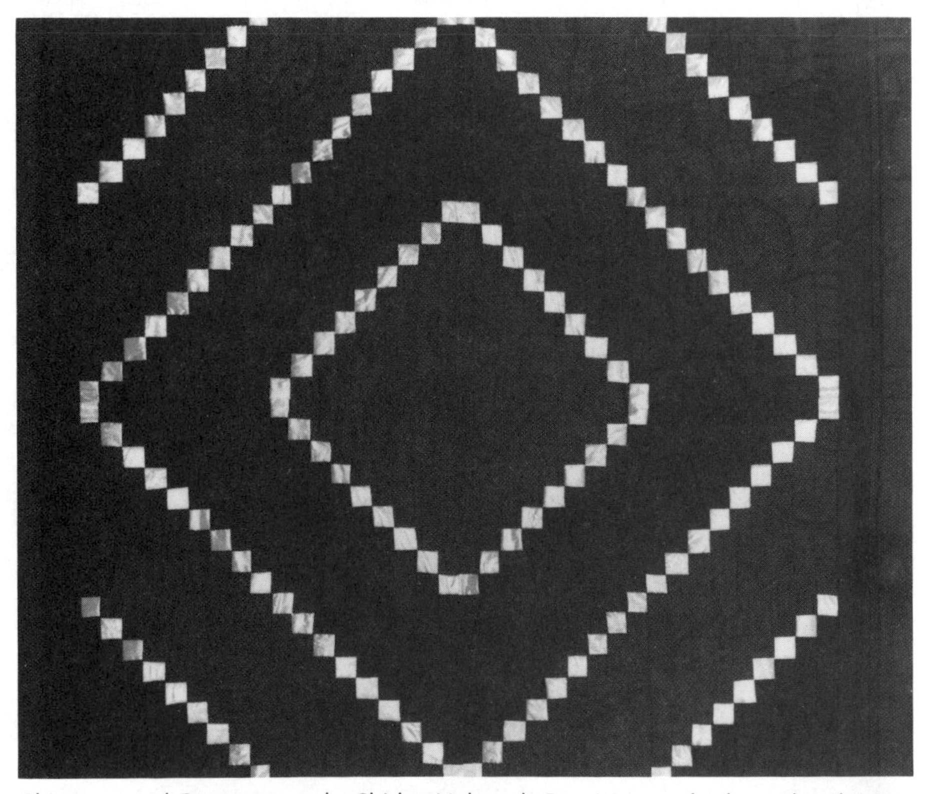

Chimneys and Cornerstones, by Shirley Halstead. Creative use of color makes this Log Cabin variation in black and silver stand out. Photograph courtesy of Buzzard Studios.

satisfying is a balance in which small areas of intense colors are combined with larger areas of neutral colors.

Quilt artist Judith Larzelere deliberately puts an understanding of the emotional effect of color to work in her art:

> *I begin a new piece because I want to express my reaction to the world of nature, or to communicate an emotion that is too strong to keep inside myself. I use colors to gain a mood response from a viewer. I appreciate the way light breaks up pattern when it passes through water or flickers in a fire or comes through leaves on a tree. I put moving color into my quilts to resemble the natural beauty that I see. I have been influenced by the abstract Expressionist painters who used color, texture, and gesture to represent emotional states. I feel I am exploring the same problems as if I were a painter using oils or acrylics.*[1]

COLOR SYMBOLISM

Every culture has its own traditional color associations. In addition, every person has personal likes and dislikes regarding color that may be based on positive and negative experiences. Russians traditionally hold red in high esteem. This is reflected in their use of the word *krasnyi* to mean both "red" and "beautiful." To many Americans, however, red is a symbol of blood or violence. It takes on the meaning of passion on Valentine's Day and of sacrifice in our country's flag. In Western cultures, white is a symbol of purity. In China, white symbolizes mourning. In America, on the other hand, black is the symbol of mourning.

Colors can evoke certain moods. Many people find cool colors calming, warm colors exciting. We also symbolize specific moods by certain colors. An angry person "sees red," a depressed person "feels blue," a jealous person is "green with envy." These are color clichés, and yet because they have found their way into the public consciousness, they influence us in how we react to color.

COLOR RELATIONSHIPS

For the most part, we have looked at colors individually. Yet colors do not exist alone. They exist in combination with each other. Indeed colors affect each other very much. Try this experiment. Select a colored sheet from a pack of construction paper. Cut out two squares. Lay each square in the center of a different colored sheet from the pack. For instance, cut two identical red squares and lay one down on a white sheet, the other on a black sheet. How is the color and apparent size of each square affected?

Earlier in this book we considered the relationships of visual elements in design. The way in which colors relate to each other parallels the workings of visual elements. For instance, we can speak of balance, proportion, movement, mood, contrast, and rhythm in color use just as in the placement of visual elements. Knowledge of the effect of colors upon each other is useful to quilters. Color can be used to influence the viewer's reaction to our fabric art.

When color is used symmetrically, the colors on one-half of the design mirror those used on the other half. The placement and area of color are exactly the same but reversed. Many traditional patterns feature a symmetrical balance not only of elements but of color as well. A symmetrical use of color like a symmetrical use of design has an appealing solidity about it. On the other hand, a design may be symmetrically balanced in terms of its visual elements and its color may be treated asymmetrically. In this case the balance of equal parts in unequal placement is visually appealing. The introduction of an asymmetrical color balance adds interest.

In a design we use the term proportion to talk about ratios—mathematical sizes or areas—within a design. The principle of proportion applies to color, too. For instance, if the proportion of red to the whole of a design is overwhelming, the design itself may be unsatisfying. Generally, a small amount of an intense color may be balanced by a larger area of a more neutral color. It is more visually appealing to have one color predominate rather than have several colors of equal intensity fighting for attention.

Artists speak of dominant and subordinant colors. In quilts, often there is more of one color featured than any other. This color is the dominant color. Conscious use of a dominant color can be an important tool in design. For example, in a quilt made up of the complementary colors orange and blue, it would be important to have one of those colors clearly dominant and the other subordinate. What would happen if you used as much orange fabric as blue fabric? The two complementary colors would have to fight it out for attention. The viewer's eye would be confused, bouncing from one overstated use of color to the other. The result would not be harmonious.

A harmonious balance between warm and cool colors may also be established. Often, a small amount of a warm color enhances a design that is done mostly in cool colors. A small amount of red balances out a design made up mostly of blues and greens. Is the reverse true? Generally not. Cool colors tend to recede while warm ones move toward the viewer. A design made up mostly of reds and yellows would be a very powerful design. A small blue accent, therefore, might just be lost. A violet accent might work better in this case because it would contrast sharply with its complement, yellow.

It may sound strange to talk about colors having movement. However, intense colors appear to generate more energy than colors of lower intensity. Warm intense colors almost seem to vibrate with movement and vitality. Cool colors and those of less intensity suggest tranquility and lack of movement.

The use of contrast in colors is also important. Contrast is what

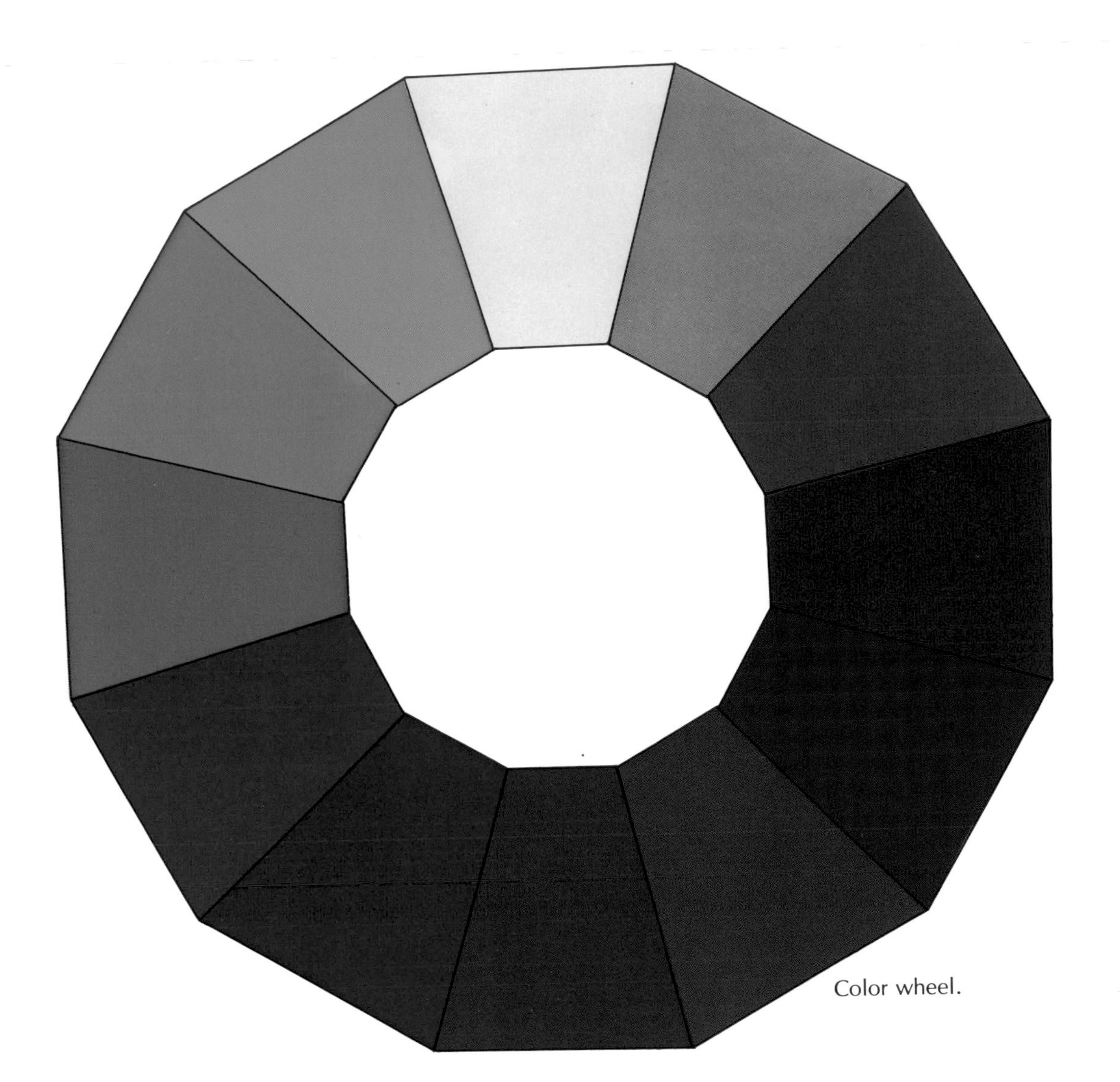

Color wheel.

Jacket by Char Russell and Billie Gunderson of Tabitha Quilts.

Undersea World, by Debora Konchinsky of Critter Pattern Works.

Dangling Participles, by Judy B. Dales.

Mother Earth, Father Sky II, by Jo Diggs.

Snow in the Mountains (project, Chapter Eighteen), pieced by the author and quilted by Amish Goods.

Peonies wall quilt by the author (project, Chapter Eleven).

Sunset Star (project, Chapter Seventeen), pieced by the author and quilted by Amish Goods.

Hawaiian Rain Forest wall quilt (project, Chapter Twelve) by the author.

Turtles in the Grass wall quilt (project, Chapter Ten), pieced by the author and quilted by Amish Goods.

Across the Lake wall quilt (project, Chapter Thirteen) by the author.

Dolphin Jacket (front and back) by the author (project, Chapter Nine).

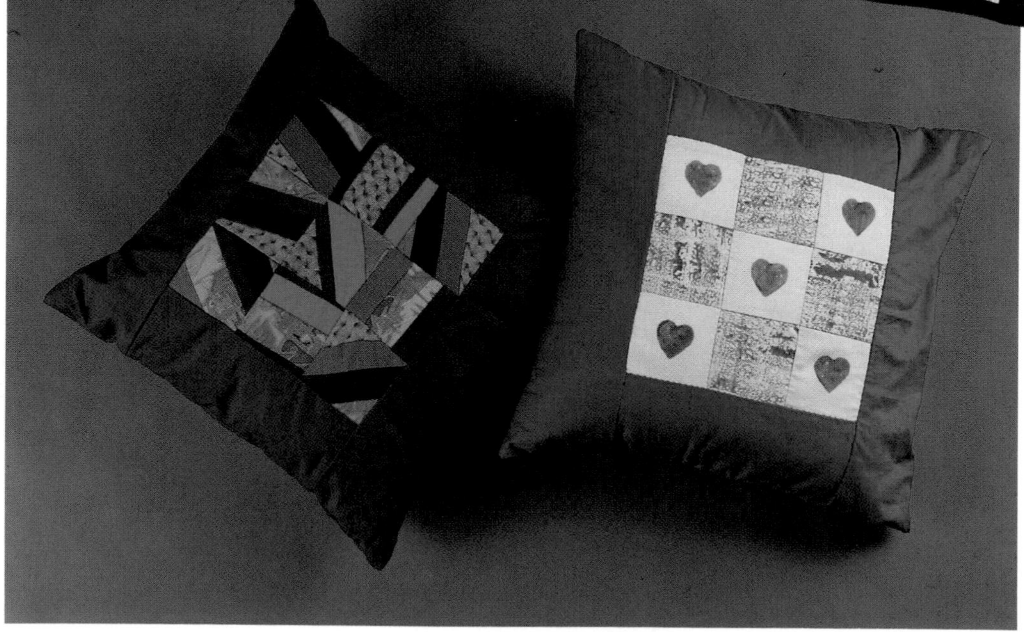

Pillows: *Spontaneous Squares* (left, project, Chapter Fourteen) and *Potato Print* (right, project, Chapter Fifteen), both by the author.

Southern California Scene, by Linda Worland.

Log Cabin, by Louise Young.

Cranes, by Kitty Pippen. This award-winning quilt features the exciting Japanese sewing technique of sashiko. Photograph courtesy of the American Quilter's Society.

Seaview wall quilt, by Sally Brown (project, Chapter Sixteen) adapted from *Attic Windows* by Diana Leone.

makes colors stand out from one another. Complementary colors placed next to one another intensify each other. Placing neutral colors between complementaries greatly lessens the intensity of the complements. An intense color placed next to a less intense color seems more intense than it would otherwise. At the same time, the less intense color appears to lose what little intensity it has. A blue fabric, for instance, placed next to blue-gray becomes an intense blue, while the blue-gray becomes almost indistinguishable from gray. As artist Josef Albers points out:

> *Imagine in front of us three pots containing water, from left to right: warm, lukewarm, cold. When the hands are dipped first into the outer containers, one feels—experiences—perceives—two different temperatures: warm (at left); (at right) cold. Then dipping both hands into the middle container, one perceives again two different temperatures, this time, however, in reversed order: (at left) cold—warm (at right) though the water is neither of these temperatures, but of another, namely lukewarm. Herewith one experiences a discrepancy between physical fact and psychic effect called, in this case, a haptic illusion—haptic as related to the sense of touch—the haptic sense. In much the same way as haptic sensations deceive us, so optical illusions deceive. They lead us to "see" and to "read" other colors than those with which we are confronted physically.*[2]

Albers's book *Interaction of Color* offers an excellent step-by-step study in color. The book is set up as if he were teaching a class and the reader were his pupil. It allows the reader the unique opportunity of making his or her own color discoveries with the guidance of a master. See his book listed in Recommended Reading.

Finally, we come to the quality of rhythm. Rhythm in color is achieved through repetition and gradation. By repeating a color throughout a design, the eye is caused to move logically from one point to another, holding the viewer's attention. Color gradations also can be used effectively to generate interest. Gradations of color from light to dark, or bright to dull, can be used successfully to create a sense of movement in a design. Amish quilts in the Sunshine and Shadow pattern often make use of rhythm provided through color gradation.

CHEVREUL'S LAWS

Most of the preceding observations on color relationships are drawn directly or indirectly from the findings of one of the most influential colorists of all time. In the early nineteenth century, M. E. Chevreul was employed as supervisor of the dyeing department of the Gobelin tapestry factories in France. As a fellow textile expert, his conclusions hold special meaning for quilters. As a color scientist, he made many notable discoveries about the properties of color.

Chevreul observed that a thread of a certain color appeared faded when used in relation to one group of colors, yet intense when used elsewhere. He learned that some color combinations appear harmonious while others do not. He worked out various rules for combining colors which he published in a volume still in print and used as a viable reference by artists today. Quilters will want to keep the following "laws" of Chevreul in mind:

- Colors are influenced by their placement near other colors.
- Light colors appear most intense when placed against black.
- Dark colors appear most intense when placed against white.
- Dark colors appear darker when placed against light colors.
- Light colors appear lighter when placed against dark colors.
- A color placed beside its complement appears more intense than when viewed by itself.
- Adjacent colors influence each other by "tinting" their neighbor with their own complement.

The last observation relates to the experiment with the construction paper squares suggested earlier. Chevreul referred to his theory as successive contrast. Today we call it *afterimage*. He observed that when one stares at a colored shape on a white background for half a minute or so, then shuts one's eyes, the complement of that color appears. The eye seeks a balance by providing the complementary color. With this in mind,

Amish Inspirations, by Sally Brown. Variation of color intensity makes this quilt striking even in black-and-white photography.

many recent artists have explored the use of complementary color to produce unique effects.

WORKING TOWARD COLOR HARMONY

We often think of harmony as a quality of music, but there is color harmony as well. When the colors used in a quilt create a feeling of completeness, the result is one of harmonious balance. Let's consider some ways to begin exploring color harmony.

Before you start choosing colors, take a thorough inventory of your fabric collection. It can be helpful to organize your fabrics, not by solids, prints, and stripes, but by color from lightest values to darkest ones. Feel justified in filling in any gaps in the color range. Your fabrics are your palette. Would a painter set out to create a painting with a limited color range? Perhaps by choice, but not by accident. Don't let your design choices take place by accident either.

Be clear about what you want to achieve with your design before planning the colors for it. Know what mood you want to evoke, what kind of effect you want your design to have on the people who look at it. Do you want to convey a peaceful feeling? Do you want to shock viewers out of a complacent attitude with a quilt of conscience? Do you want to preserve the memory of an exciting place or time? Colors are important in conveying your message, but you need to be clear about the message before you begin choosing colors.

Choose the background color or colors first. How the main elements of your design appear will depend on what background they are set against. Then, when you are deciding on what colors to use in the main part of the design, consider limiting your colors. This is not the same as limiting the number of fabrics you use (although you will probably want to do that to some extent as well). When you are starting out, consciously limiting yourself to three or four colors will help ensure that you remain in control of the situation. It can also be helpful to use intense colors sparingly. Too many brilliant colors will compete for attention and steal the show away from your main design theme. You may well want to introduce neutral colors—black, gray, tan, or white—to provide greater harmony in your color selection.

COMBINING COLORS

If you are wondering how to begin choosing colors, try working with the colors you see in nature every day. Blues, greens, and neutrals may not be the most original choices, but they can provide you with a foolproof starting point until you gain more confidence in color selection.

If you are comfortable with choosing your own colors, but would like to experiment in order to develop a more personal style, begin with analogous color combinations. Try designing a quilt that uses three colors situated next to each other on the color wheel. Analogous colors provide a good starting point for color exploration. Each color actually has a little of the other colors in it, so you do not have to be as concerned about which is dominant or how each is used in relation to the others. Even with such a simple approach to color use, you are sure to develop a new appreciation for the ways in which colors work together and affect each other.

Next, you might want to try working with a monochromatic color scheme. This is one in which you use variations of only one color. The exercise is challenging because one's palette is deliberately limited. Such an experiment can provide you with a new understanding of the relationship between value and intensity.

You will also want to become familiar with the use of complementary colors. Complementary colors require sensitive handling. They strongly contrast with each other. Careful attention has to be paid to establishing one of the complements as dominant. The old saying "opposites attract" does not quite apply to colors. When the same proportion and intensity of complementary colors are used in one quilt, the result can be chaos. The eye becomes confused by being pulled violently from one direction to another. The answer is to establish one of the complements as the dominant color, using a small amount of its opposite to provide an accent. Intensity of complements is also an issue. Using two complements of the same intensity can be boring or, in the case of highly saturated colors, exhausting. A brilliant yellow with a deep violet, for instance, can be less than appealing. A rich purple with a pale yellow, however, might be just right, or a medium blue with peach (rather than a vivid orange).

Another combination to experiment with is that of split-complements. In this kind of color scheme, a theme color is put together with two colors that lie next to its complement. A quilt pattern that features red with yellow-green and blue-green is an example. The complement of red is green. The two colors that lie next to green on the color wheel are a green with lots of yellow in it and a green with a great deal of blue in it. The thought of such a combination of these colors in their full-intensity state may be repulsive, but keep in mind that a color has a broad range in value. With sensitive choices as to value and intensity, a combination of split-complements can be quite successful.

In your color explorations, keep in mind that neutral colors can be important tools. Using a large amount of a brilliant color can easily overwhelm the viewer. Intense colors placed side by side often have too much impact to produce a pleasing sense of harmony. Introducing moderate areas of neutral colors into your pattern provides rest for the eye. It also adds balance to the design as a whole.

Transparency is a color technique being used by many contemporary quilters. Transparency is the effect produced when two colors appear to overlap and produce a third. For instance, where a blue square and a red square were to overlap, the shared area of the squares would appear as purple. The use of transparency involves an illusion. In this example, we would know that the purple area was a separate fabric shape. Yet, it would appear as if the two squares had intersected and that the darker one below was showing through the lighter, transparent one on top. Transparency is an exciting color technique that can be used to create a dynamic sense of movement in a design.

Quilters seldom take color for granted. Yet most of us still have a lot to learn about the properties of color. The best way to find out more is by reviewing what other artists have observed about color and experimenting on your own.

Notes

1. Setsuko Segawa, ed., *New Wave Quilt: Setsuko Segawa and 15 American Artists* (Kyoto, Japan: Mitsumura Suiko Shoin Publishing Company, 1991), p. 91.

2. Josef Albers, *Interaction of Color* (New Haven, CT: Yale University Press, 1975), p. 8.

Fabric

What makes a creative person choose to express herself or himself in fiber instead of some other medium? For some the appeal lies in the inviting softness of fabric. For others, it is in the combination of color and print. For still others, it is in the familiarity of cloth. Artist Anne Healy has observed, "Cloth is something we all relate to from birth to death. It is associated with every event of our lives . . . It's a magical medium which is itself and yet appears to be so many other things."[1] Many quilters find the tactile quality of cloth especially rewarding. Some enjoy the option of dyeing their own fabric to get just the right effect. What makes a fiber artist choose quilting? Quilt artist Judi Warren gives us a glimpse into her selection of quilting over other fiber arts when she says, "Working with hand-dyed colors is somewhat like painting, and the quilting creates subtleties much the same as embellishments in a drawing. In the quilt I find an added quality of contrast between the soft light-and-shadow of the quilting and the clean edges of the pictorial statement."[2]

Quilts seem to embrace contradictory qualities at one and the same time. They are precise as well as soft. They represent both reality and a dream world. With quiltmaking, we enjoy the painter's palette in our wide range of colors. Patterned fabrics provide detail similar to the cross-hatching of a pen-and-ink drawing. We even have low relief sculptural effect provided by the quilting stitch. You might say quilters have it all.

Many of us simply fell into quilting because our relatives or friends were quilters. It is important, therefore, to remember that many fiber artists deliberately choose the medium of fabric. As Caryl Bryer Fallert explains: "For as long as I can remember, I have expressed myself through artwork. After many years of painting and trying other artistic media, I discovered that fabric, as an artistic medium, best expressed my personal vision. I love the tactile qualities of fabric, and the unlimited color range possible through hand dyeing."[3] Whatever our fascination with fiber, it is helpful to develop an awareness of the vast potential of pure fabric as a medium for self-expression.

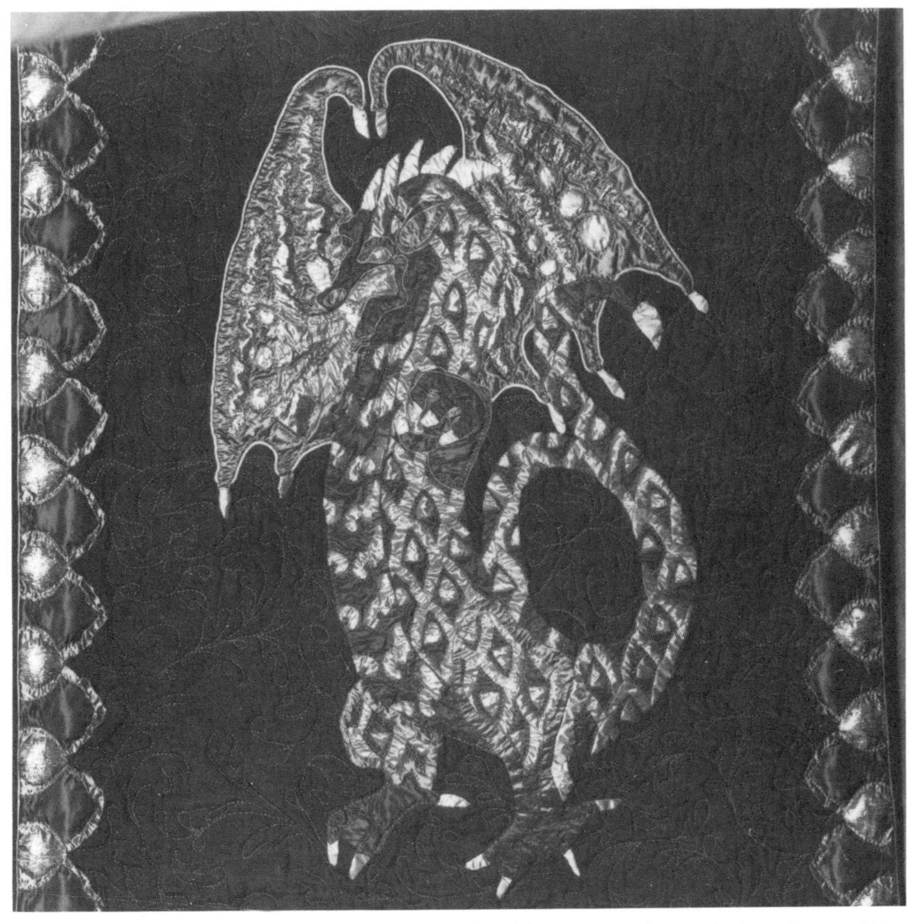

Dragon Quilt, by Laura Walsh. Unusual silky fabrics give this wall hanging a shiny appearance. Photograph courtesy of Buzzard Studios.

CHOOSING COLORS

For the quilter, fabric *is* color. As we collect fabric to work with, we often tend to collect heavily in the area of one or two colors. It can be helpful to branch out and make some deliberate new color choices.

The way in which we match fabric colors in quilts is often influenced by fashion and culture. At this moment, black clothing for women is fashionable. At the same time, there have never been so many quilts with black accents (aside from Amish quilts) at regional quilt shows. Similarly, in our Western culture, one seldom puts red and pink together. A pink shirt with red slacks just would not do. Yet look at textiles or patterned paper from Japan. Combining red and pink is common. In fact, such a combination can be used to lend a distinctively Japanese flavor to a design. In combining fabric colors in quilts it can help to step outside our cultural bias and our preconception of what looks good.

Often the most pleasing balance in fabric choice arises when a solid and one or more prints, plus one or more neutral fabrics, are used. Choosing all solids can give a bold, contemporary look to a design. If the pattern is an especially busy one, using all solids can help to tone it down and lend it a quality of stability. Solid color fabrics in gradation can be especially powerful. A quilt that features a single color presented in a range of values can be quite appealing.

Some quilters prefer to dye their own fabric to achieve just the right color. Dyeing fabric is also useful when you want to get a variety of colors in one section of fabric, perhaps to represent the changing colors of the sky. Tie-dyed, tea-dyed, and marbleized fabrics are related options as well. (We will discuss more about personalizing one's own fabric in Chapter Fifteen.)

PRINTED FABRIC

When we think of the color of a print fabric, it is important to consider not only the background color, but the color or colors of the printed motif as well. The background color in a fabric is the color on which the print is placed. (This is not the same, of course, as the background or setting fabric used for the entire quilt.)

Color and print are united in fabric. They work together. Print color influences how we perceive the background color. For instance, solid navy blue fabric appears darker than does navy blue with a tiny white print in it. Red calico with printed yellow flowers appears lighter than red calico with a black print.

In a fabric print, the motif is the main visual element. The motif can be tiny or enormous. It can be anything in between. It may be a collection of contrasting specks of color. It may be an enormous printed flower. Print size affects design. A delicate pattern like the traditional Palm Leaf is usually more effective in solid fabrics or a tiny print. A large print fabric, in which the motif is still recognizable, would draw attention away from the thin, narrow triangles that make up such a dainty pattern. On the other hand, if the quilter were to cut thin, narrow shapes from an unusually large print, the motif of the print might be lost. It would appear instead as a combination of abstract lines and would no longer detract from the delicate pattern shape. In this way it is sometimes possible to use large prints in an innovative way. It takes a practiced eye to recognize when this approach will work.

Prints add interest, but they can also add busyness. They need to be handled carefully, often balanced against a solid and/or one or more neutral fabrics. Fabric prints can be roughly divided into three categories: random prints, directional prints, and pictorial prints. In a random print, the motifs face in different directions. These prints are easy to work with because the template may be placed at any position to achieve the same visual effect. Many calicoes are examples of random print fabrics.

Untitled, by Judy Shea. A striped fabric produces a unique medallion design in this quilt. Photograph courtesy of Buzzard Studios.

In a directional print, the motifs repeat in a regular line or otherwise suggest movement in a specific direction. Some small prints can be deceiving. They appear at first to be random, but a closer look reveals that rows of small design elements repeat evenly in columns. Other directionals involve motifs that face in a certain direction, for instance, butterflies that all face up. If the butterfly motif were an integral part of your design, you would not want to have the butterflies in all but one part facing the same direction unless you had deliberately planned it that way. Plaids and stripes are obvious examples of directional fabrics. Directionals require care in their use to achieve a balanced visual effect. For instance, in a four-patch block, you would not want three squares to run horizontally and the fourth to run vertically.

Pictorial prints are those that portray scenes—landscapes, tropical scenes, and large leafy motifs like the kind one might use for *broderie perse* cutouts. Pictorials can be used to add boldness to a design. They are often directional, too. For instance, if you were to cut out printed flowers from a floral fabric, they would need to be placed on the background so as not to appear upside down. Many elements from pictorial prints give

The Pasture, by the author. Detailed broderie perse cutouts for the sheep in the foreground of this design enhance the sense of distance, especially when combined with simple, undetailed appliqués toward the background.

up their directionality the moment they are cut out of the fabric, but a few do not.

Chintz and other pictorial fabrics can be used to create a sense of depth in a design. Picture images that lend themselves to being cut out and appliquéd in broderie perse style are easy to locate. Your own painted fabric motifs can substitute for the printed chintz. Either way, solid-color appliqués can contrast effectively with chintz cutouts in a fabric picture to create a sense of perspective. The eye goes immediately to the attention-getting chintz with its suggestion of three-dimensionality. Then it travels to the two-dimensional silhouette motifs—bold in their own way for their clear, crisp outline. The result can be an intriguing balance of realism and illusion, of perspective and flat silhouette. Mixing the two perspectives can lend a fabric picture a dreamy, ethereal quality.

DENSITY

Density is another important element of printed fabric. It refers to how closely the print motifs are arranged on the background of a fabric. A busy calico is very dense. There is little space between the motifs. Such a print suggests liveliness, agitation. A print in which the motifs have a greater amount of space between them provides more of a feeling of calm. A design made up entirely of dense fabrics may appear too full of movement. One design approach that guarantees good results is to provide a balance of solids, space-filled prints, and dense prints.

Dense, small-print fabrics can be used successfully in landscapes. The tiny motifs seem to break up, creating color expanses with a shimmering effect. Contrasted with solid-color motifs in the foreground, such a backdrop can add interest to a simple landscape design.

Many quilters deliberately choose prints of several different densities to create a visual texture within a single work. The variation of densities makes for added interest. A very tiny, subtle print may be used as a background fabric rather than a solid color or muslin. Some of the newer white-print-on-white ground or black-print-on-black ground fabrics are especially effective for this. Like in an Impressionist painting, the tiny print adds an almost iridescent effect.

Larger, more distinct print motifs can be used to provide a different effect. Often it is possible to use a specific portion of a print as the main element in a single shape. For instance, an Irish Chain pattern using calico squares on muslin background squares looks agreeable. Yet, how much more dynamic would be an Irish Chain in which each of the squares forming the chain featured a printed motif at its center. To capture the motif in the center of each square, you would need to place clear plastic templates on the fabric selectively to get the motif right in the center of each square. You might also need to resign yourself to cutting the squares from the fabric in such a way that lots of square holes would be cut out leaving much of the fabric wasted. Waste is anathema to quilters. Yet the dynamic design results are often worth the waste.

The issue of wasting an amount of fabric is a difficult one for quilters. Sometimes waste is needed to create an exceptional design. We have no difficulty throwing away a perfectly recyclable aluminum can, but a few inches of fabric? Never! Next time you are faced with such a decision, be daring. Explore that extravagantly wasteful design.

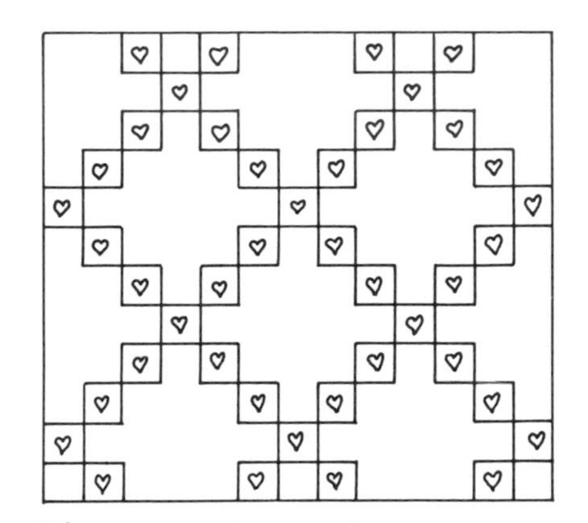

Fabric waste is sometimes necessary when focusing attention on a specific fabric motif for emphasis, as seen in this Irish Chain.

WEIGHT AND TEXTURE

Most quilters use good quality 100% cotton in their quilts. Generally, fabric purchased at a quilt shop will have a fuller, heavier feel to it than that bought at a discount or general fabric store. Loosely woven or lightweight fabrics may allow quilt batting to seep out through the surface. These fabrics can lose their shape over time. Synthetics are an option, but most quilters find that natural fibers are more pleasant to work with. Natural fibers breathe and, as more than one quilt historian has commented, we know what cotton will do in the years to come. No one has yet seen a 100-year-old quilt made from polyester fabric.

What of fabrics other than traditional quilter's cotton? Today's quilter has the opportunity to experiment with a wide variety of fabrics including velvets, velveteens, taffetas, metallics, felts, flannels, polished cottons, unbrushed corduroys, linens, satins, and more. Makers of wall hangings have a little more freedom in their fabric choices. There is less need to prewash fabric used in a wall hanging, particularly if you never plan to wash it. This way the fabric retains its sheen and sizing, making it especially pleasant and manageable to work with. Quilted garment expert Virginia Avery does not recommend washing fabrics to be used in a piece of quilted clothing that is likely to be dry cleaned. Unbleached muslin is the only fabric she insists on washing "because it shrinks so much, even when dry cleaned."[4]

Being innovative about fabric choice means taking some risks. Often the wrong side of a piece of fabric is the most appealing. Creative quilters need to be open to breaking this kind of conventional rule, the kind that says there is a right side and wrong side to the fabric being used. If the wrong side is "right," use it! In instances where you want a tint of a hue you are already using, the wrong side of the fabric can be just what you need.

When choosing fabrics, you will also want to give consideration to physical texture. Quilt weight 100% cotton has a delightfully smooth texture to it. Velveteen is smooth in a different way. It is soft and cool on the fingers. Metallic lamé appears smooth and shiny, yet may have a slightly scratchy feel to it. Exotic fabrics like ikat, yukata, or block-printed cloth can give exciting results. When designing a quilt that is to be quilted, keep in mind the difficulty of quilting through heavyweight fabrics. Heavyweights like velvet and corduroy are fine for unquilted wall hangings, but quilting through these fabrics is difficult.

Try to be open to experimenting with fabrics of all kinds. It is possible to combine fabrics of different weights and textures to create innovative effects. If you run into trouble with fabrics that will not hold their shape well, you can often stabilize them with a light muslin backing. Through variations in color, print, weight, and texture today's fabrics allow quilters an almost unbelievable range of design options. Exploring them can be quite a challenge—and full of reward.

Notes

1. Anne Healy, quoted in *The Art Quilt* by Penny McMorris and Michael Kile (San Francisco: Quilt Digest Press, 1986), p. 53.

2. Judi Warren, quoted in *The Quilt: New Directions for an American Tradition*, edited by Nancy Roe (Exton, PA: Schiffer Publishing for Quilt National, 1983), p. 33.

3. Caryl Bryer Fallert, quoted in *New Wave Quilt: Setsuko Segawa and 15 American Artists*, edited by Setsuko Segawa, (Kyoto, Japan: Mitsumura Suiko Shoin Publishing Company, 1991), p. 91.

4. Virginia Avery, *Quilts to Wear* (New York: Charles Scribner's Sons, 1982), p. 36.

8

Quilting

We call our medium *quilting,* yet how much consideration is usually given to the quilting in a quilt? Typically, we devote pages and pages of books and magazines to patchwork patterns, sewing techniques, and tools, with comparatively little space given over to the art of making our quilting line as interesting as possible. The term *quilting*, of course, refers not only to the occupation itself, but to the stitching used to hold the three layers of a quilt together. When today's quilters focus on their quilting, it is usually to lament that their technique is not all it should be. Since we will consider only the design qualities of quilting here, quilters who need a few pointers on improving their quilting stitch may want to read *Fine Hand Quilting* by Diana Leone, listed in Recommended Reading.

Quilting is worthy of attention. It has an ancient history. Some of the earliest quilts that survive are whole-cloth quilts featuring exquisite quilting. Among them is the famous Sicilian "Tristan" quilt, separate panels of which are preserved at the Victoria and Albert Museum in London, and the Museo della Casa Fiorentina Antica in Florence, Italy. Yet quilting may have even earlier antecedents. The earliest example of "quilting" is said to exist in the form of a small ivory statue made in Egypt about 3,000 BC. It portrays a pharaoh wearing a quilted robe. Archaeologists in Mongolia have found a quilted floor covering that is believed to be 2,000 years old.

Many medieval references to quilts exist such as in the *Itineraries of William Wey*, published in 1458, in which travelers were advised to purchase bedding for their shipboard journeys including "a fedyr bedde, a matres, too pylwys, too peyre scehtis and a qwylt."[1] We often hear that the European knights of the Crusades brought quilting back to the West from their sojourn in Moslem lands. Whether they discovered quilting or, perhaps, rediscovered it remains to be determined. (Certainly the Arabic world preserved learning of all kinds that was lost to the West during the Dark Ages.) Moslems may have preserved the art of quilting because it is equally conceivable that quilting was known to the Romans and to the European tribes they subjugated at the height of the Roman Empire. Our own word "quilt" comes from the Latin word *culcitra*, meaning bed or mattress.

Quilting deserves attention if only by virtue of its venerable heritage. From a design standpoint, it also has a lot to offer. Quilting is more than something to be gotten through in order to finish a quilt. Quilting adds dimension. It creates texture. It offers light and shadow. When you look at a single-layer patchwork of fabric, there are no sculptural highlights to catch your eye. When you look at the same patchwork after it has been quilted, all kinds of once-hidden patterns rise to view.

Quilting is what makes us want to touch a quilt. It calls our tactile sensibilities into play. It makes the difference between a flat surface image and a multi-faceted one. Quilting provides a subtle three-dimensional relief quality that reminds us of our need to touch and be touched.

Wholecloth crib quilt, designed by John Degge and quilted by his wife, Mary Frances, Petersburg, Illinois, c. 1850–1853. Collection of the Illinois State Museum. Gift of Mrs. Catherine Degge Mars.

As fiber artist Anni Albers points out:

> *We touch things to assure ourselves of reality. We touch the objects of our love. . . . All progress, so it seems, is coupled to regression elsewhere. We have advanced in general, for instance, in regard to verbal articulation—the reading and writing public of today is enormous, but we certainly have grown increasingly insensitive in our perception by touch, the tactile sense. No wonder a faculty that is so largely unemployed in our daily plodding and bustling is degenerating. Our materials come to us already ground and chipped and crushed and powdered and mixed and sliced, so that only the finale in the long sequence of operations from matter to produce is left to us: we merely toast the bread. No need to get our hands into the dough.*[2]

The quilting in quilts provides an antidote to civilization by awakening our tactile sense and by its own quietly meditative process. (Indeed, many needleworkers turn to quilting in troubled times expressly for its calming repetitive motion.) Quilting is also important for the visual possibilities it excites in us. Quilting can form an appealing design of its own. Or it can echo and enhance the motifs in a design. Quilting can add detail, much as an artist's pen might do. Quilting can make a leaf come alive with tiny veins. It can make a night sky sparkle with the suggestion of gentle breezes. It can portray the ripples on a pond or the crashing surf of an ocean.

TECHNIQUES

A line of quilting in a design creates movement. It gives the viewer a direction to follow. It leads the viewer's eye from one area in the design to another. It can pull us into a design, or suggest movement that radiates outward, even beyond the confines of the quilt itself. Quilting can provide balance and solidity through vertical lines; calm and gentleness through horizontal ones. Diagonal quilting lines suggest liveliness and tension. Curving, flowing, swirling lines hint at playfulness or sensuousness. First and foremost, the quilting line is a line. It has the attributes of a line. (See Chapter Three, Visual Elements.)

The quilting line is a tool. It may be used in an innovative way or not. It can be successfully exploited to add rhythm, balance, contrast, and sculptural effect to surface design. The choice is up to the quilter. We do not always keep the full illustrative, tactile potential of quilting in mind. There are many ways in which quilting enhances surface design. There are also many styles of quilting. Let's take a look at them.

OUTLINE QUILTING

Outline quilting, a traditional favorite, is done by stitching about ¼″ from each seam line in pieced quilts. Generally, a row of quilting is done

Example of outline quilting.

on each side of every pieced seam line where this style is used. In pieced designs, outline quilting works best when the individual shapes that make up the design are fairly large, at least 2″ or 3″ across. When the shapes are much smaller than this, the result is too busy, with lots of tiny shapes and their outlining stitchery competing for attention. Outline quilting along straight seams is made easy with the use of quilter's masking tape. The tape is placed with one edge against the seam line of the shape to be quilted and a line of quilting is sewn along the opposite edge of the masking tape.

Outline quilting is also used in appliqué. The quilting line is sewn about ¼″ from the edge of the appliqué and follows its contour exactly. It is often done freehand, making it an easy and convenient style in which to work. For both piecing and appliqué designs, outline quilting provides a reliable way to enhance the surface design. It offers no surprises and therefore no pitfalls. It is a suitable way to add a quality of subtle relief to a design without distracting from the main theme.

QUILTING IN THE DITCH

Stitching in-the-ditch, that is, right in the seam line of a pieced geometric pattern, is another traditional means of providing low relief within a quilt design. It is a style that appears deceptively easy. Because the lines of the quilting are the seam lines of the pattern itself, no marking is involved. There is also no question of removing the marking lines when the quilting is done—a quilter's nemesis. In-the-ditch quilting, however, is more difficult than it may at first appear. All seams must be carefully ironed in one direction, allowing the stitching to be done through one top fabric layer (plus batting and backing). If this requirement is not observed, the result can be difficulty in quilting and unbalanced stitches. Another disadvantage to in-the-ditch quilting is that occasionally the quilter must cross areas where there are extra layers of seam allowance, which makes sewing difficult. In-the-ditch quilting can provide an appealing sculptural quality to a quilt without complicating the design with lines of quilting.

STUFFED QUILTING

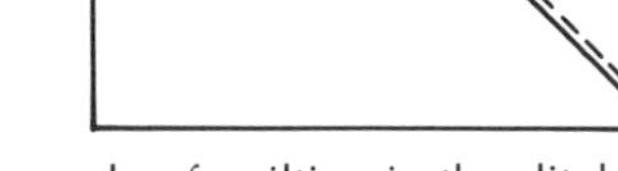

Example of quilting in the ditch.

Stuffed quilting, or trapunto, is a dramatic style of quilting in which the unquilted area between two lines of stitching is filled to make it stand out. There are two styles of filling. In one, the item is first quilted. Then a small opening is worked between the threads on the back of the quilted piece using a pointed sewing awl. Through this opening, small amounts of cotton or other batting are stuffed into the area inside the lines of stitching to make it stand out. The opening is then closed simply by working the threads of the backing fabric back and forth. The hole may also be cut and closed with stitching, but many quilters prefer the method that does not involve cutting and weakening the backing.

Another style of stuffed quilting is called channel quilting. In this

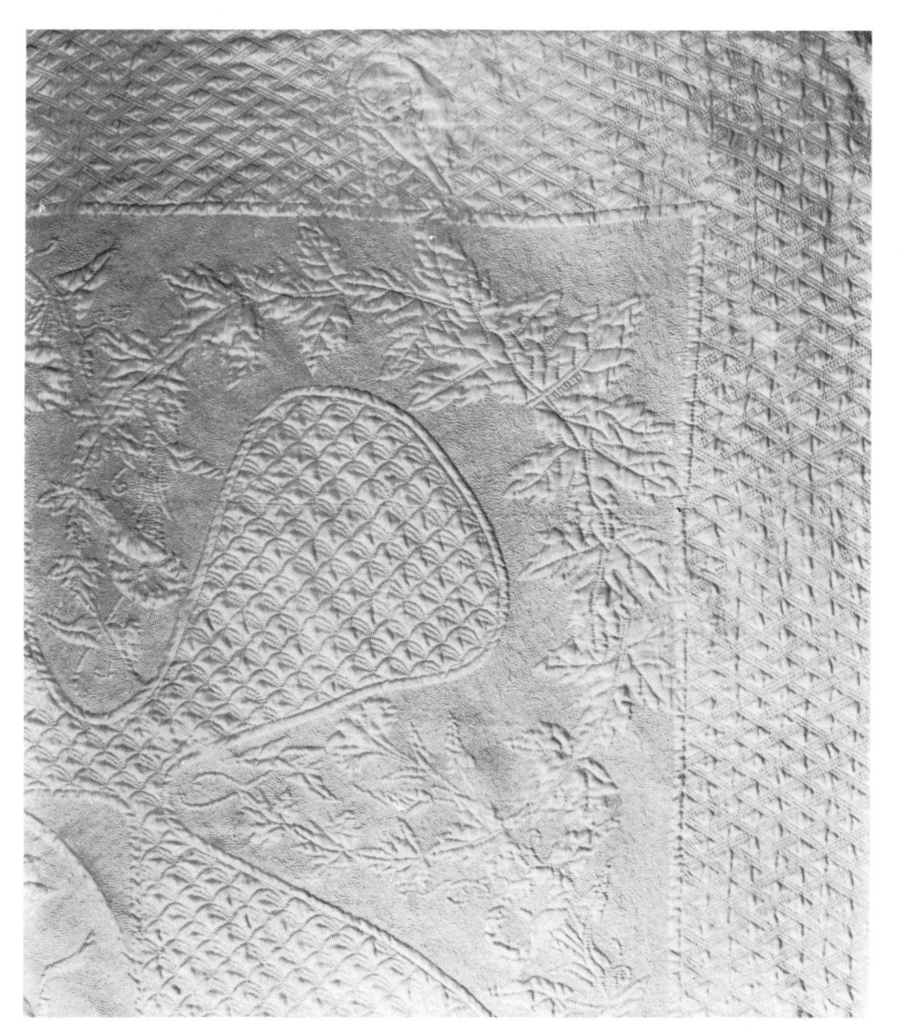

Detail, *Marie's Garden,* by Louise Young. A contemporary trapunto quilt.

method, usually only two fabric layers are quilted together. Parallel lines of quilting are sewn with ¼″ to ⅜″ between them. Each channel made by the lines of stitching is then stuffed by running a large, yarn-filled needle through it between the two layers of fabric. The yarn is cut, leaving a thick strand between the lines of quilting to make the channel stand out.

Stuffed quilting is used in many venerable Baltimore Album quilts, and more and more contemporary quilters are developing an appreciation for its emphasis and rhythm. Stuffed quilting adds an appealing quality of high relief to a design. It can provide a dramatic effect, making stuffed motifs stand out significantly from other motifs. Combining stuffed and unstuffed quilting can be effective too. The viewer's eye is immediately drawn to the stuffed areas first, continuing on to other unstuffed areas of the design second. Channel quilting can provide an appealing rhythm of repeated elements in a design. Rows of channel quilting around a square, for instance, reinforce the solid impression of the square. Repeated channels surrounding one or more design motifs add emphasis and, again, direct the viewer as to where to look first.

Echo quilting.

ECHO QUILTING

Related to channel quilting is echo, or contour, quilting, the style most often associated with Hawaiian quilts. Indeed, echo quilting is often called Hawaiian quilting. It is somewhat like channel quilting that has been left unstuffed, a style in which row upon row of parallel quilting lines repeat. Often the quilting lines repeat around a single central motif, but they may be used to enhance other design motifs as well.

Interestingly, the earliest Hawaiian quilts were not quilted in echo style at all but rather in allover patterns—straight vertical lines, diagonal lines, or variations of these. Before long, Hawaiians developed quilting styles rooted in their own traditional craft patterns that recalled the natural forms around them—seashells, fish scales, and turtle backs, for instance. Eventually, what we think of as the traditional style of Hawaiian quilting evolved. In this style, the stitching echoes the lines of the central motif, providing an appealing quality of emphasis through repetition. As curator Lee S. Wild notes, this style of quilting also ". . . gives a three-dimensional quality to a quilt, a quality often described as resembling the waves in the ocean. Such wavelike rows of quilting (ideally measuring half an inch apart) give life to the piece and create a complementary motif."[3]

STIPPLE QUILTING

In stipple quilting, the line of stitching is extremely dense. Stippled areas in a quilt provide a dynamic contrast to areas in which this technique is not used. Stipple quilting usually does not follow any pattern outline but rather is used to fill in areas in a random style. Stippling is done in close, often wavy lines, so close, in fact, that the integrity of the lines may be lost entirely. The stippling may appear as an area, rather than a line, of stitching. Stippling is an intensive process that deeply flattens the background area, allowing alternate areas to rise slightly and stand out.

When doing stipple quilting, the stitching line needs to be even closer than in echo quilting—ideally ¼″ or less apart—to make the area recede and the alternate, unquilted areas come forward. Stippling may be done in extremely close, straight lines as well as wavy, random-moving ones. The wavy line style has the advantage of requiring no measurement or marking while ensuring appealing results. Stippling is the visual opposite of stuffed quilting. A combination of stuffed and stipple quilting on the same quilt can highlight a surface design dramatically.

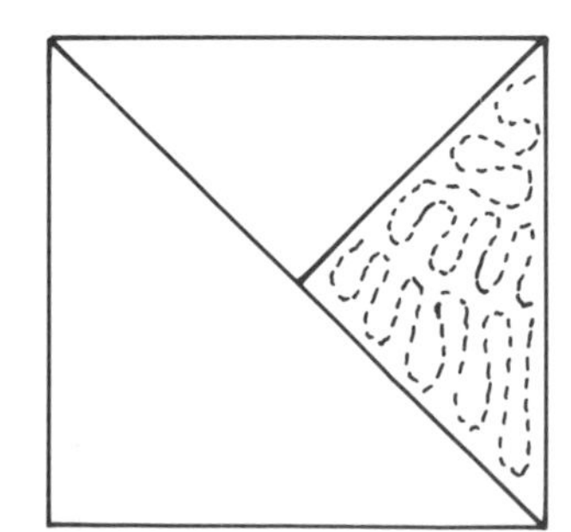

Stipple quilting.

ACCENT QUILTING

Lines of quilting stitches, like an artist's pen, can be used to add vivid and appealing accents to surface design. Quilting may be used to give the illusion of multiple seams, even curved seams, where there are really only a few simple straight ones. The optical effect is greatly heightened when, for instance, a simple eight-pointed Star block is quilted using four circles, breaking the star up into four sections and creating a sense of curved lines juxtaposed with straight seams.

The quilting line may extend beyond the boundaries of a pieced pattern to suggest movement beyond the field of vision. By using lines radiating out from the center of a Star pattern, a strong sense of movement is created. Closely running parallel lines can be used to form an accent against a surface design. The repetition of lines running closely together in parallel also suggests movement that extends beyond the field of vision. Combining horizontal lines and vertical ones creates an appealing tension in a design.

Accent quilting.

PICTORIAL QUILTING

When lines of stitching are used to suggest the outlines of picture images, we call it pictorial quilting. We noted earlier that lines do not really exist. They are a kind of symbol by which we suggest the outlines of forms. An example of picture quilting would be the quilted outline of a cat. Such picture outlines may echo motifs in the surface design of a quilt. They may also be used in borders to illustrate the name of an abstract geometric pattern (Cats and Mice, for instance). They may be superimposed onto abstract geometric patterns to produce a unique contemporary statement with a hint of realism.

One approach to quilting is to concentrate on a pattern name, especially one that suggests pictorial motifs such as Pine Tree, Lobster, Pineapple, and so on. The quilting can be used to portray the object represented by the pattern name. In the case of abstract geometric patterns with a picturesque name, this can be especially effective. (A border of quilting mice, for instance, might be used with the Cats and Mice pattern.) In this way, pictorial quilting can add a whimsical contemporary touch to a traditional pattern. If you need help drawing simple pattern outlines, try looking through children's coloring books or books of silhouettes. The patterns you find can easily be reduced or enlarged on most photocopy machines. Often the design forms a closed loop, which means you can cut out a single paper template, pin it on the quilt, and quilt around the outside of it as a stitching guide.

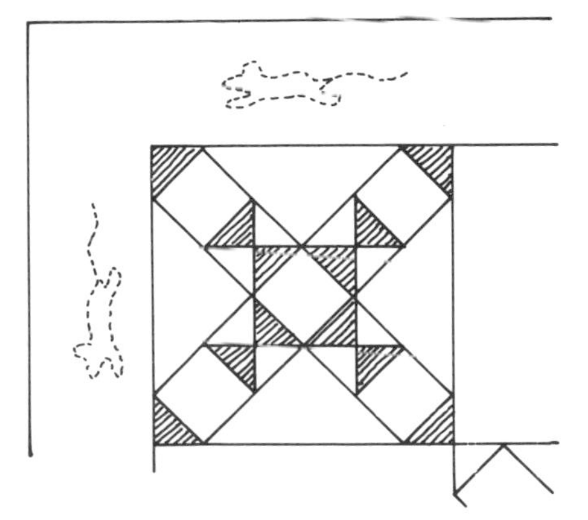
Pictorial quilting.

ALLOVER QUILTING PATTERNS

Traditional allover quilting patterns include parallel diagonal lines, cross-hatching, and the clamshell design. These quilting patterns provide a regular linear statement of their own. Because quilting provides a subtle design, generally these patterns do not compete unfavorably with

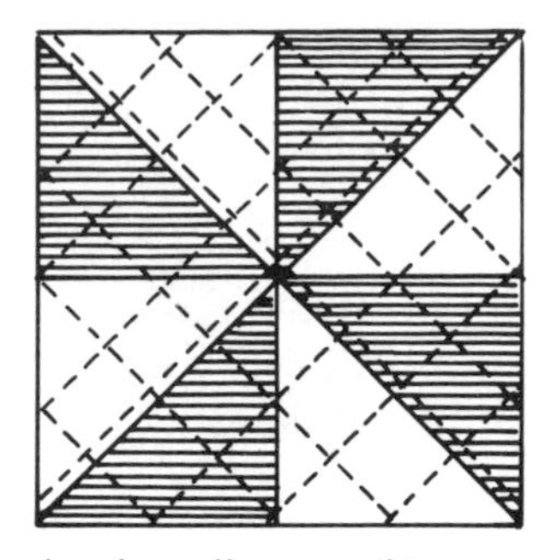

Example of an allover quilting pattern.

a surface design pattern. On the contrary, they enhance a simple allover quilt pattern by adding an appealing secondary design.

Contemporary quilters often make use of random allover quilting designs. Unlike traditional allover patterns, random designs appear to have a mind of their own. They are not dependent on the surface pattern design. The secondary design that they establish in the work is not a rigidly repeating one. They broaden the surface design by providing contrast. Like a madrigal in which the different voices are independent of each other, yet provide a pleasing harmony, random quilt designs stand on their own, while adding interest to the design as a whole.

Today's contemporary designs offer plenty of opportunity for experimenting with random lines of quilting. For instance, a strip-pieced landscape can be enhanced by quilting lines that run contrary to the straight horizontal strips. Random quilting lines may be used to suggest atmospheric qualities in landscape designs—zigzag lines for storms, softly curved lines for gentle breezes, and so on. A strongly geometric pieced design can be softened and enhanced by the use of contrasting quilting lines that run in random curves across its sharp, straight seams. Quilt artist Nancy Halpern is especially known for her crisp, straight-seamed contemporary appliqué designs that feature sensuously curved whorls and ripples of quilting. Her curved, fluid quilting lines provide a distinct contrast to her sharply defined surface designs.

One way to approach a more random, contemporary style of quilting is to try to see your quilting design as a whole, instead of as a group of parts or blocks. Rather than focusing on small sections to be quilted, imagine a fluid series of quilting lines that work their way over the entire surface. Do not try to fill in an entire section before going on to another section. Try to quilt a few lines that cover the entire quilt or large areas of it. Consider mapping out a general design on paper. Concentrate on establishing a main theme—the details can be quilted in later. Decide what mood you want your quilting to evoke. Do you want to use rigid, repeating lines to suggest firmness and stability? Do you want to use random, fluid lines that parallel each other in a rhythmic procession? Use your quilting line to further express themes or feelings already inherent in the surface design.

QUILTING THREAD

Colored quilting thread has the ability to enhance a design in many ways. Today's options for colors in quilting thread are tremendous. In addition to colorful options provided by cotton and cotton/polyester quilting thread, there are some exciting metallic threads, strong enough for hand quilting, on the market. Some are even variegated so that the quilting line changes color as it proceeds. Variegated thread looks especially well on solid-color fabric to which it adds a lively sparkling effect. Thicker threads like buttonhole twist can also add appealing accents.

Colorful quilting is an exciting way to add a dynamic quality to an overall design. Quilting thread in a contrasting color can be used to bring out a certain fabric or to tone it down. If you plan to densely quilt an area, you should keep in mind that the color of your quilting will influence the color of the fabric against which it is displayed, particularly if the fabric is solid. The eye tends to blend the stitching and fabric together. If you want your quilting to show up, be sure to choose colors that contrast well with each other. Light thread on dark fabric, dark thread on light fabric, or complementary colors offer particularly high contrast for high visibility in quilt stitches.

Today, polyester batting, as well as the newer needlepunched cotton batting, offers quilters wide flexibility in their stitching. These materials provide us the option of leaving some areas unquilted because there is little worry about the high-tech battings shifting or disintegrating with wear. Indeed, many of us produce wall quilts that show virtually no wear, despite our enjoyment of them in our homes. Even with full-size quilts that are to be used, we no longer need to fill in areas of close stitches just to keep the quilt sandwich held together. This freedom can lead to laziness. Many of us tend to look at quilting as the ancillary part of making a quilt, rather than an integral part of the process. We need to challenge ourselves to revitalize our quilting.

Quilting has much to offer modern designers. It excites our tactile sensibilities. It adds texture, highlight, and provides contrast. It creates a subtle three-dimensional quality in an otherwise flat design surface. As quiltmakers we are already painters in fabric. The quilting line allows us, in a sense, to be sculptors as well.

Notes

1. William Wey, quoted in *Memoirs of a Medieval Woman: The Life and Times of Margery Kempe* by Louise Collis (New York: Harper and Row, 1983), p. 73.

2. Anni Albers, *On Weaving* (Middletown, CT: Wesleyan University Press, 1979), p. 62. Anni Albers was an exceptional fiber artist whose weavings invariably offer an exciting textural statement and provide inspiration to craftspeople and artists alike. Her works are to be found in many leading museums including the Museum of Modern Art in New York City. She was married to painter Josef Albers whose "Homage to the Square" series is so popular with many quilters.

3. Lee S. Wild in the introduction to *The Hawaiian Quilt,* catalog of an exhibit curated by Reiko Mochinaga Brandon (Honolulu: Honolulu Academy of Arts, 1991), p. 13.

Projects for Practice

9

Two-Dimensional Design

Like many quilters, you may have been limiting yourself to traditional patterns until now, enjoying the creativity involved in harmonizing fabrics and colors. There is nothing wrong with that! Traditional patterns have survived for a reason. They are time-tested and they work. Now you have reached a point where you are ready to move on, not abandoning the traditions of the past, but taking what you have learned along with you as you move into a new realm. Perhaps you have had an experience that cries out to be expressed, and traditional patterns are not flexible enough to enable you to say what you want to say. Or maybe you simply feel a need to branch out.

For a quilter who has never tried designing original patterns before, you may be at a loss as to where to begin. One possibility is to try your hand at combining simple, two-dimensional appliqué motifs. It is an approach that, historically, many creative quilters have used in America.

Today, the three-dimensional approach dominates almost everything we look at. Pictures in magazines and books are characterized by photographic realism. Before the invention of the camera, two-dimensional folk art was the norm. Instead of a snapshot, a young woman might keep a silhouette of her beau. Instead of a painting on the mantel of a fashionable home, there might be an elaborate papyrotamia, a paper cut-out scene. Many barns carried a silhouette-style weathervane on the roof. And, not surprisingly, silhouette appliqués found their way into many one-of-a-kind quilts. Two-dimensional designs allowed for a simple folk art style to emerge. Although the majority of quilters continued to make quilts in geometric traditional patterns, a few exceptional quilters gave free rein to their creativity and made unique two-dimensional fabric pictures.

Cotton crazy patchwork with two-dimensional appliqués. From the collection of the Shelburne Museum.

SILHOUETTES AND SHADOWS

Even if your drawing skills are somewhat limited, you can use silhouettes to make your own quilt design. Begin gathering ideas for silhouettes at your local library. Two books that will give you some ideas are *Silhouettes* and *More Silhouettes,* edited by Carol Belanger Grafton. (For these and additional books see Recommended Reading.) At your library investigate books of weathervanes, gravestone rubbings, antique cookie cutters, and symbols from ethnic cultures from around the world. A wide variety of silhouette animal motifs for quilting can be found in *Making Animal Quilts: Patterns and Projects* by the author.

Go on a silhouette hunt through your newspaper. You will be surprised at how many advertisements rely on the bold graphic image of a silhouette to get their point across. We think of silhouettes as being old-fashioned, but modern graphic artists often make use of the silhouette concept, giving their designs a sleek, angular line to make a strong contemporary statement.

Make it a point to discover the gouache and paper cutouts of French artist Henri Matisse. Near the end of his life, Matisse grew too weary to stand at his easel. He turned a disadvantage into an advantage by exploring a new art form. While his assistants covered sheets of paper with brilliant colors of gouache, he spontaneously cut out the dried sheets, arranging and rearranging them as his imagination dictated. Many of his

Gouache-on-paper cutout by Henri Matisse. *The Horse, the Equestrienne and the Clown,* 1947. Photograph courtesy of the National Gallery of Art, Washington, gift of Mr. and Mrs. Andrew Keck.

designs were reminiscent of the sunny tropical islands he had visited earlier in his life. Rich plant and animal forms, as well as human figures, burst with energy in his famous cutouts. His colorful undulating forms are sure to provide inspiration.

Try tracing your own silhouettes. Rather than the standard profile, experiment with a wide range of tracings. You might trace leaves, shells, or your own hand, for instance. In working with silhouettes for the first time, you will probably want to make a paper pattern to work from. Remember to cut out silhouettes by working with both fabric and paper pattern wrong side up on your work surface. Otherwise you may get a motif that is facing the opposite direction from what you had planned.

CONTRAST

When planning a quilted project based on silhouette motifs, be aware of the importance of contrast. This is what makes a silhouette work. In true silhouette art, only two colors are used—silhouette and background. Your silhouette may combine more than one color, but in finding a background fabric, it will need to be treated as a single color. High contrast between silhouette motif and background fabric is imperative. The space surrounding the motif is as important as the motif itself.

Keep in mind that contrast does not just refer to the difference between light and dark colors. Opposites on the color wheel also contrast well. It is also often possible to make use of a high-intensity color in contrast to one of low intensity.

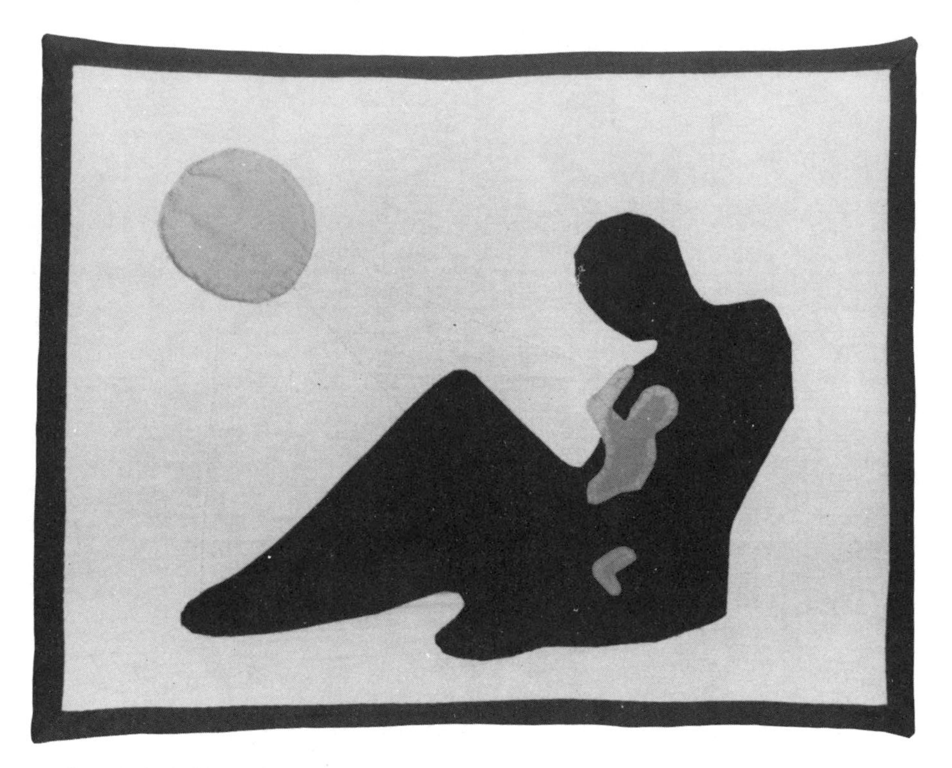

Mother and Child, appliqué wall hanging by the author inspired by the paper cutouts of Henri Matisse.

DOLPHIN JACKET

DIFFICULTY LEVEL: Moderate to Challenging

FINISHED SIZE: Optional

About the Project. This short kimono-style jacket is made using only three rectangles of fabric. The rectangles are quilted separately in "quilt-as-you-go" style and joined last. If you do not feel comfortable making your own jacket pattern, you may want to purchase a commercial pattern. Also see *Wonderful Wearables* and *Quilts to Wear* by Virginia Avery or *Weaving You Can Wear* by Jean Wilson with Jan Burhen (in Recom-

mended Reading) for suggestions on making your own clothing patterns based on fabric rectangles and squares.

MATERIALS

(Note: Exact fabric dimensions cannot be given for this project since you must determine your own garment measurements and, consequently, your own fabric requirements. The measurements used here are for a woman's small jacket size 6–8.)

2 or more yards blue ocean print fabric for jacket outer layer

2 or more yards solid black for jacket lining

Additional 1 yard solid black for jacket trim

Two 1½″ × 18″ strips of each of the following: royal blue print, lavender, metallic gold, mulberry, and red print for Seminole piecing

¼ yard turquoise

¼ yard pink

¼ yard sky blue

¼ yard green ocean print

One 24″ strip each of medium green and light green

One 12″ × 12″ square slate blue (for dolphins)

Thread to match appliqués

White quilting thread

Three navy blue frogs or other closures

DIRECTIONS

1. The jacket includes a large rectangle folded in half (for back and front) for the body of the jacket and two smaller sleeve rectangles, also folded in half. To determine the basic dimensions for your jacket, make a paper pattern first. Use a sweater or loose-fitting top garment as a general guide in sizing. In making this simple jacket based on rectangles, you will need to take into consideration the following measurements: the length from shoulder to hem (slightly below the waist); the width between the tip of one shoulder to the other; the width of the extra-wide sleeve; and the desired sleeve length from the joining place at the shoulder of the jacket to the sleeve hem. Use newspaper or tissue paper for your paper pattern. Work with the jacket body first. Fold the rectangle in half top to bottom. Make the width 2″ to 3″ wider on each side than that of your guide garment. Tape the open sides of the paper pattern together up to, but not including, the armhole, cut a slit up the front of the folded taped rectangle and put it on. If it does not fit, adjust accordingly.

2. Next, make the paper patterns for the sleeves. Be sure to make the sleeves extra wide. This gives the jacket its distinctive kimono-style effect. Extend the sleeves to just below the elbows. Again, the rectangle is folded top to bottom to make the front and back of the sleeve.

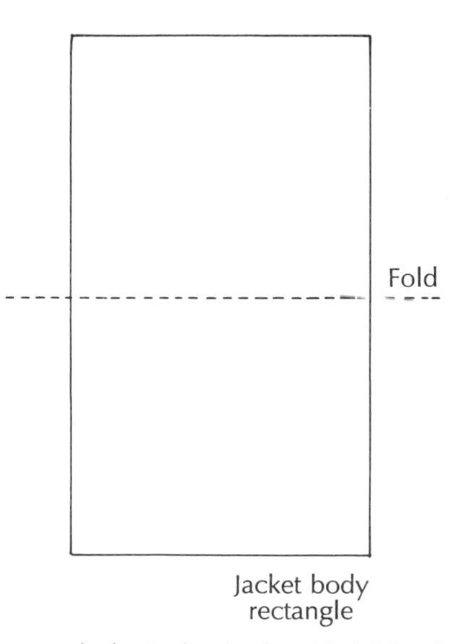

Rectangle for jacket body with fold indicated.

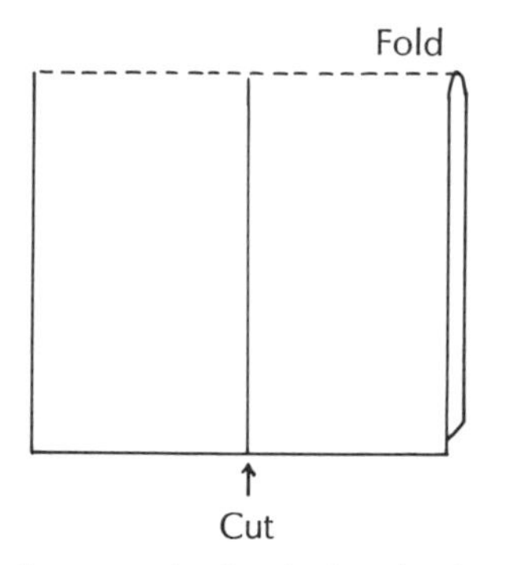

Folded rectangle for jacket body with front cut out.

Tape the paper sleeve where it should inset at the armhole and along the open sleeve bottom.Try the paper kimono jacket on. If it does not work, adjust it. Peel off the tape so you again have three flat, unfolded rectangles. Using the paper pattern, cut the rectangles for the jacket. You will need a lining, batting, and front fabric rectangle for each paper pattern. Iron the fabric rectangles. Organize all of the rectangles on a work surface. Place the lining right side down, the batting on top of this, and the front fabric right side up. Pin in place. On the jacket body rectangle, cut the slit for the front opening of the jacket just as you did earlier for the paper pattern. Cut a triangular neck hole as in the diagram.

3. Cut enough 4″-wide strips of black fabric to make one long strip that is roughly four times as long as the jacket body rectangle. (For instance, if the length of the unfolded jacket body rectangle is 40″, you will need a black strip roughly 160″ long.) Machine stitch the black strips together to make one long strip. Iron and set aside. This will be the binding for the raw fabric edges of the jacket.

4. Decorate the jacket body. Begin with the Seminole-pieced strips. This jacket makes use of the simplest style of Seminole piecing, although you can easily substitute more complex piecing if you are experienced at it. Using a rotary cutter, cut five strips 1½″ × 18″ each. Machine stitch the first two strips together along one long edge. Join the remaining strips to make a band with five long horizontal stripes. (Note: Take special care in working with any metallic fabric as it often melts upon being touched with an iron.) Then cut the resulting band vertically into new strips 1½″ wide. This will yield a series of strips made up of small squares. Sew the new strips into one long Seminole-pieced strip to be cut as needed. Iron, but do not iron any metallic fabric to be used.

5. Cut two strips from the long Seminole-pieced strip. Each should be the length of the jacket body rectangle. Set aside. Cut two strips of turquoise and two of pink, each the same length as the two Seminole-pieced strips you just cut.

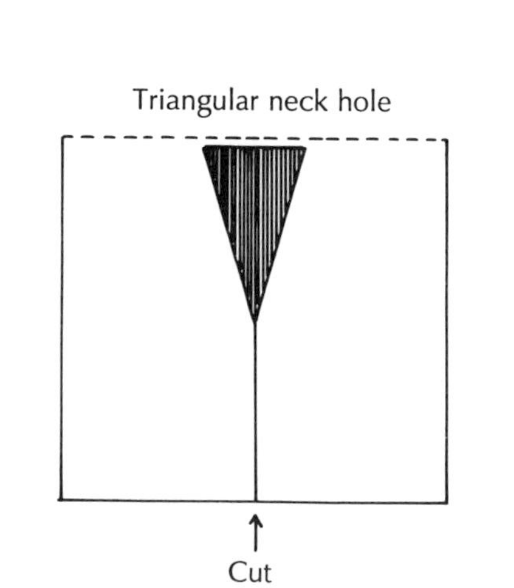

Jacket front showing triangular neck hole.

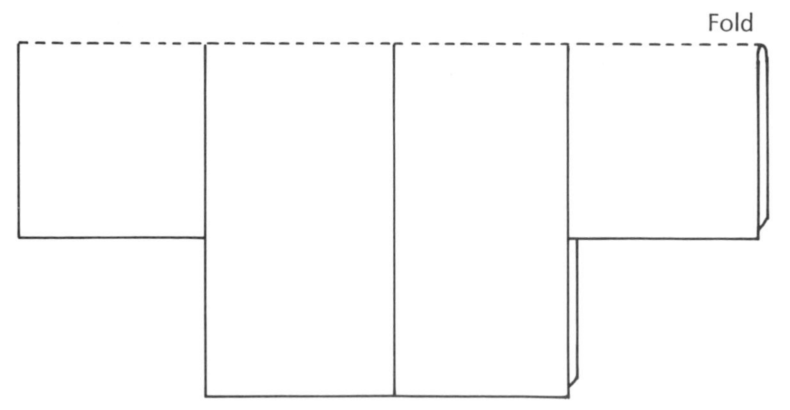

Whole paper pattern showing jacket body and sleeves.

6. Fold one of the turquoise strips in half lengthwise. Fit the ragged lengthwise edge of the turquoise strip to one ragged edge of one Seminole-pieced strip. Machine stitch together lengthwise. Do the same for the pink strip on the other side of the Seminole-pieced strip. Now repeat for the other Seminole-pieced strip. This will give you two bordered Seminole-pieced strips. Iron them carefully to avoid melting the metallic fabric.
7. Decorate the jacket body rectangle with the two bordered Seminole-pieced strips as shown. Pin the strips in place and top stitch.
8. Make similar bordered Seminole-pieced strips for the jacket sleeve rectangles. Pin the strips in place and sew.
9. To make the decorative back panel, machine stitch the following strips lengthwise for the background of the picture (each strip should be the width of the jacket body): one 1½″ strip black, one 5″ strip sky blue, one 3½″ strip green ocean print, one 1″ strip medium green, one 1½″ strip light green, one 1½″ strip black. On the actual project, the top of the green ocean strip has been cut to form curves. It has then been appliquéd to the sky strip so that curved ocean waves are suggested. You can do this or simply piece the straight strips together. Iron and set aside.
10. Trace or photocopy the pattern piece for the dolphins. Mark and cut two dolphins from the slate blue fabric. Appliqué them to the center of the background panel. (See the photo in the color section of the finished project for general placement.) Pin the picture background to the jacket back. (Again, see the photograph of the finished project for general placement.) Tack in place by hand and quilt along the edges of the strips.
11. Quilt the jacket body rectangle and the sleeve rectangles before sewing them together to make the completed jacket. Be sure to leave at least ½″ to 1″ unquilted along the edges that are to be sewn together when the jacket parts are joined. Use the project photograph as a guide in your quilting. The quilting follows the detail lines

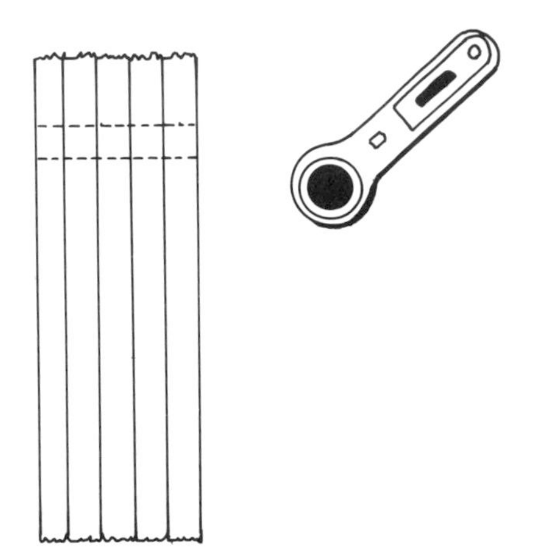

Horizontally placed color band being cut vertically.

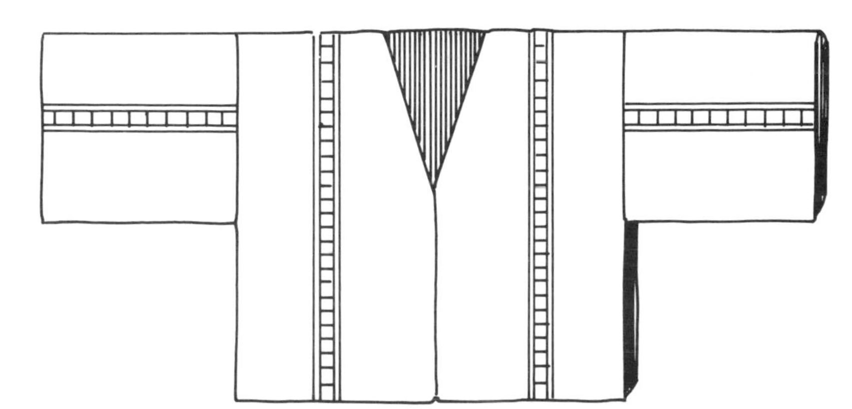

Jacket front showing placement of Seminole-pieced strips.

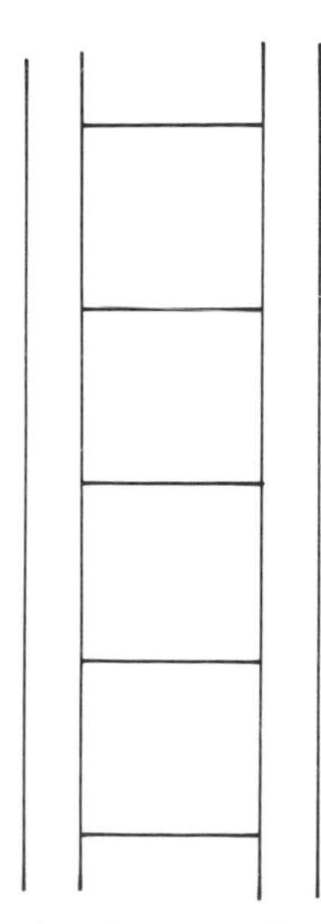

Seminole-pieced strip with color strips joined to either side.

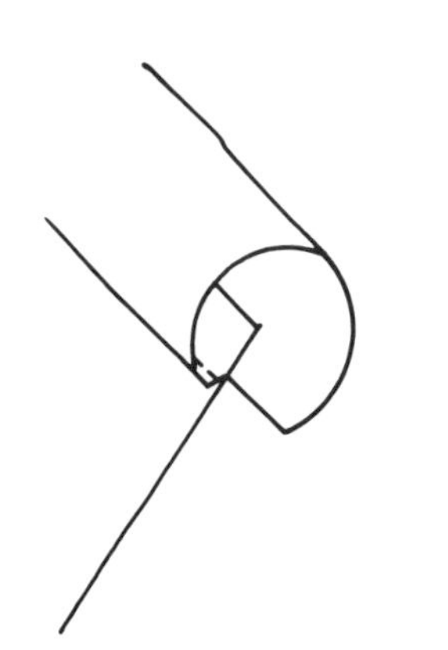

Detail of jacket binding being folded over ragged jacket edge.

of the fabric and, on the sleeves, is done simply in straight lines. You might want to vary the quilting by using a combination of straight lines on the sleeves and cross-hatch quilting elsewhere.

12. Sew up the sides of the jacket, leaving the armholes unsewn. To do this, machine stitch the lining edges together; clip the batting so that it does not extend as far as the fabric edge. The batting edge should be about ¼″ short of the fabric edge. Then hand sew the front edges of the jacket together. Do the same to sew the sleeves in place and iron.

13. Take the 4″-wide black strip that was sewn and set aside earlier. Place one of its ragged edges against the ragged edge of the bottom of the front jacket opening. Pin in place all along the opening, up along the neck, and down the other side of the front opening. Cut off the excess black strip and set aside. Working from the right side of the jacket, machine stitch the black strip in place. Bring the strip over the ragged edge of the jacket opening as if you were bringing over binding on the edge of a quilt. Note: For binding a quilt, you would use a doubled or folded strip. Here the strip should not be doubled. Working from the lining side of the jacket, pin the other side of the black strip in place and hand sew as you would for quilt binding.

14. Take the remaining black strip fabric and use it to bind the jacket bottom and the sleeve edges. Bind as you would a quilt, folding the binding strip in half lengthwise so that the fabric is doubled. Place the ragged edge of the binding strip against the ragged edge to be bound. Pin in place. Working from the right side of the jacket, machine stitch the binding in place. Bring the doubled binding strip over the ragged edge to be bound. Working from the lining side of the jacket or sleeve, pin the other side of the black strip in place and hand sew as you would for quilt binding. Iron all black binding edges and sew the frogs or other closures to the jacket front to complete the project.

10

Contemporize Those Blocks

Uniquely American. That is how many of us think of those wonderful old block quilts that were the mainstay for generations of quilters. Why do we think of patterns like Basket, Schoolhouse, and Grandmother's Fan in this way? Jonathan Holstein offers an explanation in his discussion of "functional design":

> *The pioneer-settler, in a way perhaps difficult now to envision, was on his own. Solutions to the problems he faced often could not be found in previous experience, but rather, through an open approach to the situation from which would come the appropriate new tools and methods. These tended to be the simplest and most expedient possible—for he had no labor or materials to spare. This will be reflected in architecture, tools and household furnishings, and work systems as well as political and social institutions. There was an attitude toward design which emphasized functionalism "without any blind adherence to old established forms or precedents," one which shaped both the everyday objects of the house and the products of technology.*[1]

Block-style quilts are an example of a functional approach to design. Traditionally they were easy and inexpensive to produce, could be made up quickly, and were stored conveniently (with the blocks in an accumulating pile) as they were being made. They often represented familiar objects reduced to their simplest terms.

DEFINING BLOCK QUILTS

Generally, what we think of as block quilts are made up of identical patterned units or identical patterned units interspersed with plain ones. In this chapter we will focus on block patterns that can stand alone as

Detail of late nineteenth-century *Rose of Sharon* quilt.

individual units, as opposed to allover designs that are actually made up of blocks, but in which the block construction is not always obvious (examples include Irish Chain and Robbing Peter to Pay Paul). Block quilts in which each unit can stand on its own are powerful visually for their repetition.

THE VITALITY OF CONTRAST

Traditionally, block quilts were often constructed using a single bright calico and white muslin. The powerful contrast of light and dark that resulted was nearly always captivating. We can take a tip from these traditional quilts and maintain the quality of high contrast while putting some contemporary design considerations to work as well.

White muslin was once the all-purpose background for blocks. With white squares interspersed between calico-on-muslin blocks, the visual effect was to isolate the colored pattern in the design. The result was often startlingly impressive, with bright floating stars or other motifs appearing to rise out of a sea of white. Plain muslin blocks became visually interlocked with the white background of the patterned blocks, creating a static plane. A more contemporary visual plane that adds emphasis to the motifs of your patterned blocks can be created using a print background fabric. Using a nondirectional fabric in a medium-to-large print causes the background blocks to connect visually. The seams between the blocks quickly disappear when the quilt is viewed from any distance. The result can be a delightful effect in which the motif is made to stand out distinctly from the background and yet remain thematically linked by the choice of print used.

Just how can color and fabric print be used to provide contrast in a quilt? Instead of contrasting white and a brilliant calico, we can, for instance, contrast a dark fabric featuring a small, delicate print with a light fabric in a large, bold print. An example is the project for this chapter, *Turtles in the Grass.* The turtles are made from a dark "feathered" print that is delicate enough for the eye to register as a solid color. The light background fabric, on the other hand, provides contrast not only by being lighter in color, but by being bolder in its print. It features prominent twisting leaves and grasses.

The use of a print background, rather than a solid-color background, can provide a block-style quilt with a strong pictorial quality. The design becomes scene-oriented, instead of block-oriented. The result is a combination of symmetry (since the blocks are identical) and naturalism provided by the randomness of the printed background.

Color contrast is an important way of providing a strong visual statement in our quilts today just as it was in the nineteenth century when block-style quilts were at the height of their popularity. Today, however, we can make use of a wide range of color contrasts—gray-muted colors with light ones, saturated colors with complementary saturated colors, colors chosen with an emphasis on the mood they evoke rather than the constraints of fabric availability, and more. Color contrast is as important as ever.

Structure of individual units in block quilts also offers endless possibilities for contemporary designers. Where many of our grandmothers pieced identical square blocks, today's quilters are experimenting with blocks of different shapes and sizes in the same quilt. Quilts featuring identical units probably developed not only because they were easy to make, but because the repetition of the blocks provided a bold visual image. Today, we are more likely to put together blocks of different shapes and sizes. Blocking-in a motif adds visual emphasis. Disparate motifs can be combined in a single design by using blocks. Those same motifs might appear out of place were they put next to each other on the same background. Block construction can provide a way to let the viewer see something the way it appears in the artist's memory, in a group of separate, clustered visual impressions.

Wildlife Blocks, by Debora Konchinsky. This wall hanging features an interesting asymmetrical, yet balanced, combination of blocks. Critter Pattern Works offers a variety of contemporary block patterns featuring different animals (see Sources). Photograph courtesy of Critter Pattern Works.

Venice Under the Stars, by the author. A combination of different-sized blocks is stabilized by an overall square construction in this contemporary wall hanging. Photograph courtesy of Emily Jayne.

EXPERIMENTING WITH BLOCKS

Block quilts in which the blocks are different sizes can be visually exciting. They require slightly more planning than quilts whose blocks are all the same size. One relatively easy method for experimenting with different-sized units is to combine blocks that are divisions of each other, for instance, a 10″ × 10″ square combined with four 5″ × 5″ squares. Different pieced designs may be combined in the same quilt this way without difficulty. A wall hanging made up of units of different sizes may be easily planned on graph paper. Many art stores carry graph paper with larger units than the standard four-squares-to-the-inch style available at an office supply store.

Appliqué quilts in which the background blocks are of different shapes and sizes also present an intriguing challenge for today's quilter. Try combining simple two-dimensional shapes appliquéd to blocks of different sizes. Again, if you encounter difficulty, try making the smaller blocks a division of the larger ones. Although blocks of unrelated size can

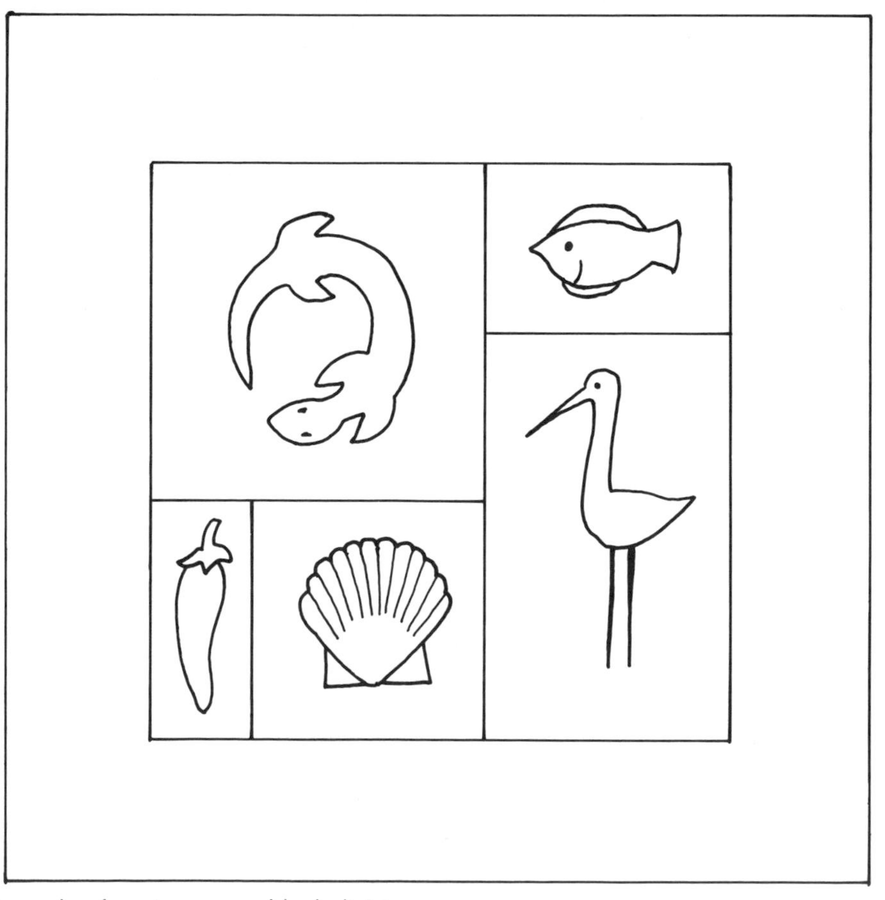

Example of contemporary block divisions.

Inspiration can be found in anything! Photograph courtesy of Ann Bryan.

provide an interesting use of spatial divisions, they often take more practice to produce successfully.

When working with blocks of different sizes, whether pieced or appliqué, remember to exploit contemporary fabrics. Metallics, hand-dyed cloth, and exotic prints can provide a bold, contemporary look.

TURTLES IN THE GRASS WALL QUILT

DIFFICULTY LEVEL: Moderate to Challenging

FINISHED SIZE: 36″ × 36″

About the Project. While visiting relatives in Florida, I had an enjoyable encounter with two large land turtles. They were busily eating grass at the side of the road, entirely undisturbed by my presence. Their large pink tongues looked surprisingly human as they curled around the tasty morsels of grass. I was fascinated by these calm-looking creatures whose home was also their food. They not only ate the grass around them, but were obviously designed to hide in it as well, as their coloring indicated. The experience inspired *Turtles in the Grass.*

The design is fun because it uses the popular traditional pattern Drunkard's Path in an unusual way. By adding two appliquéd shapes, the Drunkard's Path pattern is transformed into a turtle. The quilt also features a technique often used today in graphic design, that of including a motif that extends beyond a border. The grass blades and flowers along the bottom seem to defy the limits of the wide border, which makes for a playful reconsideration of what the function of a border really is.

Drunkard's Path is a more challenging pattern because it features curved piecing. If you are not familiar with curved piecing, you might want to see *Quiltmaking* by Susan Denton and Barbara Macey, or *The Second Quiltmaker's Handbook: Creative Approaches to Contemporary Quilt Design* by Michael James listed in Recommended Reading. Both of these books feature exciting contemporary methods for using curved seams in original designs and include basic techniques for sewing curved seams.

If you have done curved piecing before, the following tips are probably all you need before getting started. Remember to clip the concave curves of the L shapes before sewing. Also sew the pie shapes to the L shapes from the center out, not from edge to edge. That is, pin the pie shape and the L shape together and sew from the center of your seam line to the end where the two raw fabric edges of the shapes meet. Then turn the half-sewn pieces over and complete the sewing of the seam from the center out on the other side. This ensures less give and fluctuation in your piecing.

Also, if you are experienced in piecing the Drunkard's Path, you may want to sew the appliqués as you piece the blocks. Turn under just two edges of each appliqué. Then let the raw fabric edge where each appliqué attaches to the turtle's body fall under the seam where the turtle's body and the background of the pieced block join together. If this process does not appeal to you, just follow the simpler directions for turning under the appliqué shapes all the way around and joining them to the turtle body/background block after it has been pieced together.

MATERIALS

1¾ yards solid yellow fabric

1½ yards patterned background fabric in leaves and grasses print (fabric A)

¾ yard patterned "turtle" fabric in dark green feather print (fabric B)

One "fat" quarter each: kelly green feather print fabric (fabric C), similar muted yellow print fabric (fabric D), similar muted red print fabric (fabric E)

One 44″ × 44″ square batting

One 44″ × 44″ square backing fabric

White quilting thread

Green quilting thread

DIRECTIONS

1. It is best to choose nondirectional fabrics for this project. If you decide to use directional fabrics, consider how it will look to have the background and/or the parts of the turtle in fabrics going in different directions.

2. Mark and cut all the pieces for the five turtle blocks. In the case of curved piecing it is especially important to mark and cut the seam allowance around the entire shape accurately. One quarter of the Drunkard's Path pattern (which makes the turtle's body) is made up of two shapes. These two shapes are joined to form a square. Four small squares are then joined to make the full Drunkard's Path block or, in this case, the turtle block. Instead of labeling the shapes used in the turtle block by letter or number, we will give them names. The turtle block shapes are the pie shape (which has a rounded, convex curve), the L shape (which has an inward-turning, concave curve), the turtle head, and the tail. You will need:
   Pie shape: 10 in fabric A, 10 in fabric B
   L shape: 10 in fabric A, 10 in fabric B
   Turtle head: 5 in fabric B
   Turtle tail: 5 in fabric B
3. Be sure to clip the inward-turning concave curves on all of the L shapes. Clips should be perpendicular to the fabric edge and should go up to, but not into, the marked sewing line.
4. Mark and cut four large blocks from fabric A.
5. Mark and cut out the grass blades, stems, and flowers. You need not have an exact number of grass blades, stems, and flowers. Make as many as you feel will look appealing with the print fabrics you have chosen, or eliminate these additions to the border entirely if you prefer. Roughly, you will need:
   12 short grass blades from fabric A
   12 short grass blades from fabric C
   6 long grass blades from fabric A
   6 long grass blades from fabric C
   4 short grass blades from fabric D
   2 stems from fabric A
   5 flowers from fabric E
6. Remember to clip the inward-turning or concave curves of the grass blades.
7. Mark and cut out the four small borders from fabric A. Each should be 4½" × 28". There will be some excess border fabric left over after the borders are joined, which should be trimmed.
8. Mark and cut the four large borders from the solid yellow fabric. Two should be 6" × 40". Two should be 6" × 46". There will be some excess border fabric left over after the borders are joined, which should be trimmed.
9. Mark and cut the four binding strips from fabric A. Each should be 3" × 46". There will be some excess binding fabric left over after the binding is joined to the quilt.
10. Begin sewing the turtle blocks. First sew all of the pie shapes to an L shape. All of the pie shapes in fabric A should be sewn to an L shape

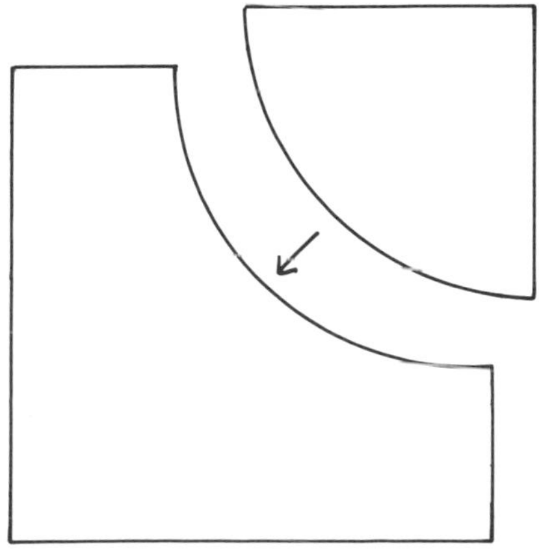

A pie shape is joined to an "L" shape.

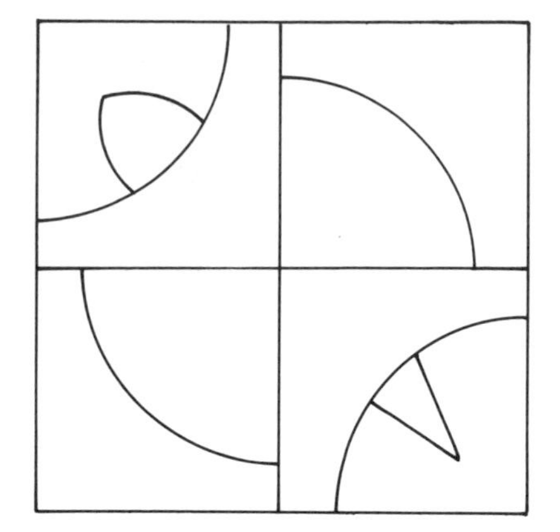
Completed turtle block.

in fabric B. All of the pie shapes in fabric B should be sewn to an L shape in fabric A. Remember to sew the pie shapes to the L shapes from the center out, not from edge to edge. That is, pin the pie shape and the L shape together and sew from the center of your seam line to the end where the two raw fabric edges of the shapes meet. Then turn the half-sewn pieces over and complete the sewing of the seam from the center out on the other side. When you finish, you should have twenty small squares.

11. Join your twenty small squares into five large turtle squares, using the piecing diagram as a guide. Then appliqué one head and one tail to each turtle and iron the finished turtle blocks.

12. Join the turtle blocks into a unit of nine blocks, with the plain fabric A background blocks in between the pieced squares. Iron the pieced nine-block unit.

13. Join a small fabric A border to the top and bottom of the pieced nine-block unit. Trim the excess border. Join the remaining two small fabric A borders to the left and right of the nine-block unit and iron.

14. Join the two shorter yellow border strips to the top and bottom of the pieced nine-block unit. Trim the excess border. Join the remaining two large yellow border strips to the left and right of the pieced nine-block unit. Trim the excess border fabric and iron the project.

15. Turn under and appliqué all of the grass blades, stems, and flowers, using the project photo in the color section as a general guide.

16. Lay out the backing fabric right side down, center the batting on top of this, and center over these the pieced and appliquéd wall hanging top right side up. Baste and quilt the project, using the project photograph as a guide. Note that the inner section of the design is quilted in green thread, while the borders are quilted in white. You will need the circular templates for quilting in the turtles' shells and the small turtle template for quilting the borders.

17. Trim the excess batting and backing fabric. Bind the project, using the four fabric A binding strips.

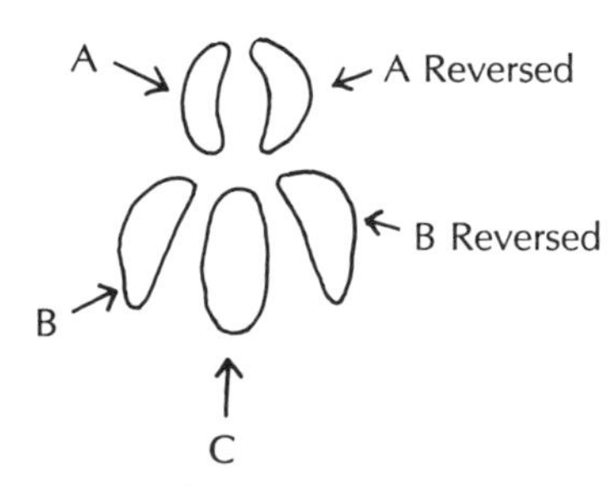

Iris construction.

Note

1. Jonathan Holstein, *The Pieced Quilt: An American Design Tradition* (Boston: Little, Brown and Company, 1973), p. 49.

Fabric Inspirations

11

As quilters, fabric is our most important tool. It can also be our greatest inspiration. To be inspired by the very medium with which we work is somewhat unusual in the arts. It lends our designs a quality of directness. Consider the observation of Henri Matisse, who, in speaking of his own expressive paper cutouts, observed: "The cut-out paper allows me to draw in color. It is a simplification. Instead of drawing an outline and filling in the color—in which case one modified the other—I am drawing directly in color. . . ." Like Matisse, quilters are engaged in "drawing with scissors."[1] When we allow ourselves to be inspired by pure fabric, the results can be truly amazing.

Being open to working in new ways with fabric often means discarding some of our preconceptions. Allowing oneself to waste some fabric is a challenge for some quilters. Learning to isolate print motifs and use them innovatively is another. How can you set about the task of encouraging your own fabric inspirations? Try following one of the paths suggested below. We are all moved by a special print or fabric color at times. The potential for growth lies in what we do with that response.

PUTTING FABRIC INSPIRATION TO WORK

One method for putting a fabric inspiration to work is to extrapolate on a particular motif. Think of ways to isolate the motif by cutting it apart from its background and repositioning it in a new design setting. Does the motif lend itself to being cut out in the shape of a square, a triangle, or some other shape? Once you have decided on a basic shape for your motif cutouts, combine the same shape in different ways and different sizes to create your own design. Position the shapes so that they have a different orientation—up, down, right, or left—in different parts of the design. If you are using triangles to isolate the motif, include triangles of

A wide fabric range featuring small, medium, and large prints, as well as different textures and characteristics from soft to metallic.

different sizes from colors used in the original fabric. Repeat the motif to achieve a sense of rhythm and movement in your design.

Another method is to combine fabric motif cutouts with appliqué versions of the same image. Design motifs such as animals, flowers, or leaves may be cut out from a length of fabric and turned under in broderie perse style. At one time whole quilts were made using the broderie perse technique in which an expensive colored chintz was used—its flowers, animals, and other images cut out, turned under, and appliquéd to a (usually) solid white background in a pleasing design. The technique made the most of costly and, in some cases, illegally imported exotic fabrics. Contemporary quilters more often use broderie perse as a jumping-off point for their own unique designs that combine traditional appliqués with printed fabric motifs. The result can be an appealing mix of soft tradition and sharp realism.

Yet another approach is to experiment with a wide variety of disparate fabrics, especially those from other countries. A consistently Western fabric collection can be limiting. Experiment with printed and painted cottons from Africa, block prints from India, yukata from Japan, batik from Indonesia, and other fine fabrics from different parts of the world. (For fine foreign fabrics, see International Fabric Collection and Kasuri Dyeworks listed in Sources at the back of the book.) Cloth from other countries can help revitalize your creative vision. A tropical scene may be inspired by fabrics from regions where warmth and sunlight abound. A scene depicting a specific animal—the endangered African elephant, for instance—may be given a subtle flair by the use of hand-dyed African cottons. What about a quilt with a theme of world peace that uses fabrics from many countries?

Trading fabrics is a great way to broaden your creative inspiration and get to know other quilters. Quilter Trudy Billingsley tells us: "I enjoy using other people's fabrics; it is fun when they look at my finished quilt and say, "I remember that piece." One's fabric stocks can become quite limiting. If you use a fabric selection in one quilt and then in another and another, they all take on a sameness. It really is necessary to refresh your fabric stock."[2]

Why not instigate a fabric trade with quilters from other countries through the "pen-pal" section of your favorite quilt magazine? If you belong to a guild, a sister guild may become an outlet for exotic fabric options. All too often we get in a fabric-collecting rut. We tease ourselves about being "fabriholics"—the worst part of fabriholism is that each of us tends to collect similar prints and colors. We are drawn to the same things again and again. To break out of that rut, deliberately try adding some out-of-character fabrics to your collection. Try using a few prints that seem weird or ugly at first glance. A small amount of them in your design may accentuate what you especially like about your usual fabrics. Also, be sure to experiment with using the wrong side of fabrics. The wrong side of a fabric print often features a muted motif that provides the perfect subtle effect.

When allowing fabric to guide your creativity, you need to analyze cloth patterns more closely. We have a tendency to glance at fabric without taking in all that it has to offer. Next time you visit a fabric store or fabric vendors at a quilt show, try focusing on patterns in the fabric as individual design elements. See all that the fabric has to offer, not just the

Peace Cranes, by the author. This wall hanging features cloth origami cranes made from Japanese block print fabrics.

Veg-Star-Bles, by Judy Mathieson, makes the most of an unusual fabric print.

tiger in the jungle pattern, but the *leafy green background* as well. See the pattern, not just as motif on background, but as pattern on pattern. Ask yourself, What design elements are used? What geometric shapes do the motifs remind me of? What shapes would complement those of the fabric motif?

To help you begin seeing the hidden properties of pattern, try cutting out a 6″ square from black oaktag or construction paper. Out of the center of it, cut a 4″ square. Now you have a 2″ black frame around a 4″ square hole for viewing fabrics. Hold your viewing square up to the same pattern in different positions. What new elements within the design leap to view with this method that were hidden before? By investigating the full possibilities of the medium of fabric, we can stretch our creative limits further than ever before.

PEONIES WALL QUILT

DIFFICULTY LEVEL: Easy

FINISHED SIZE: 42″ × 42″

About the Project. Line, form, and space are the basic design tools with which the quilter works. This project combines square form and fluid line in a seemingly random pattern. A closer look, however, shows an underlying structure of elements—printed flower blocks, solid squares, and squares made up of triangles—repeated on the diagonals. The juxtaposition of solid and linear-print fabric provides added interest.

The flowers are cut from two Japanese-style fabrics called Naomi prints. (See International Fabric Collection listed in Sources.) One of the fabrics depicts large flowers that fill a 5″ × 5″ square block; the other features smaller flowers that fill a triangle made by folding a 5″ × 5″ square in half on the diagonal. The first fabric features larger flowers that filled the square completely. The flowers from the second fabric are in the same color range as the first, but are smaller in size, which suggested the use of two sizes of triangles. You will want to substitute fabric motifs of your own choosing. You may want to use a similar oriental print, or a fabric that features an entirely different cultural statement, but the size of the motifs will need to be in the range discussed previously, or they may not work as well with squares and triangles of the sizes indicated in the project. A fine variation for this project would be to paint or print your own flowers, using fabric paints.

Cutting out the flowers means taking them from wherever they appear in the fabric, leaving gaping holes, a wasteful process that any quilter abhors. In this case, however, a little waste produces a bold flowered effect. You can cut some of the binding strips from the remaining cut-up "waste" fabric or you can set aside the extra for later strip-pieced projects. The wide black borders give the design emphasis. The printed fabric binding helps to lighten up those borders. Black is a powerful color and a little goes a long way.

MATERIALS

¾ yard printed "peony" fabric from which are to be cut ten red and magenta flower squares

¾ yard printed "peony" fabric from which are to be cut six red and gold flower triangles (Optional: additional ½ yard "peony" fabric from which 3″ strips may be cut to make four 3″ wide × 48″ long binding strips, or cut strips from the leftover flower print fabrics to make the binding)

½ yard gold

¼ yard each: black, magenta, red, royal blue, and turquoise

Scraps of each: green, light pink, and medium pink

One 45″ × 45″ square batting
One 45″ × 45″ square backing fabric
1 yard solid black fabric for border

DIRECTIONS

1. On the gold fabric, mark one 10″ × 10″ square. Add a ⅜″ seam allowance all the way around to yield a 10¾″ × 10¾″ square to cut out. Cut out the gold square for the center.
2. Photocopy or trace the pattern pieces for the large and small triangle and the square. Cut them out to make templates. Note that the seam allowance is included for these templates. Using the templates, cut out ten flower squares and six flower triangles, positioning the template directly over the center of each flower so that as much of the flower as possible is included.
3. Using the square template, mark and cut the following squares: two magenta, one red, three royal blue, one turquoise, and two gold. Cut down the square template and using the smaller square as a guide, mark the seam allowance on all cut-out squares.
4. Using the larger of the two triangle templates, mark and cut the following triangles: two black, four magenta, four red, two royal blue, five turquoise, and one gold. Cut down the template and mark the seam allowance on the large cut-out triangles.
5. Using the smaller of the two triangle templates, mark and cut four small triangles: one magenta, one red, one royal blue, and one turquoise. Cut down the template to mark the seam allowance on these smaller triangles.
6. Photocopy or trace the pattern to make a template for the four center leaves. Mark and cut out the leaves from green fabric. Generally, when doing appliqué, you turn under the appliqué shapes as you sew them in place. For this center block, however, you may find it easier to turn under all of the component parts first, pin them in place, and then sew. Turn under the outer edge of the leaves, using matching thread.
7. Photocopy or trace the patterns for the petals. Mark and cut out the following: Petal A: 11 magenta; Petal B: 12 medium pink; Petal C: 3 magenta, 4 medium pink, 14 light pink; Petal D: 11 magenta. Turn under the outer edge of all petals, using matching thread.
8. Position the leaves and petals of the center peony block, using the piecing diagram as a guide. Position first the leaves, then the outermost ring of petals, then the inner rings, and finally the center. Pin all of the shapes in place to make the flower, and appliqué. Iron the finished center block and set aside.
9. Join the two sets of small triangles to make large triangles. Join the small red and the small blue triangle along one short side. Join the

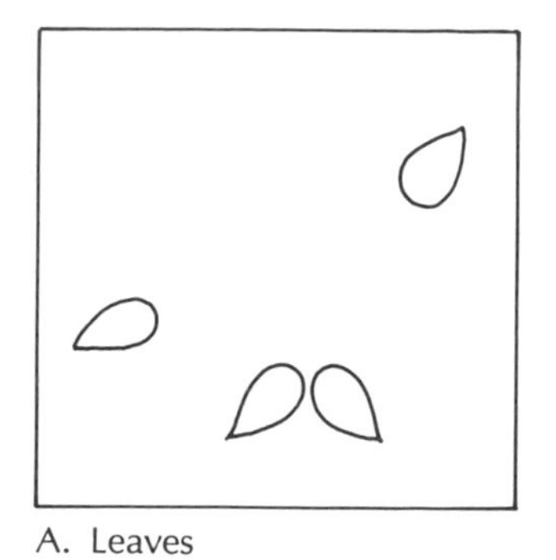

A. Leaves

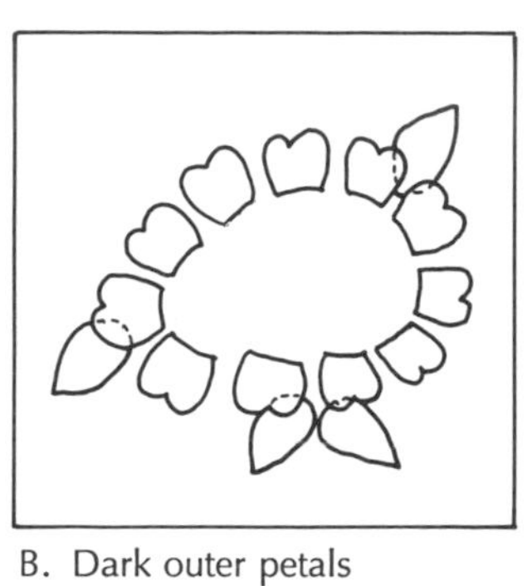

B. Dark outer petals

C. Medium inner petals

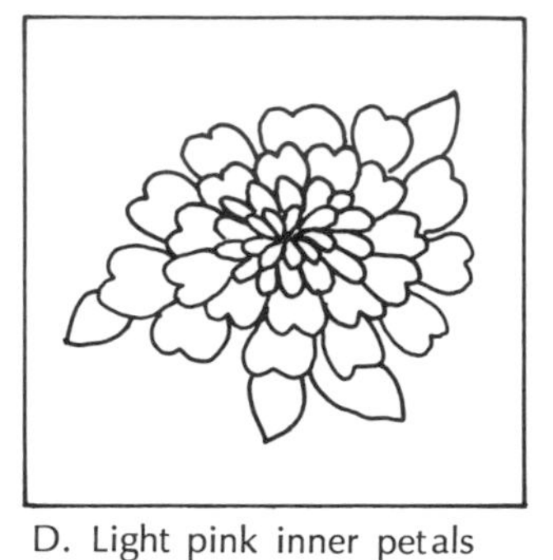

D. Light pink inner petals and medium center petals

Center flower diagram.

small turquoise and small magenta triangles along one short side. Iron and set aside. Each of these may now be treated as you would a large triangle.

10. Join the remaining large triangles to make squares, using the color photograph as a guide. Iron and set aside.

11. Lay out all of the squares in the proper sewing order. Use the project photo in the color section and the piecing diagram as guides. In the

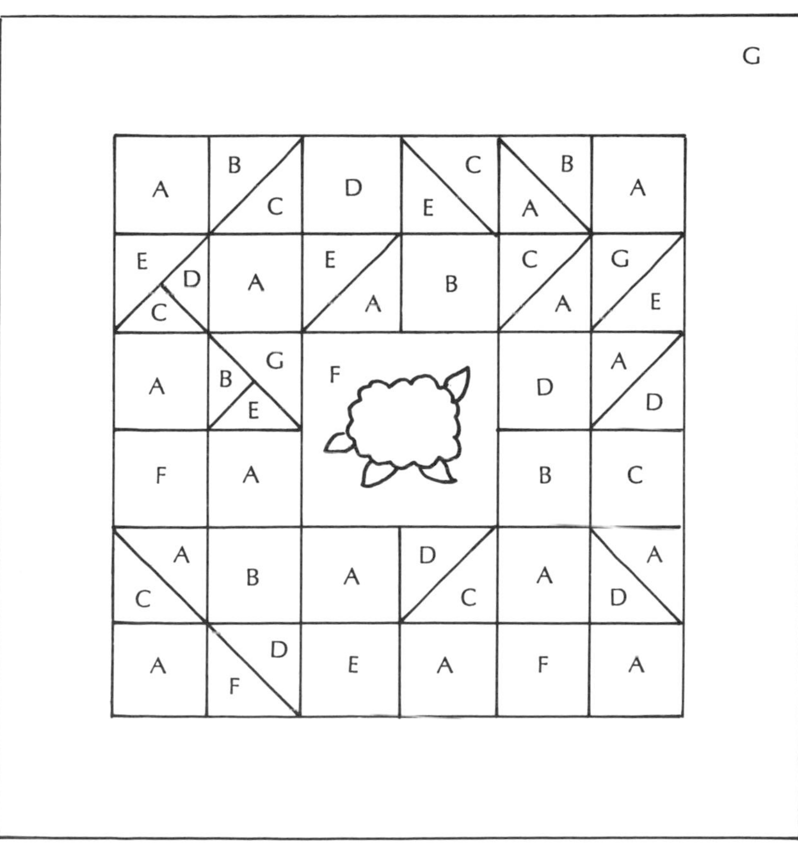

Peonies piecing diagram. Fabric A = print fabric, fabric B = royal blue, fabric C = turquoise, fabric D = magenta, fabric E = red, fabric F = gold, and fabric G = black.

diagram, fabric A refers to any print fabric you are using. The remaining fabrics used are solid colors. Sew the squares together, being careful to match seams as you go. Sew the squares together in groups of four, rather than sewing them in strips. Then join together the groups of four, including the large center square. Iron the sewn block unit.

12. Cut two 44″ × 7″ border strips and two 33″ × 7″ border strips from black fabric. Join the two short border strips to the top and bottom of the sewn squares patchwork. Trim the excess border fabric. Then sew one long border strip to each of the remaining sides to form the complete border. Trim the excess border fabric; iron.

13. Lay out the backing fabric right side down, center the batting on top of this, and center on these the pieced and appliquéd wall hanging top right side up. Baste and quilt the project, using the project photograph as a guide.

14. Trim the excess batting and backing fabric. Bind the project, using four 3″ × 48″ binding strips cut from the "peony" fabric—either from a length of uncut fabric, or from the "waste" fabric cut into short strips and sewn together to make longer ones.

Notes

1. Henri Matisse, quoted in *The Cut-outs of Henri Matisse* by John Elderfield (New York: George Braziller, 1978), p. 22.

2. Trudy Billingsley, quoted in *Piece by Piece: The Complete Book of Quiltmaking* by Dianne Finnegan (London: Blandford Books, 1991), p. 49.

12

Technique-Inspired Design

We live in an exciting time in which the sewing techniques of cultures from all around the world are accessible. The different ways in which one idea may be presented in the quilter's medium are almost endless. Perhaps that diversity plays a part in the widespread appeal of quilt-making.

Fish on Coral/Hukilau, by Elizabeth Akana.

Hmong patchwork, made by a needleworker at a refugee camp in Laos.

A WORLDLY APPROACH

The cultures of the world have given us an immense storehouse of fabric techniques upon which to draw. Many quilters enjoy borrowing from the colorful molas of Panama, the distinctive mosaic style of Polynesian tifaifai, as well as the delicate relief of Italian trapunto. Other inspiring techniques from around the world include Japanese sashiko, broderie perse, and intricate Hmong patchwork.

Our own country is the birthplace of a wide variety of techniques and styles, as well as being home to all the wonderful styles brought to this nation by people from other cultures.

PUTTING TECHNIQUE TO WORK

Before designing your next quilt, take the time to become familiar with some different sewing techniques from other parts of the world. The motifs associated with techniques from far-away places are inspiring in themselves. But that is another story. Try focusing primarily on the construction methods and ways they can be adapted to your own work to broaden your personal style. See if you cannot become inspired to take your self-expression into new avenues by exploring one or more tech-

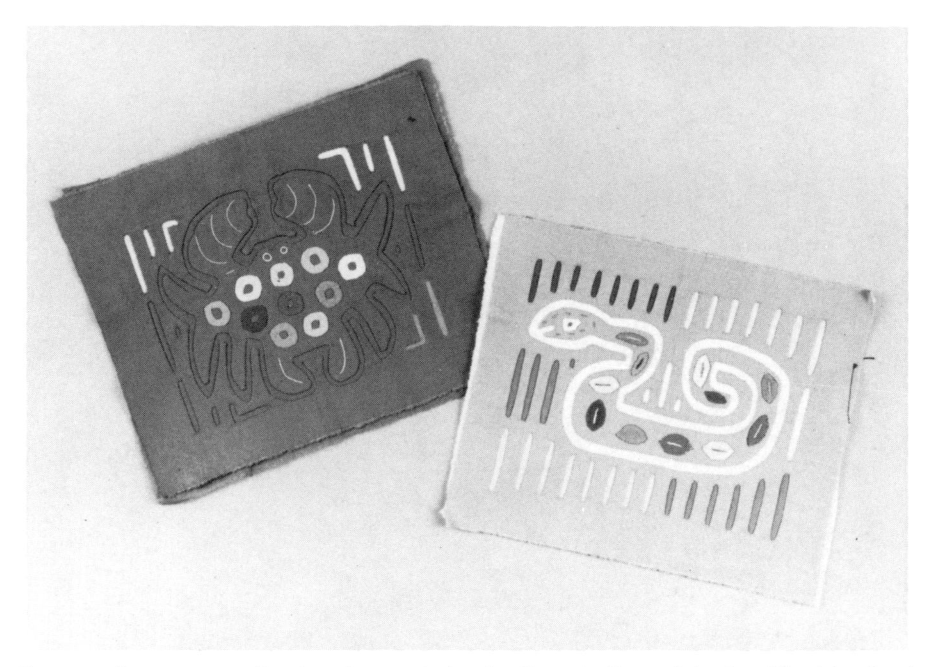

Two small reverse appliqué molas made by the Cuna Indians of the San Blas Islands of Panama.

niques from around the world. Be like the painter who practices working in different mediums in order to be able to draw on the right technique at the right time. To a painter, a misty seascape might be better portrayed in transparent watercolor than in opaque gouache or acrylic. Similarly, a subject of *your* choosing can benefit from the use of a different quilting technique.

It is one thing to look at, say, a mola and feel inspired by it. It is yet another thing to learn the method of constructing molas. A further challenge is required in applying the techniques of mola construction to your own unique designs. How do you go about making use of what different quilting techniques have to offer? Let's take a look at some examples.

The Cuna Indians of Panama design and sew molas—a kind of layered fabric picture—as part of their traditional apparel. On first glance, the mola appears to be done in reverse appliqué only. It is actually a construction of reverse, regular, and layered appliqué. It is built up from the back as well as from the front. Such an approach to our own quilts, in which reverse and layered appliqué are combined, can provide exciting results. The mola style is intricate, but not necessarily geometrically precise—wherein lies much of its appeal.

Try designing "mola-style." Choose a simple subject, a flower or animal, for instance. Using colored paper, and with one background sheet as a foundation, practice creating a layered design. Place one cut out shape on top of another. Work freehand. Next, try an echo effect in which the same basic shape is cut out three times, each time in a different color and each time a little larger than the one before. Place the three

The Dance of the Salamanders, a contemporary mola made by Louise Young. Photograph courtesy of the artist.

shapes one on top of the other so that the edge of each extends a little beyond the smaller one in front of it. The result is an "echo" effect. Try adding one or two motifs in reverse appliqué. You might do this by adding a block with a cutout in the center. Be flexible. Let your subject and its background, including landscape elements, change as you go. If your finished design appeals to you, translate it into fabric (with an extra seam allowance for turning under) and layer in the same way as you did the paper version.

Trapunto or stuffed quilting was once popular in Italy. Elements of stuffed quilting add emphasis to an otherwise flat design. The repetition of channel quilting can be especially pleasing. In channel quilting, lines of contour quilting repeat, each stuffed with a single strand of yarn. The effect can be used to enhance waves, clouds, or other natural elements.

Try applying a similar technique in making a simple landscape. Use fairly large expanses of colored fabric for land masses, sky, or bodies of water. Avoid detail. Then enhance the large, plain natural forms with trapunto. Use curved, repeating lines of quilting for the ridges on a hill. Fill the areas between the quilting lines with loose batting. Or, if the channels between the quilting lines are narrow, run a strand or two of yarn between them with a blunt tapestry needle. Use widening circles of quilting to simulate the ripples on a pond. Quilt in waves for an ocean scene. The trapunto will provide detail to the plain shapes and heighten interest in your design.

Broderie perse is the art of cutting out printed fabric motifs, turning them under at the edges, and applying them to a background. This technique developed in Europe about the time printed chintz fabric from India began to be exported on a large scale. The import of exotic printed chintz was suppressed by European governments to keep indigenous textile production alive and well. Nonetheless, the colorful fabrics made their clandestine way into France and England and other nations. Women responded by cutting out the leaves, animals, flowers, and other figures in a piece of chintz and reapplying them to a (usually) white background fabric to produce a bed covering. The broderie perse technique was popular because it squeezed the most use out of a single piece of costly printed fabric.

We can use the technique of broderie perse to add interest to pictorial and other designs. Try mixing regular appliqué motifs with broderie perse cutouts. A vase of flowers in which traditional appliqué flowers are mixed with ones done in broderie perse style has a quirky, fun feel to it. Or cut out a printed fabric image of your favorite animal. Place it in the foreground of a simple landscape—just earth and sky. Add a couple of simple two-dimensional appliqué animals to the mid-ground of your design. Regular appliqué is better for these. They are less detailed to the eye because they are farther away from the viewer. The result can be charming and simple.

We know it is important to explore all the design possibilities of the fabric we use. It is just as important to be open to using less orthodox methods of fabric construction. There is nothing wrong with traditional piecing and appliqué techniques. But how much more rewarding to investigate the wide variety of options that exist.

Before tackling a construction method that is new to you, be sure to read all you can about it. There are many books currently available that focus on individual styles from different countries. Some of them are listed in Recommended Reading. For an overview of many techniques from other cultures, see *Quilting the World Over*, by the author, also listed in Recommended Reading.

RIGHT AT HOME

Our own quilting heritage also provides a multitude of technique options. U.S. quilters can draw upon a wide variety of indigenous quilting styles such as crazy patchwork, Amish quilting and color use, and Seminole strip-piecing. In addition, Hawaiian quilting offers a distinctive approach to design that is part of our country's heritage.

In the early nineteenth century, a group of missionaries sailed from Boston to Hawaii. Fortunately for quilters, their wives traveled with them, and it was these women who first introduced basic patchwork to the women of Hawaii. Soon after, it is suspected that Pennsylvania Dutch missionaries shared their own appliqué style with the islanders as well. The appliqué style of the Pennsylvania Dutch featured small cut paper snowflake-style appliqués. These were turned under and appliquéd to individual fabric squares to produce a block quilt, usually one appliqué to a block. Hawaiians took this idea, expanded upon it (literally), and made it distinctively different.

Traditional Hawaiian quilts feature a single large fabric motif cut in a snowflake-style in an extremely intricate pattern and appliquéd to a full-quilt-size background. A similarly cut-out border may also be added. The result is one of almost incredible variation and precision. The approach holds special appeal for anyone seeking a new design method. The paper snowflake approach ensures geometric precision and a pleasing symmetry. The style also offers a method for presenting your own favorite motifs in a new way. Hawaiian quilts are distinctively Hawaiian not only because they feature an indigenous technique, but because they portray the plants and animals of the quiltmaker's beautiful island home in a unique design.

Quilters who live in places other than Hawaii can rely on their own environments to provide design motifs. Hawaiian-style quilting gives us a special way in which to portray nature. It also encourages us to observe our natural world closely. What is truly exciting about any art form is not just that it allows us to produce an appealing product or even that the process of making that product is enjoyable, although for quilters usually both of these are true. One of the demands of art is that we become careful observers.

Professional artists have developed their sense of seeing so that they really see the world around them most of the time. The rest of us have to rely on glimpses of our world, in between going to work at the office, making dinner, tying a child's shoelace, and taking the dog for a walk. As amateur or semiprofessional fabric artists, we may not feel we have the luxury of being full-time observers. Our artistic endeavors become all the more important. They change and enhance our lives. They can also help us learn to cherish our fragile natural world—a necessary endeavor if we are to preserve its beauty and diversity for future generations. Perhaps John Ruskin best expressed this idea when he observed: "The greatest thing a human soul ever does in this world is to see something, and tell what it saw in a plain way. Hundreds of people can talk for one who can think, but thousands can think for one who can see. To see clearly is poetry, prophecy, and religion, all in one."[1]

Whatever quilting technique you choose to work in, let it stimulate your ability to see and appreciate your surroundings. If you decide on Hawaiian quilting, try some of the ideas that follow to enhance your appreciation of the natural world all around you.

HAWAIIAN RAIN FOREST WALL QUILT

DIFFICULTY LEVEL: Moderate

FINISHED SIZE: 30″ × 30″

About the Project. Although you may not live in a lush, tropical region, your own natural surroundings offer a wealth of motifs for Hawaiian quilting. Try using the basic project directions provided here with your own design. Take a walk outdoors and look for small natural forms to incorporate into your pattern. Collect a number of them—leaves, seeds, flowers, brambles, twigs—anything that interests you. Don't eliminate items to consider for your design until you have had a chance to return home and lay them all out. Try drawing them individually to gain a fuller appreciation of their unique qualities—their angles, smooth edges, or fuzzy surfaces. Then, when you are ready, make some simple small-scale drawings incorporating the elements you have chosen to include. You may need to make more than a few drawings before you are satisfied with the result.

From your drawings, work out a small-scale simplified version of your design. Fold the paper in eighths or fourths and cut it out. Then do a full-size version in paper. You can use large sheets of lightweight sketch paper taped together. Even a sheet of newspaper will do, although you will need to be careful not to transfer newsprint from your hands to your fabric. To transfer your full-size version to fabric, fold the cut paper template into eighths. Then fold the fabric into eighths, place the folded paper template on top of the folded fabric and trace. Be sure to leave an extra ⅛″ to ¼″ seam allowance as you go along. You may find it useful to mark both sewing line and seam allowance. Then cut out the fabric version. When your fabric is opened, it will equal the paper version plus seam allowance.

Two gadgets are particularly helpful with this project. One is a two-pencil marking device for appliqué. A piece of plastic holds the pencils securely at exactly ¼″ apart at both top and bottom, ensuring even turning-under lines for precise appliqué. The other item is a pair of lightweight, black nylon, razor-sharp Gingher™ scissors. They cut through many layers of fabric, which is what you need when cutting out fabric in paper snowflake style, and are relatively inexpensive. Both are available from many quilt suppliers, including Cabin Fever Calicoes, listed in Sources.

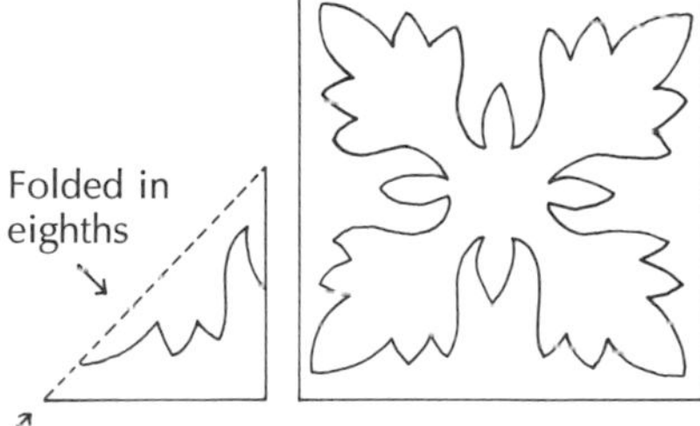

Folded fabric triangle with appliqué template positioned on it for marking and cutting.

MATERIALS

2–3 yards* solid magenta fabric
36″ × 36″ square muslin

*See directions for specific fabric requirements.

40″ × 40″ square batting
40″ × 40″ square backing fabric
White quilting thread

DIRECTIONS

1. This design is in two parts—a center motif and a decorated border. It is possible to cut both the center motif and the border from the same fabric square. But it requires careful planning and cutting. If you are new to Hawaiian-style quilting or appliqué in general, you may want to follow the directions for tracing and cutting the center motif and border from two separate same-size squares of fabric. In this case, you will need about an extra yard of magenta fabric. This will leave a significant amount of waste but will ensure good results. If you are more experienced, trace and cut both the center motif and the border from the same square as described below, but be attentive to places where there may be shared cutting lines between the center motif and border.
2. Begin with the center motif. Trace the pattern pieces for the center motif onto tracing paper. Cut them out and tape them together to make a single tracing paper template. Use this tracing paper template as your pattern, or make a firmer template from heavier paper. Follow the same procedure for making the border template.
3. Cut out a 36″ × 36″ square from the magenta fabric. Fold the magenta fabric square three times (into eighths) to get a triangle. Line up the base point of the center motif template with the base point of your fabric triangle. Position the border template at the opposite end of the fabric triangle from the base point. Mark the design on the fabric triangle. Only the sewing or fold line for the appliqué is indicated by the template so you will need to add a consistent ¼″ for turning under as you go.
4. With the fabric triangle still folded, cut out the marked appliqué for the center motif and the border. Open them out. At this point, you will have only one-eighth of your appliqué pattern of each marked with a fold line. Draw in the fold line on the rest of the two appliqués.
5. Clip all concave (inward-turning) curves on the center motif appliqué and border appliqué. Fold the two appliqués back up into eighths as they were when you cut them and iron. Then open them out again and set aside.
6. Fold the muslin background square into eighths and iron. Open it out again. Position the center motif and the border on the background fabric, using the ironed fold marks as a guide. Match the center point of the center motif to the center point of the muslin background. Position the border around the outside of the center motif; be sure it lies flat. Pin both appliqués in place, then baste the design tightly to avoid having them shift as you sew.

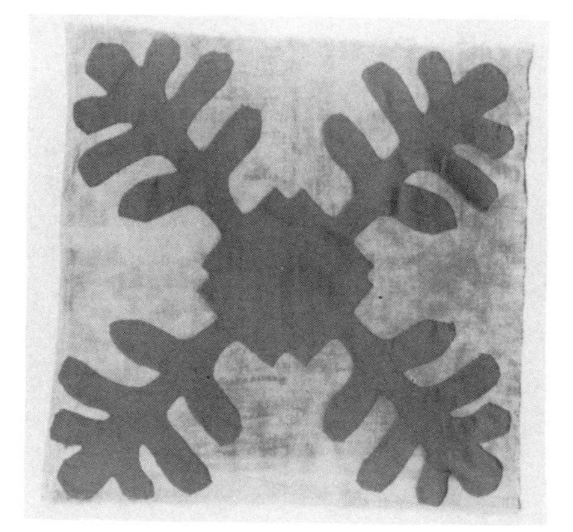

Antique block appliqué similar to that believed to have been introduced in Hawaii by Pennsylvania Dutch missionaries in the nineteenth century.

7. Sew the appliqués in place, turning under the raw edge of each appliqué as you go. Sew the center motif first, then the border. When you get to the border, be sure not to sew the outer edge that is even with the background fabric edge—just sew the inner edge that will show as part of the design. When the appliqués are sewn in place, remove any basting stitches and iron.
8. Lay out the backing fabric right side down, center the batting on top of this, and center on these the appliquéd wall hanging top right side up. Baste and quilt the project in echo quilting style, using the project photo in the color section as a guide. Hawaiian quilters traditionally do not mark their quilting stitches. They quilt freehand leaving only about ¼″ to ½″ between their lines of echo quilting.
9. There will be an excess of about 2″ to 3″ on each side of the quilted project. You will need to trim this excess plus the excess batting and backing fabric. Then, cut four binding strips from the remaining magenta fabric, each 3″ × 36″. Bind the project, using the four magenta binding strips.

Note

1. John Ruskin, quoted in *Modern Painters,* edited by David Barrie (New York: Alfred A. Knopf, 1987), p. 404.

Land and Landscapes

Do you ever wish that someone had given you a dollar for each time you had read the phrase "patchwork hills?" It is a worn-out cliché, but the saying tells us something. Landscape design is ideally suited to quilting. People who are not even quilters are reminded of patchwork upon looking at a scenic vista.

Modern people's experience of the land is colored by technology and an ever-burgeoning human population. Our natural world has shrunk pitifully. We must rely on little pockets of unspoiled wilderness to satisfy our craving for the expansive beauty of nature. On the other hand, technology has granted us some marvels, too. We have pictures of our world as seen from outer space. Many of us observe the land regularly from an airplane window. More people than ever can enjoy hiking to breathtaking vantage points. These things influence how we observe the land around us.

The idea of being transported by the beauty of nature is a relatively new idea in Western thought. The poet Petrarch is thought to be the first European to climb a mountain for the sake of the view. That was in the fourteenth century. So it is hardly surprising that in Western art, the landscape is a fairly young art form. Glimpses of landscapes exist in many earlier paintings, but as background rather than main subject. Not until later, during the sixteenth century, did landscape begin to be considered more generally as a subject in its own right.

Today, we live in a time when it is perfectly acceptable to portray images of land and sky as the main subject. We unquestionably regard landscapes as interesting enough in themselves to hold the viewer's attention. Whether for good or not, we have subdued the earth. Portraits of nature seldom have the awesome power to hold our attention through

Muir Woods, a landscape by the author.

fear. Gone are the days of the Romantic artists when a painter might (as Joseph Turner did) lash himself to the mast of a ship in a storm in order to better observe the dramatic effects of nature.

Many people today turn to landscape art for its peaceful quality. Given our contemporary need to balance the demands of family, work, and personal accomplishment, many individuals find a haven of calm in landscapes real and pictured. To them there is contentment in the beautiful vista that can be returned to over and over, in the image of a quiet pine forest, in the vision of an endless blue sky.

Save Us, by Jane Nettleton. An African landscape featuring endangered elephants. Photograph courtesy of Buzzard Studios.

LANDSCAPE DESIGN TECHNIQUES

A number of fabric techniques lend themselves to quilted landscape design. Strip-piecing is ideal for reproducing images of water and sky. Often a sunset produces streaks of color in the sky that vary slightly in shade. Strip-piecing allows for a gentle gradation of color from light to dark, or from one hue to another. Strip-piecing is also used by many quilters as a means for producing expanses of sky or water against which to portray figures. The repetition of strips allows for a subtle backdrop that is not so complex as to steal interest away from the main part of a design.

Another technique that is especially useful in designing fabric landscapes is fabric layering. Layering reflects a spontaneous approach in which fabric shapes are cut without a pattern and positioned on a background fabric one on top of the other. The edge of each one is extended a little beyond that of the shape before it. The shapes are then turned under and appliquéd. The result is an "echo" effect, often suggestive of hills beyond hills, or of foreground shapes that recede into the distance.

Layering is a good technique for reproducing realistic landscape designs. Many actual landscapes almost appear to be constructed of layers of light and dark. In fabric layering, colors can be used to suggest distance. Images become diffused the farther we are positioned from them. Images of land formations that are most distant should be cut from light-color fabrics. For those nearer the foreground, darker colors may be used. The result is the strong sense of depth every landscape needs. Layers themselves also enhance the visual illusion of depth. The same image repeated in three layers, with the edge of each extending slightly beyond the smaller one before it, adds dramatically to the sense of distance in a design.

The technique of contour quilting is particularly suited to landscape design. Row upon row of quilting that follows the outline of hills or shrubs can be especially effective. The repetition is pleasing from a purely aesthetic standpoint and the relief effect produced by the quilting lines enhances the sense of depth.

ON YOUR OWN

If you are new to landscape quilting, you may want to plan your own landscape design on paper first. If possible, though, cut and sew the elements of your design spontaneously as you go. Have a clear image in your mind, or in the form of a simple sketch, of the visual elements that are to make up your landscape. Keep it simple. An uncluttered background and a few hills or trees are sufficient to produce a pleasing first design. As you gain experience, you can introduce more complicated elements into your work. But for now, keep to basics to avoid getting discouraged.

Before you begin your own landscape design, you will need to make some decisions about its basic structure. Will your landscape be in the form of a rectangle, square, or some other shape? Remember, each shape has its own thrust. A horizontal landscape will send the eye from right to left. If you want to emphasize the contours of land in a wide area, this might be an effective choice. In a vertical rectangle, the eye will travel up and down. If you want to suggest the height of towering trees, this might be a good idea. A square structure tends to create a static image in which the eye does not travel much at all. If you want to portray the calm and peacefulness of a particular scene, this might be the best option.

COMPOSITION

You will want to design your composition around a focal point. Like a poem, a painting, or a symphony, your landscape needs a subject or main theme. This is the focal point. Generally, one part of a landscape stands out slightly from the others. One tree is larger, one hill more jagged, one area of land enhanced by a ray of sun or a flock of birds. The focal point tells the viewer where to look first.

The focal point of your landscape should never fall in the exact center of the picture. Positioning it slightly to one side of both the horizontal and vertical midlines will give the best results. A focal point, however, needs support. Just as a main theme in a work of music is enhanced by supporting themes, so the focal point in your landscape will benefit from the inclusion of other compositional elements.

The composition of a design relies on a visual harmony created by the tension of the lines, masses, and spatial areas. Each exerts a pull of its own that must be balanced by a pull in the opposite direction by other design elements. A hill that slopes down from right to left causes the viewer's eye to travel. The eye moves down the line created by the outline of the hill. From there, it may run into another land mass and be encouraged to move elsewhere in the design. A careful designer creates a composition in which the eye is constantly encouraged to follow one

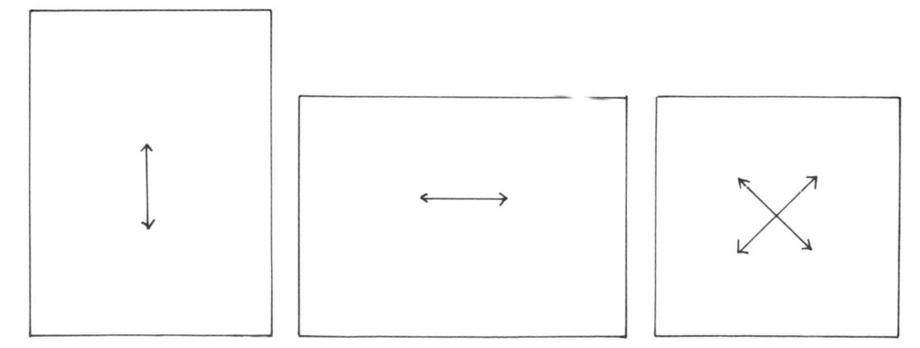

Different compositional structures each have their own directional movement.

line after another, to move all around the picture, yet always return to the focal point.

Logically, a landscape design is laid out from background to foreground. You will need to consider how you will divide the background in your design. A horizon line in the background gives the impression of distance and clearly delineates the sense of a landscape. If you are designing your own landscape for the first time, it might be well to concentrate on a simple background that includes a horizon line. If you do not already have a scene in mind, look at what nature has to offer where you live, or choose a scene from a postcard or photograph.

A single foundation fabric background can be designed in one of several ways. It can be made up of a single piece of fabric such as a tie-dyed fabric with interesting color gradations. It can also be made of two large rectangles of fabric that meet at the horizon line of your landscape. If you have some experience, one part of the background—the top or the bottom—may be made from strip-pieced fabrics to create a more interesting impression of sky, water, or land.

Never divide a background into two equal parts. Many things in nature are symmetrical, but a perfectly symmetrical background will appear unrealistic. Your landscape may be divided into two parts—just not equal ones. One appealing way to divide a landscape is 2:1—for instance, two units of sky to one unit of water or land. Likewise, visual elements throughout a landscape should not appear symmetrically balanced. A scene in which the elements are asymmetrically balanced is more appealing because it invites the eye to travel around the image.

Lake Scene, by Jo Diggs.

COLORS AND FABRICS

Once you have decided on the basic structure and composition of your design, you will need to choose fabrics and colors to work with. Selecting the right fabric for your scene is as important as creating the visual elements that make up the design. If you are just starting out, your inclination may be to work entirely in solids. This can be more difficult than it sounds. Prints complicate a design, but they also add appealing diversity. Also, the use of solid fabrics does not always lend itself to reproducing complex linear designs such as are found in forests, trees, and shrubs.

The easiest rule to follow when starting out is to mix your fabric palette. Use some solids plus prints in several different scales. Some prints are so understated that they almost look like solids. Try combining these with fabrics in solid colors, as well as a few prints with slightly larger motifs. Plan to use the fabrics with larger motifs in the foreground of your design and those with smaller motifs in the background. Avoid prints with very big, recognizable pictorial motifs, as these will distract the viewer's eye away from your landscape subject. Avoid other fabrics that do not blend well such as stripes or plaids. No one fabric should stand out from the rest. This does not mean, however, that the fabrics should all be the same style or intensity. Choose fabrics in as wide a range as your design will allow.

Color is an important factor in creating a sense of realism in a landscape. When choosing colors to represent distant visual elements, use tiny prints in the background, reserving the larger print fabrics with less subtle motifs for the foreground. Remember that the hills, trees, and other objects in the background of your landscape should appear lighter and more diffuse than those positioned toward the front.

Use intense colors for the foreground elements. This is your opportunity to put the value of contrast to work. Graphic artists often use the technique of portraying a scene as though it were shot with a camera past a highly detailed object right in front. For instance, a hill in the distance may be portrayed as if it were photographed past a tree branch in the foreground. The effect is to create a dramatic impression of depth. If you choose this approach, use intense colors full of contrast for the visual elements in the immediate foreground. The scale of prints used in the foreground should be the largest available in your palette. Save the tiny prints for more distant images.

The above guidelines should help as you try to translate your own visual impressions of nature. Study a variety of landscape paintings to get a feel for the ways in which focal point and linear perspective function in pictorial images of land, water, and sky. Then set about designing your own impression of the natural world around you whether it be wooded hills, foggy seascape, or breathtaking sunset.

ACROSS THE LAKE WALL QUILT

DIFFICULTY LEVEL: Easy

FINISHED SIZE: 20″ × 30″

About the Project. The idea for this small wall hanging came while on a special trip. The haunting beauty of silhouetted marsh grasses against a night sky is suggested through the use of dark earth tones. Strip-pieced water with wide bands to the foreground and narrow ones near the horizon line enhance the sense of distance. The marsh grasses to the foreground give the eye a point of reference and offer a further suggestion of depth.

This project calls for strip-piecing. Items you will need include a rotary cutter, wide quilter's ruler, and cutting mat. You will also need a sewing machine. Hand sewing is generally inappropriate for strip piecing. You can choose your own gradation of colors for the strip pieced water section. Be sure, however, to run the shades from darkest at the foreground to light at the horizon line to create a sense of distance.

MATERIALS

One 11″ × 11″ square black

½ yard black for marsh grasses and binding

Nine "fat" quarters water fabrics (you will need 11″-long strips. Use tiny prints and/or solids ranging from dark teal to light lavender)

Four "fat" quarters hill fabrics (Use tiny prints and/or solids ranging from dark to light green)

Two 5″ × 32″ gray borders

Two 5″ × 12″ gray borders

One 22″ × 32″ square batting

One 22″ × 32″ square backing fabric

Teal quilting thread

DIRECTIONS

1. Lay out all of your water fabric. To begin cutting, fold each length of fabric in half so that the two selvage edges are touching. One at a time, place the folded fabric lengths on the cutting mat with the folded edge at the top. Always cut in the same up-and-down direction on your mat. Line up the horizontal lines on the quilter's rule with the fold of the fabric. Trim the edge of the fabric to make it perfectly straight.
2. Measure the appropriate width of your strip at the top, middle, and bottom. Make a mark on the fabric with a silver pencil or other marker. Then cut your strip with the rotary cutter using these marks as a guide. Follow the same procedure for each fabric. Use this

method to cut one 11″ long strip each in the following widths: 2″ strip dark teal, 2″ strip medium teal, 1½″ strip light teal, 1½″ strip dark turquoise, 1″ strip medium turquoise print, ½″ strip light turquoise, ½″ strip light blue, ½″ strip blue/lavender print, and ½″ strip lavender.

3. Lay out the strips in the proper sewing order. See the color photo of the project if you need help. You will be making a band of color. Pin the first two strips to be sewn with right sides together. Machine stitch the strips together lengthwise on the sewing machine. Use a stitch setting of about ten stitches per inch. Without cutting the thread, sew the next two strips in the band. (This is known as "chain-sewing.") Do this until all of the strips in the band have been joined in pairs. Then cut apart the pairs and join one pair to another. Do this until all of the pairs and double-pairs have been joined to form a single band.

4. Press the seams on the back of your color band open. Press the band from the front as well.

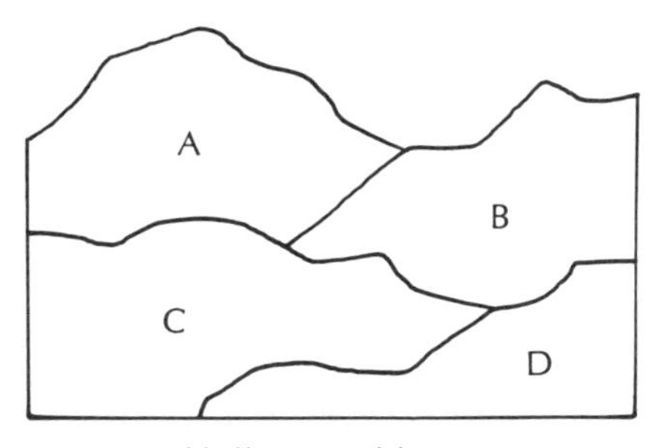

Diagram of hills assembly.

5. Photocopy or trace the pattern pieces for hills A, B, C, and D. Cut them out to make templates. Note that the seam allowance is included for these templates. Using the templates, mark and cut each hill from the appropriate fabric. Use the lightest green for hill A in the background and progressively darker colors for the hills to the foreground.

6. Photocopy or trace the pattern pieces for the grasses and cattails. Cut them out to make templates. From the black fabric, mark and cut out five grass blades. Turn the template over and use the other side to mark five more. This will give you ten grass blades, half bending toward the right and half bending toward the left. Mark and cut out three cattails from the black fabric.

7. Pin and appliqué the grasses and cattails along the bottom of the strip-pieced water unit. Use the project photograph as a general guide for placement.

8. Join the black sky to the strip-pieced water unit (with the grasses along the bottom).

9. Pin the hills to the sky fabric in order starting with the most distant hill A. Turn the edges of the hills under as you appliqué them in place.

10. Sew the two short border strips to the top and bottom of the landscape unit. Trim any excess. Then sew the two long border strips to the right and left sides of the landscape unit. Trim any excess and iron.

11. Lay out the backing fabric right side down, center the batting on top of this, and center on these the pieced and appliquéd wall hanging

top right side up. Baste and quilt the project, using the project photo in the color section as a guide.

12. Trim the excess batting and backing fabric. From the black fabric, cut four black binding strips—two 3″ × 24″ long each and two 3″ × 34″ long each. Use these to bind the project.

14

Put Some Life into It

Are you the kind of quilter who derives great satisfaction from carefully planning a quilt design? Do you painstakingly reproduce your designs on graph paper? Do you complete draft after draft before ever picking up scissors or thread? Do you cut out fabric shapes to fit your paper patterns exactly? What would be your reaction if someone were to say to you, "Don't be so pattern-bound!"

There is nothing wrong with careful planning if that is your style. But this chapter invites you to try something different, just for a change. Although careful planning has its advantages, there is something to be said for spontaneity, too. If you are in a paper pattern rut, take this opportunity to get out. Many quilters have found that the best way to create an exciting design is to cut and sew more freely. By experimenting with spontaneous style, you can begin to develop a personal approach, possibly one that blends a certain amount of planning with free-form expression.

FLEXIBILITY AND DESIGN

"There's a lot of happy accidents that take place in quilt design," says quilter Judy Shea. "You have to be open to taking advantage of a good idea, whether you planned it that way, or whether you didn't." Being flexible is part of good design. When designing spontaneously, it is especially important to be open to new ideas as you go along. Don't just design a block and leave it at that. Try turning the same block on its side, combining it with identical blocks or different ones. Try cutting it apart and sewing it back together with a different orientation.

Creative designers look at their patterns in more than one way before settling on a finished presentation. Some of us have difficulty becoming truly creative until we make a mistake. Maybe a center medallion is the wrong size or a border is too short. Then the ways in which we explore working around that mistake become creative. The trick is to

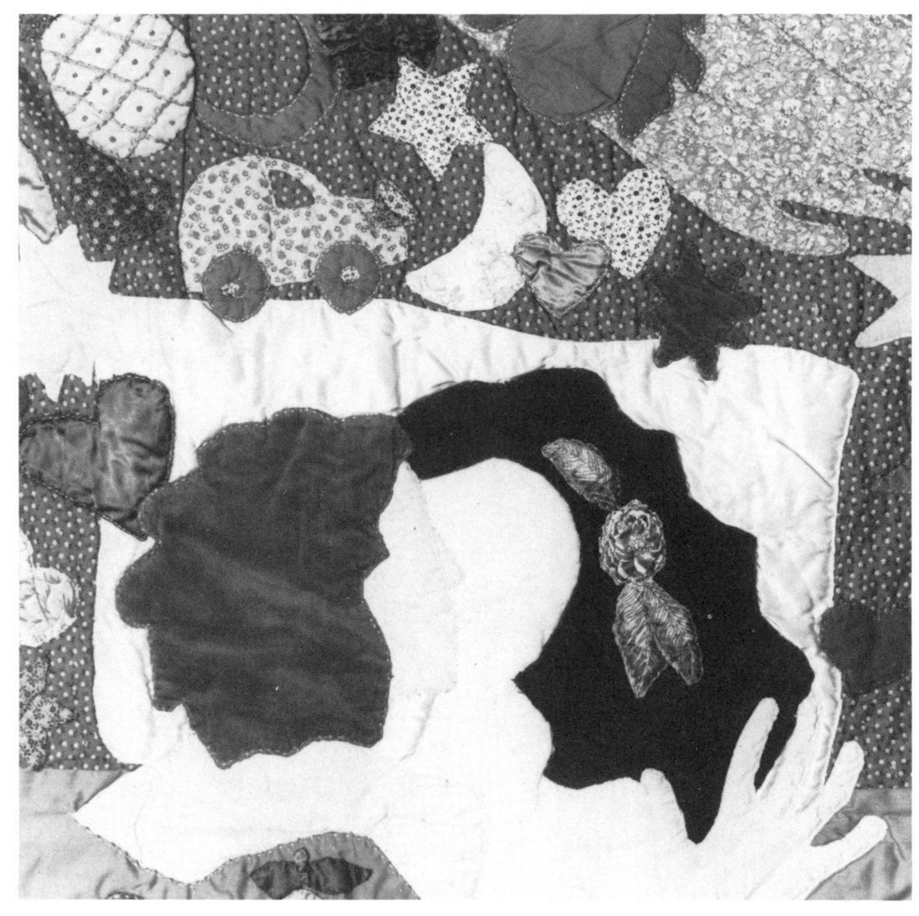

Detail, *The Dreamers,* a quilt made by spontaneously positioning appliqués as they were cut and sewn, by the author.

explore different ways of using the same design before an "accident" occurs. Being open to lots of different ways of doing the same thing is what creativity is all about.

LIVELY APPLIQUÉ

If you prefer appliqué, try cutting out and turning under appliqué fabric shapes and arranging them on a fabric background pinned on a wall or other flat surface "as you go." This method allows you to watch your design grow and lets you appreciate the spatial relationships that develop as you work. It is reminiscent of the work style of many modern painters for whom the process of creation is at least as important as the finished product.

STRIP PIECING

Strip piecing is a fast and spontaneous technique of sewing strips of fabric together in an interesting progression. It is a sewing machine technique that requires no templates and is especially fun to do with the help of a rotary cutter, cutting mat, and quilter's ruler. The cutting goes quickly and there is virtually no fabric waste. On a sewing machine, the straight-line joining together of strips is a breeze. No wonder so many contemporary quilters enjoy using this technique.

Some quilters who use the strip-piece method plan out their designs on paper first, but it is not necessary. Others begin with a general idea, whether abstract or figurative, then cut and sew strips, allowing their original plan to change somewhat as they go along. Strip-piecing may be used alone to create an entire design image or it can be used as the backdrop for an appliqué or pieced motif.

Seminole-pieced jacket made by needle-workers of the Seminole Indian Reservation at Immokalee, Florida.

SEMINOLE PIECING

Seminole patchwork is a variation on simple strip-piecing and particularly lends itself to a spontaneous method. Developed by the Seminole Indians of the Everglades, Seminole piecing involves sewing fabric strips together, cutting the strips into sections, and resewing the sections to create intricate patchwork bands. It produces a design made up of tiny squares and triangles of color, yet eliminates the need to handle small bits of fabric. It is necessarily done using a sewing machine.

Seminole piecing also eliminates the need for templates. Consequently, it is quick to do and requires little planning. A great many pattern options are possible. For a very simple Seminole-style patchwork band, strips of fabric may be cut with a rotary cutter and sewn lengthwise. The resulting multistrip is ironed, marked, and cut in perpendicular lines. This creates short strips of color squares. These sections are set on the diagonal and sewn together. The quickest method for sewing the short strips is to machine stitch them in pairs, chain-sewing from one pair to the next without cutting the thread. Then the pairs may be sewn together. This is faster than sewing the short strips one at a time into one long strip. The "diagonal squares" strip is ironed and a ruler placed over the zigzag edges. The zigzag edges are trimmed away to make a patchwork band of squares and triangles plus seam allowance. This band can quickly be made more striking by the addition of one or two coordinated color strips on either side. For more complex pattern variations, see the excellent book on Seminole patchwork listed in Recommended Reading.

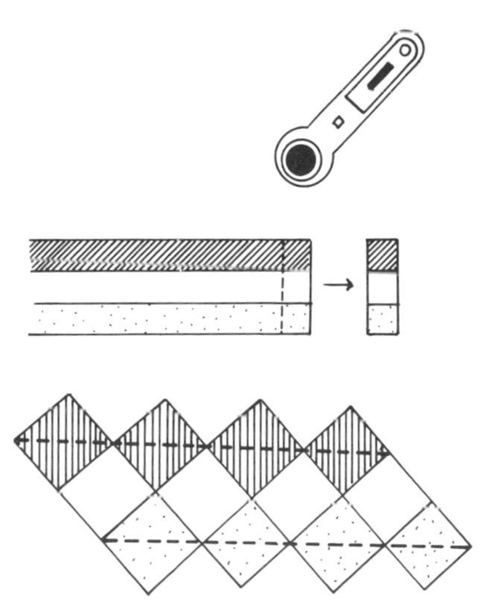
Diagrams showing simple Seminole construction.

CUT AND RESEW METHODS

Closely related to strip-piecing and Seminole patchwork techniques is the cut and re-sew method. One style of working is to sew strips or patches of fabric at random, then use a template to cut the resulting multicolored patchwork into geometric shapes—squares, rectangles, or triangles. The shapes themselves are then joined. The end product is a marriage of randomly joined patches of color and solid geometric form,

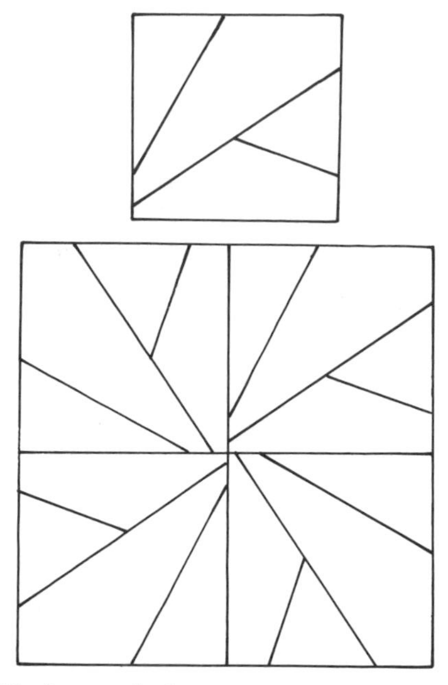

Design made from creative positioning of random-design squares.

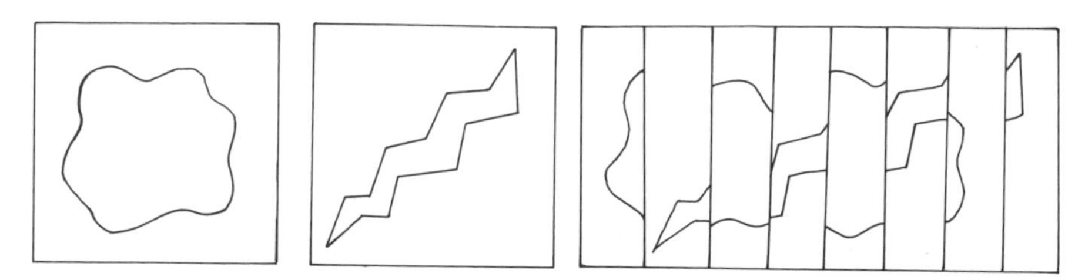

Cut and resew technique.

much like a crazy quilt. This process is used for the project in this chapter.

A second approach is to sew two large panels using separate colors and separate recognizable designs. Each panel is then cut into long strips. The strips are then sewn in an alternating pattern that allows the overall design to be viewed as a whole, while allowing the pattern of each original pattern to come through as well.

An additional approach is to divide a basic geometric shape, such as a square, randomly into different sections. For instance, a square may be divided using three or four lines running in random directions. Different colors are used for each of the sections into which the square is divided. The multicolored square is copied exactly to make many blocks in the same random design. The squares may then be placed in a symmetrical pattern or a random one to create a lively design.

SPONTANEOUS SQUARES PILLOW

DIFFICULTY LEVEL: Easy

FINISHED SIZE: 16″ × 16″

About the Project. The following project is an exercise in spontaneous design for those who have never tried it. It involves exploring random patterning to create your own unique design. The project calls for making a wide color band. The color band is then cut apart into squares and the squares sewn together to make a new design. Choose your own colors or follow the suggestions offered here. Tools recommended for this project include a rotary cutting wheel, mat, and wide quilter's ruler. You will also need a sewing machine. Hand sewing is generally inappropriate for strip-piecing techniques.

As an alternative to the pillow project, you might want to make a wall hanging using the Spontaneous Squares technique. Enlarge your color band to allow for more squares. Sew sixteen squares into a four-square unit or twenty-five squares to make a five-square unit. Add borders to complete the top. Make a quilt "sandwich" of backing, batting, and top, then baste and quilt. The resulting random design will give you a wall hanging rich in rhythm and directional movement.

MATERIALS

¼ yard each: gold print, turquoise print, royal blue solid, red solid, red print

Two 17″ × 8″ turquoise solid border strips

Two 10″ × 8″ turquoise solid border strips

One 17″ × 17″ square turquoise solid for pillow back

One 16″ square pillow form

DIRECTIONS

1. You will notice that you have one template for this project. Trace and cut out the square template and set it aside.
2. Lay out all of your fabric for the strips. To begin cutting, fold each length of fabric in half so that the two selvage edges are touching. One at a time, place the folded fabric lengths on the cutting mat with the folded edge at the top. Always cut in the same up and down direction on your mat. Line up the horizontal lines on the quilter's rule with the fold of the fabric. Trim the edge of the fabric to make it perfectly straight.
3. Decide on the width you want your fabric strip to be. It is a good idea in this project to vary your strip width anywhere from 1″ to 2½″. Measure the appropriate width of your strip at the top, middle, and bottom. Make a mark on the fabric with a silver pencil or other marker. Then cut your strip with the rotary cutter using these marks as a guide. Follow the same procedure for each length of fabric, varying your strip widths for the different colors. Each strip should be about 24″ long. You will need to cut enough strips to make a color band about 18″ wide.
4. Decide on the order in which you want to sew your strips together to form the color band. Lay the strips out in the sewing order you have chosen. Pin the first two strips to be sewn with right sides together. Sew the strips together lengthwise on the sewing machine. Use a stitch setting of about ten stitches per inch. Without cutting the thread, sew the next two strips in the band. (This is known as "chain-sewing.") Do this until all of the strips in the band have been joined in pairs. Then cut apart the pairs and join one pair to another. Do this until all of the pairs and double-pairs have been joined to form a single band.
5. Press the seams on the back of your color band open. Press the band from the front as well. Take the square template that you cut earlier and use it to mark nine squares on the front of your color band. For each square, place the template so it is facing in a slightly different direction. Then mark and cut. The resulting random patchwork pattern will be asymmetrical.

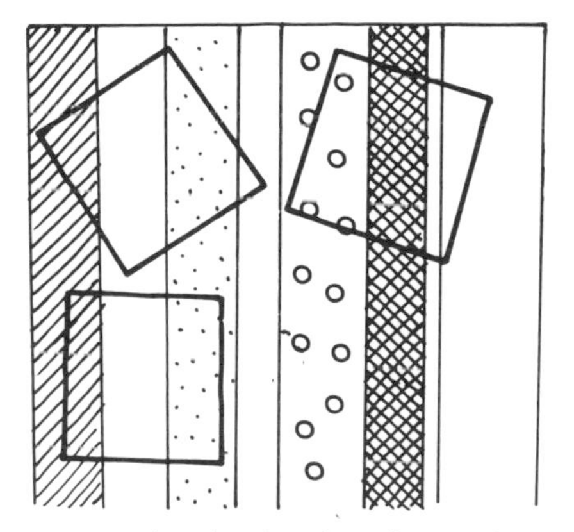

Horizontal color band with templates randomly positioned.

6. You will note that the template for this project includes a seam allowance. After cutting out the nine squares, you will need to cut down the template on the inner line. Use this new, smaller template to mark the squares from the back of the fabric to indicate your sewing line for each.
7. Sew the nine squares into a three-by-three-square unit. Pin two squares with right sides together and sew. Join three squares to make a row, repeat for each row, then join the rows to make the three-by-three-square unit.
8. Sew the two short border strips to the top and bottom of the square unit. Sew with a 3⁄8″ seam. Trim any excess border fabric. Then join the longer border strips to the right and left of the square unit. Trim the excess border fabric to complete the pillow top.
9. With right sides together, pin and sew the pillow top to the pillow back. Leave about 8″ unsewn for turning the pillow casing right side out. Turn the casing right side out and fit it over the pillow form. Then sew the opening closed by hand. (See finished project in the color section.)

15

Personalized Fabric Design

We get so much pleasure from choosing printed fabrics to work with that we often neglect the possibility of designing our own. Instead of starting out with an array of purchased prints and solids, why not start from scratch? Decide how best to express yourself using fabric that bears your personal touch.

There are numerous methods for creating fabric that meets a special need. Many quilters are put off by what they see as the mess, stress, and equipment needs of full-scale dyeing. Actually, personalizing your fabric

Stencils by Sandra Olenik of Printworks, Ltd. (see Sources). Printworks Ltd. offers custom-made stencils for quilting and other sewing projects.

can be as simple or as challenging as you want to make it. There are a number of easy methods for designing and coloring fabric yourself.

TECHNIQUES

BLEACH-DYEING

Have you dreamed of finding just the right fabric for a sky full of fluffy clouds? Try bleach-dyeing light blue fabric. You will need a bathtub or large sink, rubber gloves, and laundry soap. Wash a yard or so of light blue 100% cotton fabric purchased at a quilt shop. While the washed fabric is still wet, spread it out in the bathtub, bunching it here and there to make creases. Drizzle full strength bleach directly on the fabric so that it makes a puddle in some areas and leaves others untouched. As soon as you have achieved the amount of bleaching you want, rinse the fabric right away. Then wash it to stop the action of the bleach completely.

Bleach-dyeing can be used with different fabric colors to create innovative sky and water impressions or it can enhance fabric for an abstract design. The lines and shapes that arise from the creases and folds in the bunched-up fabric will add interest to the overall design of your quilt.

TEA-TINTING

Tea-tinting, used to give fabrics an antique appearance, is another easy, inexpensive method of personalizing your fabric. It works best with white and light-color 100% cottons. Tea-tinting, however, may cause the fibers in your fabric to weaken with age. If you want your quilt to last for generations, this might not be the method to choose. If this is not an important issue for you, though, give it a try. You will need 1 to 1½ yards of fabric, a large one- or two-gallon pot with a lid, six to eight tea bags, rubber gloves, and a wooden spoon. Pour water in the pot until it is a little more than half full. Put in the tea bags, cover, and boil for fifteen minutes. Meanwhile, wash the fabric to be tinted. Squeeze it out and set it aside. Do not dry it. Turn off the heat under the pot. Remove the tea bags and discard them. Put the wet fabric into the tea water. Allow it to simmer covered for five to fifteen minutes, depending on how dark you want the tint to be. Keep in mind that the tint will appear lighter when the fabric is dry. Stir two or three times during the simmering. Remove the fabric with the wooden spoon. Rinse in warm water until the water runs clear.

CRAYONS AND MARKERS

Fabric crayons or markers are another option. There are different kinds of fabric crayons and markers on the market. Look for them at art stores and some needlework shops. Usually they involve applying color directly to the fabric and then heat-setting with an iron. Some crayons and markers do not require heat-setting. Read the directions on the brand you are using, but be aware that 100% cotton is the preferred fabric for use with this method. White and light fabric colors will provide the best contrast for the intense crayon colors. You will need rectangles of fabric (prewashed, dried, and ironed), fabric crayons or markers, a piece of cardboard, masking tape, brown paper (a cut-open and flattened paper bag will do), sheets of white bond paper, and an iron and ironing board. Tape the dry fabric rectangles to the cardboard to hold them in place as you work. Decorate the fabric with the crayon or marker. Remove it from the cardboard. Place the brown paper on the ironing board to protect it. Place a sheet of white paper on the brown paper, the decorated fabric on this right side up, and another sheet of white paper over the fabric. Iron the block to set the color.

Be sure to use permanent, nontoxic fabric crayons or markers. Double-check the directions because heat-setting may not be required. This method is especially useful when you would like children or adults unfamiliar with sewing to contribute their own decorated squares to a group quilt.

POTATO PRINTING

Potato printing requires only the simplest of materials and is fun. Clean-up is easy when you use a water-soluble fabric paint such as Deka™, which can be purchased at most art supply stores. When you go to the art store, you will notice that you have two main choices—fabric dye and fabric paint. Dyes generally bond with the fibers of the fabric, whereas paints sit upon the surface of the fabric. When using paints, you may need to experiment to find ones that do not greatly change the feel of the fabric and that will remain easy to quilt through if that is a consideration.

To do potato printing, you will need newspapers, brown paper (a cut-open and flattened paper bag), masking tape, a small sharp knife, one or two good-sized potatoes, Deka™ or other water-soluble fabric paint, 100% cotton fabric rectangles (prewashed, dried, and ironed), waxed paper plates, paper towels for touch-ups, and a few sheets of white bond paper for practice printing. To begin, spread several thicknesses of newspaper over your work surface. Spread the brown paper over this. Place the fabric on top of the brown paper and tape it lightly in place to keep it from shifting while you print.

Cut a potato in half lengthwise. Be sure the cut surface is as flat as possible with no ridges or glitches in it. Lay the potato flat side down and cut it into a square, triangle, or other shape. Do your cutting straight up and down. Do not undercut the printing surface as this will weaken it. At this point, you can leave your potato printer as it is, or decorate the flat surface with grooves to form a motif.

To print, pour a small amount of paint onto a paper plate. Mix your colors or use them straight from the bottle or jar. Press the potato printer lightly down into the color. Pick it up and check the sides for excess paint, which you can wipe off with a paper towel. Press the potato printer down onto your practice paper or, if you are ready, onto the fabric. Apply pressure firmly and evenly, then lift up. It will take a few tries to get a feel for the correct amount of pressure required. Repeat the process to make a pattern. You might choose to make a random pattern or a directional one. Let the paint dry thoroughly. Then heat-set, with the fabric sandwiched between two sheets of white paper. Your potato-printed fabric is ready for piecing or appliqué.

You can also try printing effects with cut apple cores, slices of citrus, mushroom caps, and leaves. Treat most vegetables and fruits as you would a potato. Although you will not be able to carve most of these to create a pattern, the surface pattern they already have may be as much as you need. Dip leaves one at a time in the fabric paint, shake lightly to remove the excess and lay down on the fabric to be printed. You can place a sheet of white paper on top of the leaf and press gently. Then lift up the paper and remove the leaf. Unlike a potato printer, which can be used many times during the course of a day's printing, a leaf will usually print well only once or twice. Then you need to use a new leaf. Try combining your potato or leaf prints with other commercially printed fabrics for an exciting new look.

SPONGE-PAINTING AND MORE

Fabric paint can be used in other ways, too. Create a textured pattern for use as treetops or hills in a landscape by printing with a small piece of damp sponge pressed lightly (never rubbed) over an entire area of fabric. Cut out the shapes from the sponge-painted fabric and turn them under for use in a pictorial landscape design. Try a spatter effect in browns and golds to simulate a sandy beach in an ocean scene. Use a brush or cotton swab to hand paint an abstract pattern to be cut apart and resewn in a geometric pieced pattern. Paint more detailed foregrounds for your landscapes. The motifs in the foreground of such a scene appear more detailed, being closer to the viewer. (Avoid using highly detailed images in the distance of your landscapes.)

MOCK BATIK

You can create a web-pattern effect in your fabric similar to that of batik, but without the effort that is entailed in a full-scale wax resist dyeing process. Follow the directions on the box for melting a single block of paraffin in a double boiler over low heat. (*Always be careful when melting paraffin as it can catch fire.*) Meanwhile, mix a washing pan full of dye. A commercial fabric dye purchased at an art supply store will give the most lasting results, although your options also include Rit™ dye or vegetable dyes from plants you collect yourself. Use light-color fabric in a hue that will blend well with the dye bath. For instance, you might use pink fabric and blue dye, resulting in a pink and purple color

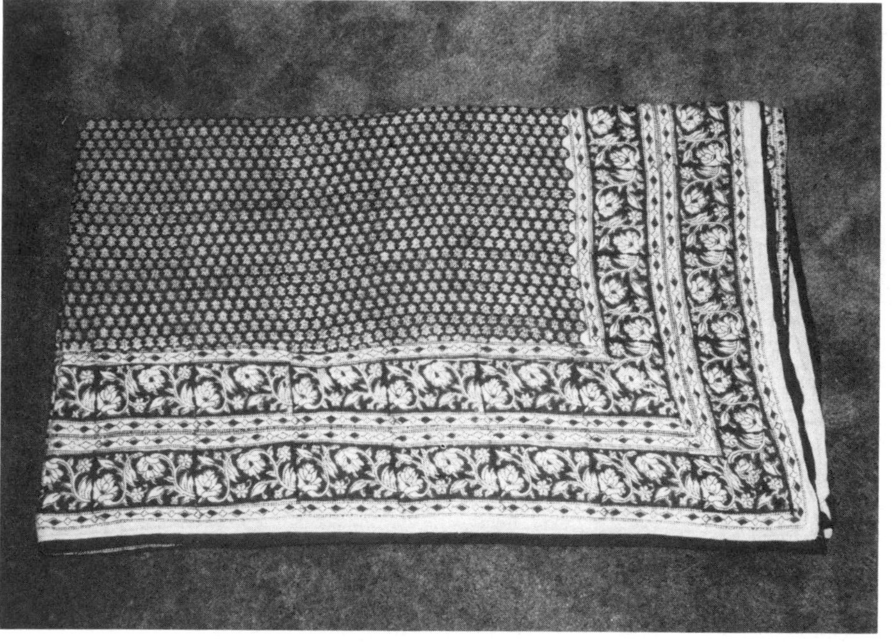

Quilt made in India from hand-blocked printed fabric.

combination. Using a wide brush, paint simple shapes on the fabric—circles, ovals, stars, squares, etc. Let the wax dry for a few minutes and repaint the areas. Then scrunch up the fabric, making cracks in the wax shapes. Immerse the fabric in the dye bath and follow the directions for the dye you are using to get the intensity of color you want. Remove the fabric from the dye bath when you are ready. Let dry, then iron the fabric between sheets of unprinted newsprint or other inexpensive paper available at your art supply store. Iron thoroughly to remove all the wax. If you like, you can repeat the process for an additional color.

OTHER CHALLENGES

Any of these simple methods of designing your own fabric will give you unique results with a minimum expenditure of time. As you become more experienced in personalizing your fabric, you will want to take on more of a challenge. When you are ready, some exciting design opportunities await you.

Dyeing fabric with hand-picked plants or Procion™ fiber-reactive dyes offers a wide range of colors to quilters who want to have greater control over their palette. Dyeing your own fabric requires more of an investment in terms of time and equipment, but the sophisticated results are worth the effort. Over-dyeing preprinted fabric is another option, one that enables quilters to make use of fabric that has passed out of fashion or that no longer appeals to them. Tie-dyeing produces beautiful starburst patterns for use in vibrant sky and water scenes. It also offers intriguing patterns for cutting and resewing into abstract geometric designs. Fabric may also be marbleized for unique effects. Marbleized textiles may be cut into triangles or diamonds and resewn to form exciting radiating patterns in the form of stars or kaleidoscopic designs. (For quilters who love the look of hand-dyed fabric, but prefer not to do their own dyeing, see the suppliers listed in Sources.)

Stencils also offer an appealing way to personalize your fabric. Stenciled motifs may be cut apart into individual squares or triangles of fabric offering new options for design. A stenciled motif, such as a heart or simple flower, repeated on alternate blocks, can make a simple four-patch block or other traditional pattern come alive.

Working with fabric you have designed yourself offers the opportunity for a powerful personal statement. It gives you a new kind of control over your work. It allows you to express your creative vision exactly as you see it. If you are happy with the range of colors and prints available to you commercially—well and good. But if you are seeking for a way to create in a style that is uniquely yours, personalizing your own fabric is a great place to start.

POTATO PRINT PILLOW

DIFFICULTY LEVEL: Easy

FINISHED SIZE: 16″ × 16″

About the Project. This project allows you to explore two simple styles of personalizing one's fabric—sponge technique and potato printing. You can cut your potato print into almost any shape. A heart design is used here. Plan to print the same day that you cut your potato because it will only last about a day. Be sure to sponge and print your fabrics before cutting out the fabric squares. After you have made a number of successful prints, you can decide which ones to cut out. This may keep you from wasting fabric unnecessarily, and it is easier to manipulate medium-sized pieces of fabric than little squares.

If you prefer, this pillow project may be quilted. You will need a backing and thin batting such as that recommended for quilted clothing added to the decorative pillow top. The top should be basted and quilted before it is joined, right sides together, to the pillow back.

MATERIALS

⅓ yard prewashed, unbleached muslin
Two 17″ × 8″ green border strips
Two 10″ × 8″ green border strips
One 17″ × 17″ square green
One 16″ square pillow form
Bottle pink fabric paint
Bottle sage green fabric paint
Waxed paper plates

Piece of sponge approximately 2″ × 2″
Utility scissors
One or two potatoes
Small kitchen knife
Paper towels

DIRECTIONS

1. Note that you will be using the square template from the *Spontaneous Squares* project in Chapter Fourteen. If you have not already done so, trace and cut out the square template and set it aside. Also see the sections in this chapter on potato printing and sponge printing.
2. Cut a potato in half. Using the knife, carve the heart shape from one of the cut surfaces. Let the potato stand for a few minutes on a paper towel to absorb some of the potato juice. The print will be clearer if your block is fairly dry.
3. Pour a small amount of the pink fabric paint onto a paper plate. Press the block carefully, but not too hard into the paint. Make a few trial impressions on your fabric to get a feel for how much pressure is needed to print a clear image. Recolor the potato block for each impression. Complete your printing (you will need five clearly printed heart motifs) and let the printed fabric dry.
4. Next, pour a small amount of the sage green fabric paint onto another paper plate. Take the little piece of sponge, dampen it, and dip it lightly in the paint. Then press the sponge onto another area of the muslin. You will want to make a light print with lots of white showing through for a textured effect. Never rub the color into the fabric. Recolor your sponge as needed. When you have sponged as much fabric as you will need to cut out the four squares, let the fabric dry.
5. Follow the instructions on your fabric paint for setting the colors properly. If you are in doubt about setting the colors, iron the sponged and printed fabric from the back onto unprinted newsprint or other inexpensive absorbent paper available from an art supply store. Using the square template from the *Spontaneous Squares* project in Chapter Fourteen, mark and cut five heart squares and four sponged fabric squares.
6. You will note that the square template includes a seam allowance. After cutting out the nine squares, you will need to cut down the template on the inner line. Use this new smaller template to mark the squares from the back of the fabric to indicate your sewing line for each.
7. Sew the nine squares into a three-by-three-square unit. See the project photograph in the color section if you need help with the order of the squares. Join the squares into rows of three squares each. Then join the rows to form the three-by-three-square unit.

8. Sew the two short border strips to the top and bottom of the square unit. Sew with a ⅜″ seam. Trim any excess border fabric. Then join the longer border strips to the right and left of the square unit. Trim the excess border fabric to complete the pillow top.

9. With right sides together, pin and sew the pillow top to the 17″ × 17″ green pillow back. Leave about 8″ unsewn for turning the pillow casing right side out. Turn the casing right side out and fit it over the pillow form. Then hand sew the opening shut.

16

Three-Dimensional Design

One quilter I know recently lamented, "Why must quilts always be flat? Quilts are made to cover people. And *people* aren't flat!" Although we usually think of quilts as being flat, many are not. (Indeed, some quilts do not turn out flat even when we intend them to be!)

Where quilts are concerned, the term *three-dimensional* has a number of meanings. A quilted sphere has three dimensions. It is a kind of quilt sculpture that has depth as well as length and width. It is not flat. Yet it is still a quilt or at least a quilted creation.

A quilt may be flat and yet have three-dimensional objects or fabric elements sewn onto it. South American arpilleras are an example. These small fabric collages feature little three-dimensional dolls, animals, vegetables, and other stuffed fabric objects on a flat landscape background. The mixing of perspectives—the three-dimensional figures and the flat background—is part of what gives arpilleras their folk art appeal.

FABRIC

A trapunto design is three-dimensional. It is a relief design and consequently has a subtle degree of depth. A quilt that uses photographs reproduced on fabric has a three-dimensional quality. The photos provide a suggestion of depth through light and shadow as the camera sees it.

Many quilters are intrigued with the prospect of creating a three-dimensional image on a two-dimensional plane. The intricacies of perspective have fascinated artists from Brunelleschi to de Chirico. Perspective and how it can be used to create stunning designs on flat quilts will be the focus of this chapter.

South American arpillera featuring distinctive three-dimensional fabric dolls against a landscape background.

More and more contemporary quilters are turning to the use of perspective in designing their own one-of-a-kind quilts. Reproducing three-dimensional spatial objects on a flat two-dimensional plane is not always easy. It also is not strictly limited to modern quiltmaking. A traditional example of three-dimensional design is the pattern Tumbling Blocks.

COLOR

When color is used in Tumbling Blocks to suggest a dramatic light source, the result is startlingly three-dimensional. We know this pattern is actually made up of multiples of three diamond shapes. Yet when a hue plus a tint and shade of that hue are used consistently throughout, the result is an image that suggests real blocks as they might be seen with light shining upon them. It appears to us as if one side of each block is turned slightly to the right, one is to the left, and one is facing up. Would this pattern appear to be three-dimensional if all three sides of each

Late nineteenth-century Tumbling Blocks pattern featuring three-dimensional design.

block were the same color? No. The illusion of light is what creates the sense of three dimensions. The bright side appears to have the light source shining full upon it. The dark side appears to be turned away from the light source so that no light is shining on it. The medium side is turned slightly toward the light so that some light is shining on it.

PERSPECTIVE

The word *perspective* comes from a Latin word meaning to look through. In a sense, when you see objects in perspective, you are *looking through* the foreground to objects in the background. The art of perspective involves picturing objects as they appear to the eye with reference to their distance both from the observer and from each other.

When perspective was first discovered by architect Filippo Brunelleschi in the early fifteenth century, it caused quite a stir. People were accustomed to the nonperspective representational styles of the times. Suddenly art became a mirror for reality. The effect was revolutionary not just in terms of visual representation, but from a philosophical standpoint. Perspective placed all objects in a measurable mathematical relationship to a human viewer. As the new idea took hold, humans became the measure of all things. Painting became more realistic in style and subject matter. Art gradually became more of a vehicle for self-expression. Perspective paved the way for a new kind of thinking that centered on the human point of view. (For more about perspective and its influence in Western thought, see *The Day the Universe Changed* by James Burke listed in Recommended Reading.)

The discovery of perspective changed not only the way people viewed art but also the world around them. This Dürer woodcut is reprinted by permission of Little, Brown and Company.

Mission Accomplished, by Edith Zimmer. A brilliant manipulation of three-dimensional form. Photograph courtesy of the American Quilter's Society.

Many quilters today are still rediscovering Brunelleschi's legacy. As quiltmakers, many of us are inclined to reproduce what we see in flat two-dimensional images. Attempting to portray the world in perspective presents a challenge—one well worth the effort. To draw objects in perspective, you need a vanishing point. The vanishing point is the point at which parallel lines going away from the observer seem to come together. If you were standing in the middle of a pair of railroad tracks, for instance, there would be one track on either side of you. These two lines would run away from you into the distance. At a point far distant from you, the two lines would seem to converge. This would be the vanishing point.

Let's try a simple exercise to illustrate a vanishing point. Take a sheet of paper. Turn it on its side so that the long end runs left to right. Now draw a horizon line straight across it. The horizon line can be anywhere on the paper, but it must run straight across—not diagonally. Mark a dot somewhere on your horizon line. This will be your vanishing point. Now mark two dots somewhere on the bottom of your sheet of paper. Imagine that each dot on the bottom of your paper is the beginning of a line. Draw a line from each dot to the vanishing point. What have you got? You have drawn a simple picture in perspective. You have pictured the two train tracks we mentioned earlier. They are running away from you and coming together at the vanishing point on your horizon line.

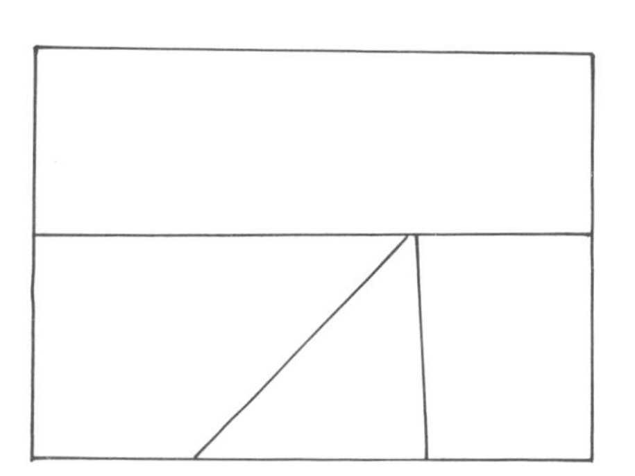

Drawing showing vanishing point on horizon line.

What if the vanishing point is positioned above the horizon line? Let's say the two lines are the two sides of a road. The two lines should come together at the vanishing point. But the horizon line cuts them off. So, you get a picture in which the converging of the lines is imaginary. This is how a road often appears when we view it receding into the distance.

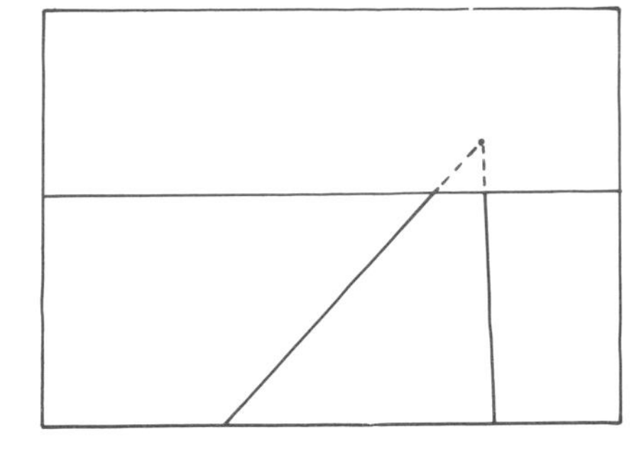
Drawing showing vanishing point above horizon line.

A cube can be drawn in the same way. Draw a flat square. Now mark a dot somewhere to the upper right of the top right corner of the square. This will be your vanishing point. Notice that three corners of the square are near to the vanishing point. One is farther away. Lightly draw lines that run from each of the three near corners of the square to the vanishing point. We will call these the vanishing point lines. You now have three vanishing point lines: a, b, and c. To make a cube, you will need to draw two more lines. The first must be parallel to the top of your square and must intersect vanishing point lines a and b. The second line must be parallel to the right side of your square and must intersect vanishing point lines b and c. You have drawn a cube in perspective. The lines of the cube are *foreshortened;* that is, the lines have been drawn shorter than they are in reality to give the impression of reality. You know that each side of a cube is really the same length. But that is not what your drawing tells you! If you were to go by your foreshortened drawing, the sides of your cube would be different lengths. You have used perspective to portray the cube, not as it really is, but as it appears.

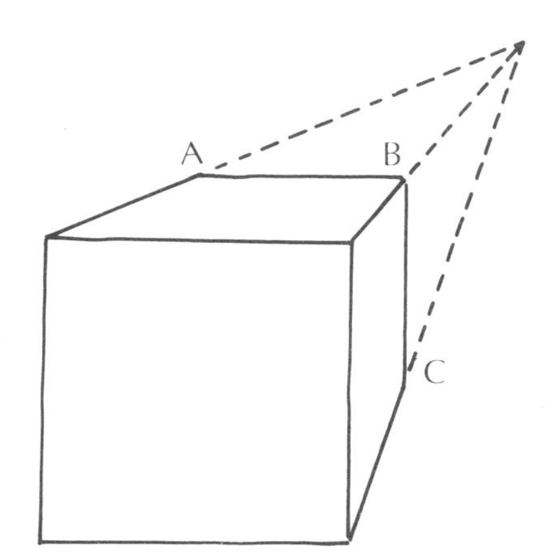

Cube in perspective.

Cubist painters in the early 1900s did just the opposite. They rebelled against traditional rules of perspective to portray the world not as it appears, but as it really is—that is, a cube portrayed with all three sides the same length, or all three sides pointed toward the viewer at once. They broke a Western artistic tradition of portraying objects in perspective that had dated from the fifteenth century. No wonder their art seemed so radical!

You can use perspective to create your own three-dimensional designs. As quilters, many of us are adept at reducing what we see to two-dimensional designs but are less accomplished in the three-dimensional approach. We need to relearn how to visualize three-dimensional objects so as to fit our design needs. A good way to start experimenting with designs in perspective is to combine simple shapes like squares and rectangles. If you have difficulty visualizing the squares, you can try looking at a small box. Look at it from different angles so that different sides are visible at a time. From there, you might want to make a design based on floating squares. Or anchor your squares securely on a flat ground, perhaps one that recedes to a vanishing point. Remember to use color to establish a light source. Sides of squares turned toward the light source will be bright. Sides of squares turned away from the light source will be dark. Those turned slightly toward the light source will be of medium intensity, just as in the Tumbling Blocks pattern.

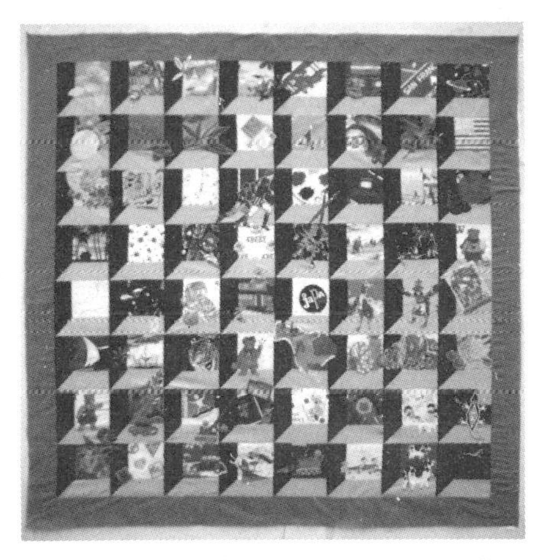
Attic Windows, by Diana Leone, author of *Attic Windows: A Contemporary View,* a good source for a variety of easy three-dimensional "window" design explorations (see Recommended Reading). Photograph courtesy of the artist.

Another possibility for beginners is to create a design suggestive of a receding tunnel. The impression of a square tunnel can be created through the use of a vanishing point and equidistant lines in a frame. To further the impression of distance, use intense colors in the forefront of the design and lighter, more muted colors in the distance. At the end of your tunnel, have something worth looking at—a pictorial image, an impression of space, maybe someone looking back at the observer. From simple designs based on three-dimensional squares and rectangles, you may want to graduate to spheres and other shapes. A good resource for practicing basic perspective is Katie Pasquini's *3-Dimensional Design* listed in Recommended Reading. The exercises she provides are especially useful in helping the novice get used to creative visualization of objects in perspective.

SEAVIEW WALL QUILT

DIFFICULTY LEVEL: Easy

FINISHED SIZE: 31″ × 28″

About the Project. The window theme offers an easy application of principles in perspective. Simple squares, strips, and trapezoids are joined to create the impression of panes of glass. Windows are fun images to work with from a design standpoint because they invite a wide range of choices as to what to place on the other side of the window. You might want to experiment with this aspect of the pattern. Instead of placing a single appealing fabric in the window space, you might want to put portions of a larger design—a scene or landscape—that is broken up by the windowpanes. Or show the window from the other side—from outside looking in, rather than inside looking out. In that case, you might portray a domestic scene on the inside, or a person or animal looking out the window. This project is based on a simple three-dimensional window pattern. For more great window patterns and project ideas, be sure to see *Attic Windows: A Contemporary View* by Diana Leone, listed in Recommended Reading.

MATERIALS

1 yard fabric A (inner window square)
½ yard each fabrics B and C (window corner pieces)
½ yard fabric D (windowpane strips)
Two 4″ × 31″ border strips
Two 4″ × 23″ border strips
½ yard fabric E (for binding)
31″ × 28″ square batting
31″ × 28″ square backing fabric
Quilting thread

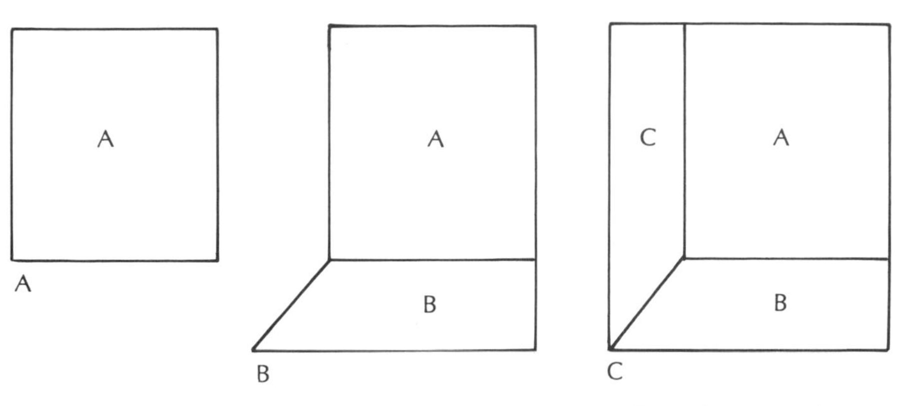

Piecing diagram for windows.

DIRECTIONS

1. This pattern uses only three simple shapes: a rectangle, a small trapezoid, and a large trapezoid. It is helpful to have a rotary cutter, quilter's wide ruler, and cutting mat for cutting the strips that form the windowpanes.
2. Trace the pattern templates and cut them out from cardboard, sandpaper, or Mylar.
3. Mark and cut nine window squares from fabric A. Mark and cut nine small trapezoids from fabric B and nine large trapezoids from fabric C.
4. Begin sewing the pattern. Use the piecing diagram as a guide. Join one window square to one small trapezoid and one large trapezoid. Iron and set aside. Do this for all nine window squares.
5. Fold the ½ yard of fabric D. Fold it so that the two selvage edges are together. Lay it down on the cutting mat so that the fold is at the top. Using the rotary cutter, mark and cut nine strips 1¾″ wide. Cut from top to the bottom—the full length of the folded piece of fabric. From one of the windowpane strips, cut a short strip 7″ long. Join this short windowpane strip to one window square along the bottom edge. Trim the short windowpane strip so that its edges are even with the window square. Iron the window square, pressing the seams open, and set aside. Do this for six of the nine window squares only.
6. Assemble the window squares and windowpane strips as they are to appear in the finished project. Then sew them together using the diagram as a guide.
7. Sew the two short border strips to the top and bottom of the pieced window unit. Trim any excess border fabric. Then join the longer

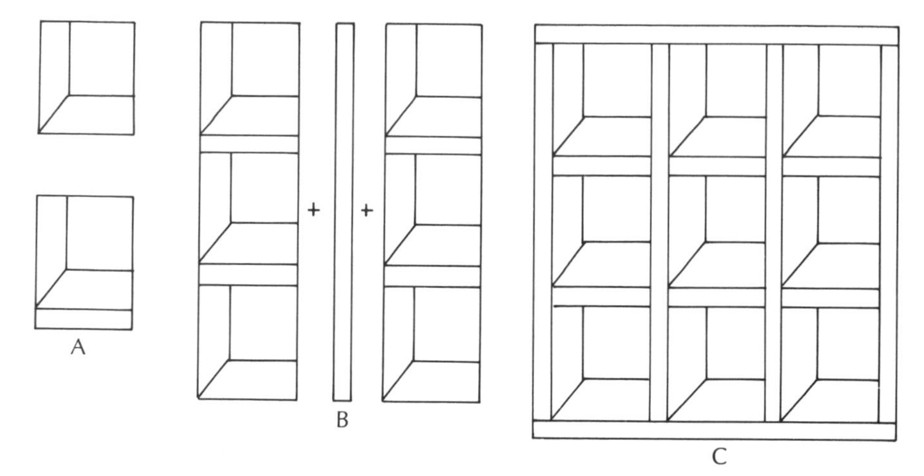

A. *Top:* Leave three window squares like this. *Bottom:* Join windowpane strip to six of the window squares along the bottom edge. B. Window units with strip-sashing before borders have been added. C. Piecing diagram for nine window quilt.

border strips to the right and left of the window unit. Trim the excess border fabric.

8. Lay out the backing fabric right side down, center the batting on top of this, and center on these the pieced wall hanging top right side up. Baste and quilt the project, using the color photograph as a guide.

9. Trim the excess batting and backing fabric. Cut four binding strips 3″ wide from fabric E. Cut from the folded top of the fabric to the selvage edge bottom as above. Use these to bind the project. (See the finished project in the color section.)

17

Color Progressions

A good deal has been said up to this point about movement in a design. One of the easiest ways to create a feeling of movement in a quilt is through the creative use of color. By paying close attention to the value and intensity of different gradations of color, it is possible to establish a feeling of sweeping movement through a design as a whole. A pattern may feature a series of tints and shades of the same color from light to medium to dark. It can feature several different colors shaded gradually from one to the other: red to orange to yellow, for instance. The result, if the color progression is logical, can be a clear, appealing directive element. The eye obediently follows the line of color from light to dark, from one color to another, without being sidetracked by a color out of sequence.

Some of the most exciting abstract quilts produced today involve creative use of color progression. While color progression quilts can conceivably be done in appliqué, generally they are executed in pieced geometric style. The progression may travel across the quilt from one corner to the corner diagonally opposite. It may move from the center out or the outer edges in. It may progress from top to bottom or bottom to top. A series of progressions may even take place in the same quilt, although in this case, the designer has to be careful not to have too much going on at once. The color progression may be a secondary theme in a design with other main components. Or it may stand on its own as the main item of interest a design has to offer.

In one-color or monochromatic progressions, the importance of color value especially stands out. Often we think an element in a design is not working because it is the wrong color, when in fact it may be the right color, but the wrong value. A single color has a wide variety of values. Green values, for instance, can range from a pearl like pastel green, through pale and lime greens, to medium grass greens, to dark spruce.

In our discussions so far, we have presented color and value as two separate entities, but it is also true that every color itself has a value. Yellow is the color lightest in value and violet is the darkest. Green can be thought of as more a middle value color. Attention to color value can

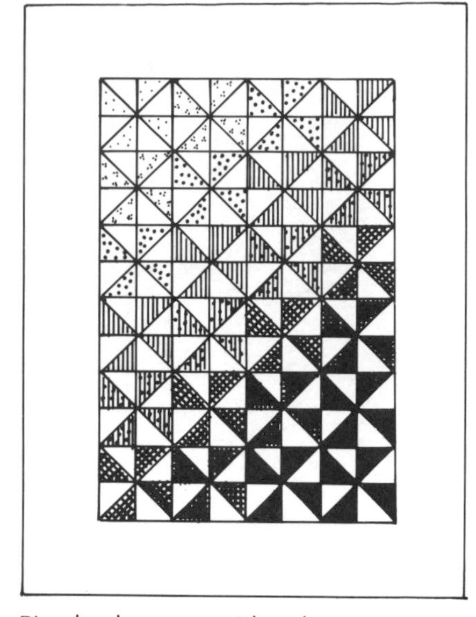

Pinwheel pattern with color progression shaded diagonally.

make the difference between a progression that works and one that does not.

PROGRESSIVE COLOR

In the chapter on color, we considered some combinations of hues that offer a starting point for color exploration. The same kinds of color schemes offer a good approach when designing color progression quilts. Analogous colors (those next to each other on the color wheel) offer a good place to begin. Each color has some of the other colors in it, offering something of a safety net to beginning designers. A monochromatic color scheme, in which variations of just one color are used, offers more of a challenge. The colors that may be used are limited, so careful attention must be paid to the qualities of value and intensity.

A progression involving complementary colors is considerably more of a challenge, yet provides especially pleasing results when it is successful. As M. E. Chevreul noted more than a century ago: "The contrast of the most opposite colors is most agreeable. . . . The complementary assortment is superior to every other."[1]

PROGRESSIVE PATTERNS

Almost any geometric pattern can be handled as a color progression. If you choose to work with a block-style design, of course, you will not want to alternate pieced blocks with plain ones as this would distract the eye from the progression. Color progressions work best if the overall pattern is fairly dense so that there is plenty of room for exercising color gradation. The goal is to shade the colors gradually in order to make the progression most effective. Avoiding too large a jump between colors is important. A dense overall pattern gives the best results. When planning a color progression quilt, try to see the design as a whole, rather than as a series of individual blocks. Work with pieced block next to pieced block and shade the color(s) gradually from block to block, horizontal row to horizontal row, or diagonal row to diagonal row.

If you are wondering how to begin designing your own color progression, try using colored pencils and graph paper to redesign in color progression a pattern—perhaps a block pattern—with which you are already familiar. Shade the colors light to dark from blocks at the top of the quilt to those at the bottom. Or shade the colors on the diagonal from the upper right corner block to the lower left one. The project for this chapter follows a third possibility that you might want to try. It shades the colors from the center of the design to the outer edges. Such a progression is reminiscent of the kind of color pattern found in traditional Amish Sunshine and Shadow quilts. As you become more comfort-

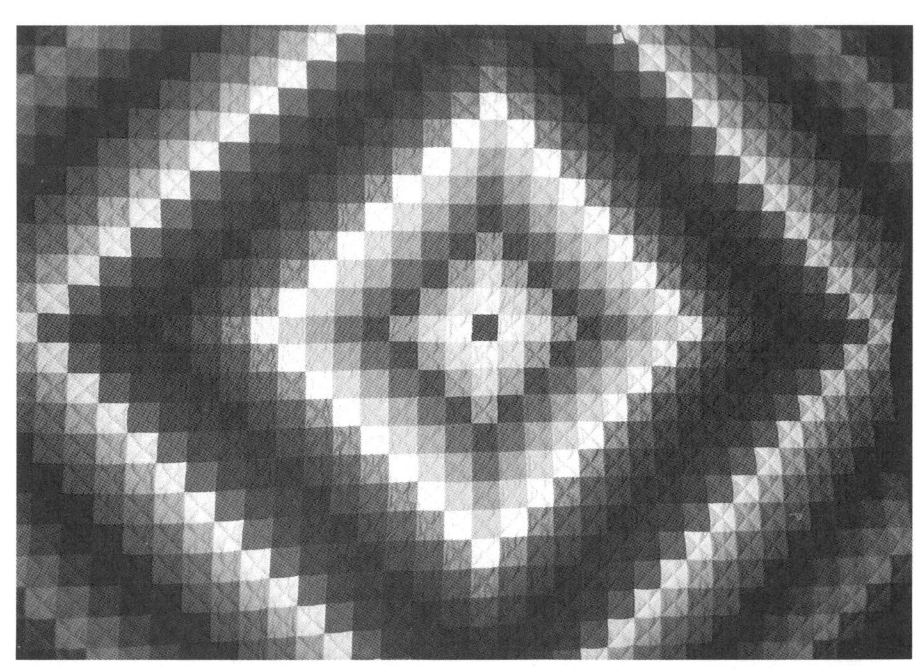

Sunshine and Shadows quilt, a traditional example of color progression.

able with creating color progressions, you will find that you can successfully combine this technique with other themes and approaches to produce exciting original designs.

SUNSET STAR WALL QUILT

DIFFICULTY LEVEL: Easy to Moderate

FINISHED SIZE: 44" × 44"

About the Project. The star theme and colors of this project were inspired by an impression of one star, barely visible, rising on one side of the night sky as the sun set in the other. Sunsets and sunrises provide a lavish palette for quilters in search of color schemes. The star pattern is based on a variation of a Rolling Star pattern from Yvonne M. Khin's *Quilt Names and Patterns*. Unlike other Rolling Star patterns, it is made up largely of squares, rather than diamonds, which makes it especially easy to piece either by hand or machine. The color progression moves from white at the center, through pinks and magentas to dark red-violet at the outer edges.

Consider using the pattern for this project with a color scheme of your own. You might try shading golds through orange into red, for instance. To suggest a snow crystal, rather than a star, try shading white, white-on-white, silver metallics, and pale pearl-colored pastels into light gray or lavender. Consider how the use of other colors might further change the pattern theme.

MATERIALS

Less than ¼ yard each: white print, pale pink solid, purple solid

¼ yard each: light pink solid, light pink metallic, medium pink solid, medium pink print, magenta print, magenta solid, dark magenta solid, dark magenta print

Two 8″ × 34″ purple print border strips

Two 8″ × 44″ purple print border strips

1¼ yards purple solid for four corner squares plus binding strips

44″ × 44″ square batting

44″ × 44″ square backing fabric

Purple quilting thread

DIRECTIONS

1. Choose nondirectional prints where prints are called for in this project. Directional prints, unless handled carefully, are likely to

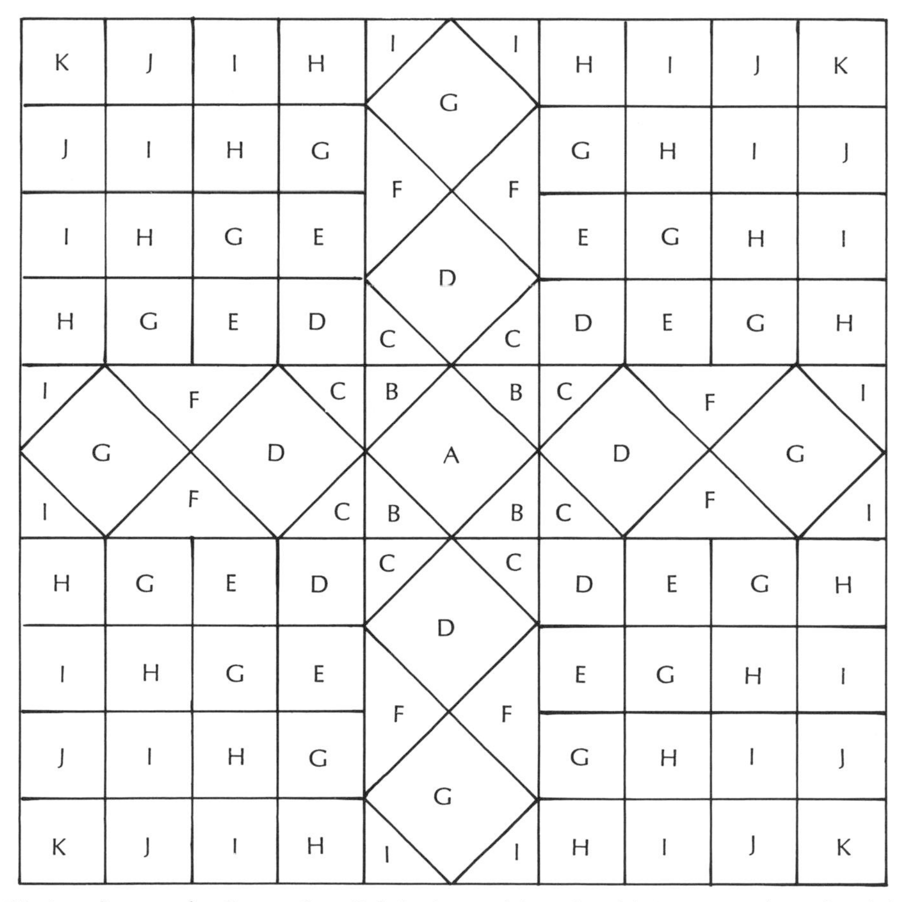

Piecing diagram for *Sunset Star*. Fabric A = white print, fabric B = pale pink solid, fabric C = light pink solid, fabric D = light pink metallic, fabric E = medium pink solid, fabric F = medium pink print, fabric G = magenta print, fabric H = magenta solid, fabric I = dark magenta solid, fabric J = dark magenta print, and fabric K = purple solid.

deflect attention away from the outward movement of the color progression.

2. This pattern uses only four shapes: a large and a small triangle, and a large and a small square. Mark and cut all the triangles and squares from the designated fabrics. You will need:
   Small squares: 4 fabric D, 8 fabric E, 12 fabric G, 16 fabric H, 12 fabric I, 8 fabric J, 4 fabric K
   Large squares: 1 fabric A, 4 fabric D, 4 fabric G
   Small triangles: 4 fabric B, 8 fabric C, 8 fabric I
   Large triangles: 8 fabric F

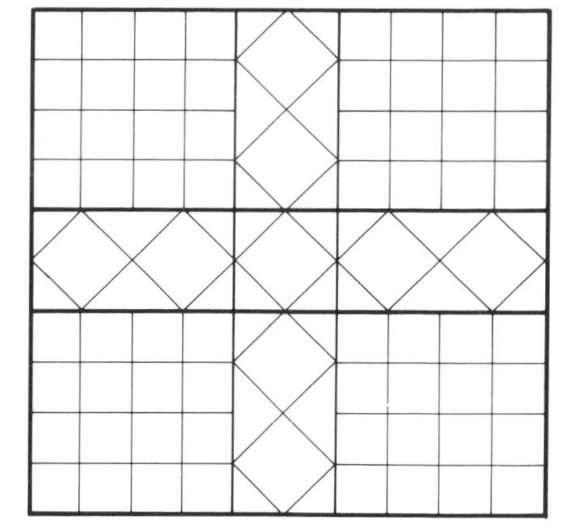

Diagram for *Sunset Star* showing piecing divisions.

3. Begin sewing the pattern. Use the piecing diagram as a guide. The pattern breaks down conveniently into nine sections: four 16-square squares, four rectangles, and the center square. Sew the 16-square units first and set aside. Then piece the four rectangular units that fall in between the 16-square units. The rectangular units are made up of eight shapes: four small triangles, two large triangles, and two large squares. Piece them and set aside. Complete the center square flanked by four triangles. Then join all of the sections together.

4. Sew the two short border strips to the top and bottom of the pieced *Sunset Star* unit. Trim any excess border fabric. Then join the longer border strips to the right and left of the unit. Trim the excess border fabric.

5. Lay out the backing fabric right side down, center the batting on top of this, and center on these the pieced wall hanging top right side up. Baste and quilt the project, using the color photograph as a guide. The quilting pattern emphasizes the radiating color progression. You may want to use your own quilting pattern to further enhance the directional movement of the design.

6. Trim the excess batting and backing fabric. Cut four binding strips 3″ × 48″ each from fabric K. Use them to bind the project. (See finished project in the color section.)

Note

1. Faber Birren, *Principles of Color,* (New York: Van Nostrand Reinhold, 1969), p. 38.

18 New Designs from Old

Years ago, women traded quilt patterns much as they did favorite recipes. The emphasis in quilting was on producing an appealing and useful product, rather than a unique creation. The quilt patterns that women copied and used over and over reveal snippets of how they lived their lives: Log Cabin, Prairie Star, Cats and Mice, Rocky Road to Kansas. Many traditional quilt patterns such as these have endured for a century or more because they are examples of good design. Their appeal stems from their adherence to basic design principles like symmetry, repetition, and balance. Often they provide an opportunity for featuring high-contrast values.

Today's quilters are producing spectacular designs by manipulating traditional block patterns in innovative ways. The creation of contemporary designs based on traditional patterns can be handled in several ways. One method is to combine two patterns in one quilt. Another option is to repeat the elements of one pattern in different sizes—using large and small triangles, for instance. Yet another approach is to use appliqué to provide a figurative representation of a pattern name like Flying Geese and add pieced elements from the traditional pattern itself. An example would be a line of pieced triangles that dissolves into a realistic representation of Canadian geese on the wing.

Midnight Sky, by Sue Tiffany, based on techniques learned during a workshop with Mary Ellen Hopkins. This contemporary Star pattern features the same star in two sizes.

MAKING PAST AND PRESENT MEET

Handling traditional patterns with a contemporary flair takes some practice. You might want to begin by looking through an encyclopedia of quilt patterns. Select one or two that are relatively easy, yet hold personal appeal for you. Using a sheet of tracing paper placed over graph paper, draw the pattern(s) you have chosen, repeating the block to form an overall pattern. Using additional sheets of tracing paper, try doubling and tripling the size of the same pattern. Combine your drawings in different ways by sliding one over another to produce different combinations. The tracing paper approach will let you experiment with the different design possibilities inherent in the altered block.

As a design develops, keep in mind the exciting options raised by color use. Pattern movement in one direction or another may be suggested by successive color use—dark violet motifs progressing to lavender ones, for instance. A transparent effect may be produced by allowing a pattern in one color to overlap a pattern in another color, creating a blended color where the two patterns come together. For instance, a line of red triangles can intersect with a line of yellow triangles, creating orange triangles where the two lines converge.

Many contemporary designs make use of unorthodox symmetry. Instead of an Irish Chain pattern in which the lines of colored squares progress in identical diagonal rows, a contemporary version might feature a diagonal row of large squares crossed by two or more rows of small squares. A night scene might be enhanced by Star blocks placed asymmetrically against a dark sky background.

Quilt artist Ruth B. McDowell is well known for her fascinating designs based on traditional patterns. She calls her style "reverberant pattern" for its strong characteristics of rhythm and repetition. By combining the same visual element (such as triangles) of different sizes, overlapping them, and varying their alignment, she creates original designs that, while based on traditional patterns, are anything but traditional. For more about her exciting style and technique, see her book *Pattern on Pattern* listed in Recommended Reading.

Lilies of the Forest, by Dorothy Bosselman, based on techniques learned during a workshop with Mary Ellen Hopkins. This contemporary version of the Irish Chain pattern features a special print motif and intersecting rows of squares in different sizes.

SNOW IN THE MOUNTAINS WALL QUILT

DIFFICULTY LEVEL: Moderate

FINISHED SIZE: 40″ × 24″

About the Project. This wall hanging combines two of the most basic traditional patterns—Pinwheel and Nine-Patch—to produce a figurative design suggestive of a winter landscape. Consider how the use of different colors would change the scene, suggesting, perhaps, a different season, or an abstract design rather than a landscape. Different values of white are used here to give the impression of the movement of falling snow. The Pinwheel pattern is repeated in both sky and land colors to add continuity to the overall image. Light greens are used for nearer mountains, while dark greens give the impression of distant mountains.

MATERIALS

¼ yard of each of the following (total eleven "snow" fabrics): gray with feather print, off-white (muslin), bright white, white-on-white (leaf print), white-on-white (maze print), light lavender, dark lavender, lavender with random spots, light gray, dark gray, gray with random spots

¼ yard of each of six different light green fabrics (allow a mix of prints and solids)

¼ yard of each of six different dark green fabrics (allow a mix of prints and solids)

Four border strips light gray fabric: two 4″ × 26″, two 4″ × 42″

One rectangle backing fabric 42″ × 26″

One rectangle batting 42″ × 26″

Four dark green strips for binding: two 3″ × 28″, two 3″ × 44″

White quilting thread

DIRECTIONS

1. Photocopy or trace the pattern pieces for the triangle and the square. Cut them out to make templates. Note that the seam allowance is included on these templates.
2. Using the triangle template, mark and cut out the following number of triangles from the designated fabrics (see the diagram code): A: 4, B: 24, E: 5, F: 4, G: 4, H: 4, J: 7, K: 4, L: 7, M: 5, N: 3, O: 3, P: 12, Q: 3, R: 8, S: 8, T: 2, U: 1.
3. Using the square template, mark and cut out the following number of squares from the designated fabrics (see the diagram code): A: 11, B: 17, C: 5, D: 9, E: 4, F: 2, H: 4, I: 2, J: 1, K: 2, M: 3, N: 2, O: 5, P: 1, Q: 1, R: 1, T: 1, U: 3.
4. Use the diagram as a piecing guide. You can do the piecing by hand or machine. To begin, join all of the triangles in pairs to form squares. Once this is done, iron the pieced squares. Lay the pieced squares and the solid-color fabric squares out in the correct sewing order according to the piecing diagram. You may want to pin them to a foundation fabric to keep them in order.
5. Piece the entire center design portion of the wall hanging. You may want to join the pinwheels first and join the remaining squares around them to form sections, joining the sections at the last.
6. Pin and sew the border strips to the edges of the wall hanging. Trim as needed.
7. Lay out the backing fabric right side down, center the batting on top of this, and center on these the pieced wall hanging top right side up. Baste and quilt the project, using the color photograph as a guide.The lines of quilting in the sky are random curved lines to contrast with

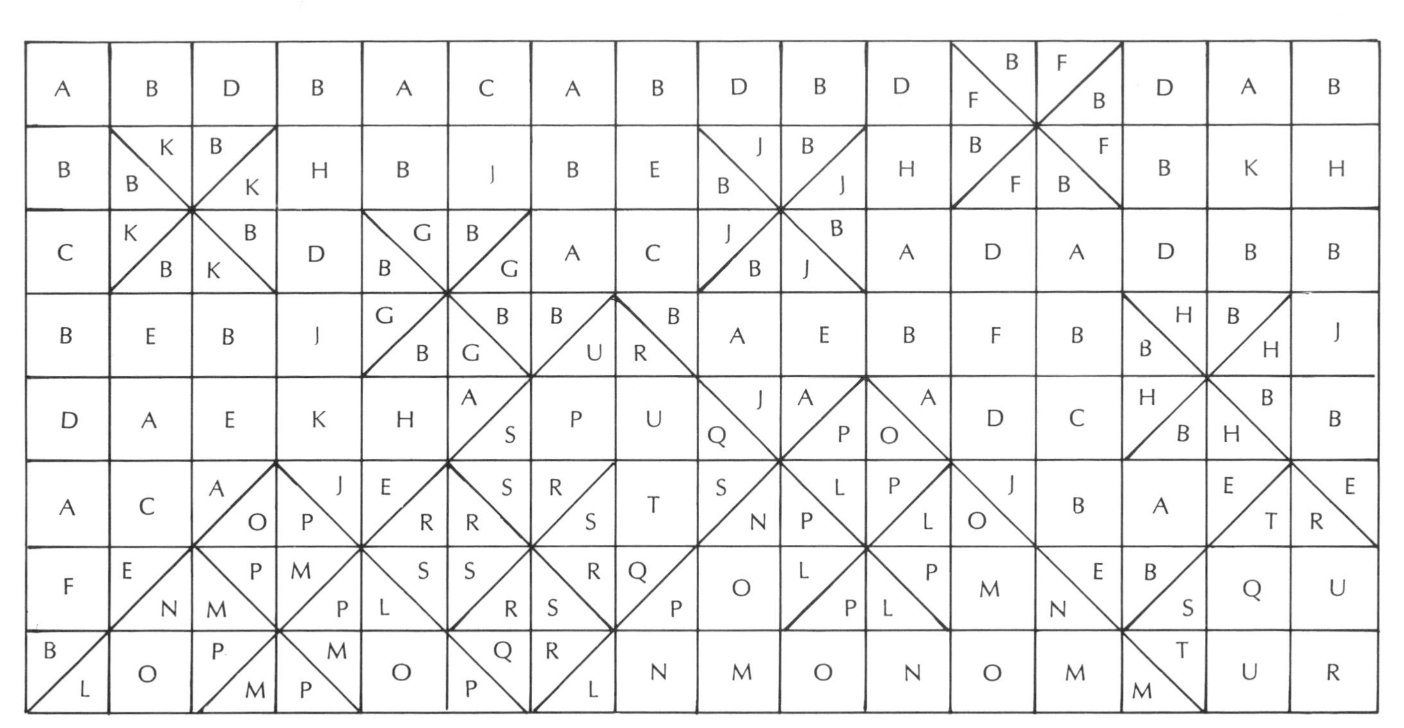

Piecing diagram for *Snow in the Mountains*.

the straight pieced seams. The quilting of the mountains echoes the straight linear forms.

8. Trim the excess batting and backing fabric. Bind the project, using the dark green binding strips. (See finished project in the color section.)

PIECING DIAGRAM

A B D B A C A B D B D F/B F/B D A B
B B/K B/K H B J B E B/J B/J H B/F B/F B K H
C K/B K/B D B/G B/G A C J/B J/B A D A D B B
B E B J G/B G/B B/U R/B A E B F B B/H B/H J
D A E K H A/S P U Q/J A/P O/A D C H/B H/B B
A C A/O P/J E/R R/S R/S T S/N P/L P/L O/J B A E/T R/E
F E/N M/P M/P L/S S/R S/R Q/P O L/P L/P M N/E B/S Q U
B/L O P/M P/M O P/Q R/L N M O N O M M/T U R

DIAGRAM CODE

A: gray print

B: off-white solid

C: bright white solid

D: white-on-white leaf print

E: white-on-white maze print

F: light lavender solid

G: dark lavender solid
H: lavender print
J: gray solid
K: gray print
L: yellow-green solid
M: pale green solid
N: lime green solid
O: medium green solid
P: medium green print
Q: dark green print with white
R: dark green print with lavender
S: dark green print with black
T: dark green print with yellow
U: dark green solid

Recommended Reading

CHAPTER ONE: QUILTS AND CREATIVITY

The Artist and the Quilt, edited by Charlotte Robinson, New York: Alfred A. Knopf, 1983.

Fiber Expressions: The Contemporary Quilt, edited by Nancy Roe, West Chester, PA: Schiffer Publishing, 1987.

Japanese Quilts, Jill Liddell and Yuko Watanabe, New York: E. P. Dutton, 1988.

The New Quilt 1, Dairy Barn Quilt National, Newtown, CT: Taunton Press, 1991.

New Wave Quilt: Setsuko Segawa and 15 American Artists, edited by Setsuko Segawa, Kyoto, Japan: Mitsumura Suiko Shoin Publishing Company, 1991.

The Pieced Quilt: An American Design Tradition, Jonathan Holstein, Boston: Little, Brown and Company, 1973.

CHAPTER TWO: STYLE AND STRUCTURE

Backart: On the Flip Side, Danita Rafalovich and Kathryn Alison Pellman, Mountain View, CA: Leone Publications, 1991.

Drawing on the Right Side of the Brain, Betty Edwards, Los Angeles: J. P. Tarcher, Inc., 1979.

Nature Drawing: A Tool for Learning, Clare Walker Leslie, Englewood Cliffs, NJ: Prentice-Hall, 1980.

CHAPTER THREE: VISUAL ELEMENTS

Basic Design, Kenneth F. Bates, New York: Funk & Wagnalls, 1975.

Picture This: Perception & Composition, Molly Bang, Boston: Little, Brown and Company, 1991.

The Zen of Seeing, Frederick Franck, New York: Vintage Books, 1973.

CHAPTER FOUR: RELATIONSHIPS OF VISUAL ELEMENTS

Design and Expression in the Visual Arts, John F. A. Taylor, New York: Dover Publications, 1964.

The Fine Art of Quilting, Vicki Barker and Tessa Bird, New York: E. P. Dutton, 1988.

CHAPTER FIVE: COMPOSITION

Composition: A Painter's Guide to Basic Problems and Solutions, David Friend, New York: Watson-Guptill Publications, 1981.

Picture This: Perception & Composition, Molly Bang, Boston: Little, Brown and Company, 1991.

CHAPTER SIX: COLOR

Color Choices: Making Color Sense Out of Color Theory, Stephen Quiller, New York: Watson-Guptill, 1989.

Color Harmony: A Guide to Creative Color Combinations, Hideaki Chijiiwa, Radnor, PA: Chilton Book Company, 1991.

A Color Notation, Albert H. Munsell, Baltimore, MD: Munsell Color Company, 1936.

The Elements of Color, Johannes Itten, edited by Faber Birren, New York: Van Nostrand Reinhold, 1970.

The Enjoyment and Use of Color, Walter Sargent, New York: Charles Scribner's Sons, 1923.

Interaction of Color, Josef Albers, revised edition, New Haven, CT: Yale University Press, 1975.

Principles of Color, Faber Birren, New York: Van Nostrand Reinhold, 1969.

The Principles of Harmony and Contrast of Colors, M. E. Chevreul, New York: Van Nostrand Reinhold, 1967.

CHAPTER SEVEN: FABRIC

Color and Cloth: The Quiltmaker's Ultimate Workbook, Mary Coyne Penders, San Francisco: Quilt Digest Press, 1989.

Pattern on Pattern, Ruth B. McDowell, San Francisco: Quilt Digest Press, 1991.

CHAPTER EIGHT: QUILTING

Fine Hand Quilting, Diana Leone, Mountain View, CA: Leone Publications, 1986.

How to Improve Your Quilting Stitch, Ami Simms, Mallery Street, Flint, MI 48504: privately printed, 1987.

CHAPTER NINE: TWO-DIMENSIONAL DESIGN

The Cut-outs of Henri Matisse, John Elderfield, New York: George Braziller, 1978.

Henri Matisse Paper Cutouts, Jack Cowart, Jack D. Flam, Dominique Fourcade, and John Hallmark Neff, St. Louis, MO: St. Louis Art Museum and Detroit Institute of the Arts, 1977.

Making Animal Quilts: Patterns and Projects, Willow Ann Soltow, Intercourse, PA: Good Books, 1986.

More Silhouettes, edited by Carol Belanger Grafton, New York: Dover Books, 1982.

The Paper Cut-Out Design Book, Ramona Jablonski, Owings Mills, MD: Stemmer House Publishers, 1976.

Quilts to Wear, Virginia Avery, New York: Charles Scribner's Sons, 1982.

Silhouettes, edited by Carol Belanger Grafton, New York: Dover Books, 1979.

Weaving You Can Wear, Jean Wilson with Jan Burhen, New York: Van Nostrand Reinhold, 1973.

Wonderful Wearbles, Virginia Avery, Paducah, KY: American Quilter's Society, 1991.

CHAPTER TEN: CONTEMPORIZE THOSE BLOCKS

Frogs & Flowers: Impressions of Ponds & Gardens Made Into Quilts, Camille Remme, Wheeling, WV: Boyd Publishing, 1991.

Quiltmaking, Susan Denton and Barbara Macey, New York: Sterling Publishing, 1988.

The Second Quiltmaker's Handbook: Creative Approaches to Contemporary Quilt Design, Michael James, Englewood Cliffs, NJ: Prentice-Hall, 1981.

CHAPTER ELEVEN: FABRIC INSPIRATIONS

Piece by Piece: The Complete Book of Quiltmaking, Dianne Finnegan, London: Blandford, 1991.

CHAPTER TWELVE: TECHNIQUE-INSPIRED DESIGN

Chintz Quilts: Unfading Glory, Lacy Folmar Bullard and Betty Jo Shiell, Tallahassee, FL: Serendipity Publishers, 1983.

The Complete Book of Patchwork, Quilting, and Appliqué, Linda Seward, New York: Prentice-Hall, 1987.

Contemporary Quilting, Sharon Robinson, Worcester, MA: Davis Publications, 1982.

Creating Pa Ndau Appliqué, Carla Hassel, Lombard, IL: Wallace-Homestead, 1984.

The Hawaiian Quilt, catalog of an exhibit curated by Reiko Mochinaga Brandon, Honolulu Academy of Arts, Tokyo: Kokusai Art, 1991.

Molas: Folk Art of the Cuna Indians, Ann Parker and Avon Neal, New York: Crown, 1977.

Patterns from Paradise, Vicki Poggioli, Pittstown, NJ: Mainstreet Press, 1988.

Quilting the World Over, Willow Ann Soltow, Radnor, PA: Chilton Book Company, 1991.

Sashiko, Bonnie Benjamin, Glendale, CA: Needlearts International, 1986.

Traditional Indian Textiles, John Gillow and Nicholas Barnard, London: Thames and Hudson, 1991.

Trapunto and Other Forms of Raised Quilting, Mary Morgan and Dee Mosteller, New York: Charles Scribner's Sons, 1977.

CHAPTER THIRTEEN: LAND AND LANDSCAPES

Frogs & Flowers: Impressions of Ponds and Gardens Made Into Quilts, Camille Remme, Wheeling, WV: Boyd Publishing, 1991.

Landscapes & Illusions, Joen Wolfrom, Lafayette, CA: C & T Publishing, 1990.

CHAPTER FOURTEEN: PUT SOME LIFE INTO IT

The Second Quiltmaker's Handbook: Creative Approaches to Contemporary Quilt Design, Michael James, Englewood Cliffs, NJ: Prentice-Hall, 1981.

Seminole Patchwork, Margaret Brandebourg, New York: Sterling Publishing, 1987.

Strip Quilting, Diane Wold, Blue Ridge Summit, PA: TAB Books, 1987.

CHAPTER FIFTEEN: PERSONALIZED FABRIC DESIGN

Contemporary Batik and Tie-Dye, Dona Z. Meilach, New York: Crown Publishers, 1973.

Marbling on Fabric, Daniel and Paula Cohen with Eden Gray, Loveland, CO: Interweave Press, 1990.

Marbling Paper & Fabric, Carol Taylor, New York: Sterling Publishing, 1991.

Natural Dyes and Home Dyeing, Rita J. Adrosko, New York: Dover Publications, 1971.

Plants & Gardens: Natural Plant Dyeing 29, 2 (August 1973) Brooklyn, NY: Brooklyn Botanic Garden.

Print Your Own Fabrics, Jutta Lammèr, New York: Watson-Guptill Publications, 1965.

Stencilling, Pamela Riddle and Mary Jane Danley, New York: Berkley Publishing Corporation, 1978.

CHAPTER SIXTEEN: THREE-DIMENSIONAL DESIGN

3-Dimensional Design, Katie Pasquini, Lafayette, CA: C & T Publishing, 1988.

Attic Windows: A Contemporary View, Diana Leone, Mountain View, CA: Leone Publications, 1990.

The Day the Universe Changed, James Burke, Boston: Little, Brown and Company, 1985.

Perspective: A New System for Designers, Jay Doblin, New York: Whitney Library of Design, 1977.

CHAPTER SEVENTEEN: COLOR PROGRESSIONS

Quilt Names and Patterns, Yvonne M. Khin, Washington, DC: Acropolis Books, 1980.

CHAPTER EIGHTEEN: NEW DESIGNS FROM OLD

The Art Quilt, Penny McMorris and Michael Kile, San Francisco: Quilt Digest Press, 1986.

Contemporary Quilts from Traditional Designs, Caron L. Mosey, New York: E. P. Dutton, 1988

Frogs & Flowers: Impressions of Ponds and Gardens Made Into Quilts, Camille Remme, Wheeling, WV: Boyd Publishing, 1991.

Pattern on Pattern, Ruth B. McDowell, Gualala, CA: Quilt Digest Press, 1991.

The Quilt: New Directions for an American Tradition, edited by Nancy Roe, Exton, PA: Schiffer Publishing for Quilt National, 1983.

The Quilt Design Workbook, Beth and Jeffrey Gutcheon, New York: Rawson Associates Publishers, 1976.

Sources

UNUSUAL FABRICS AND FABRIC-RELATED ITEMS

The Cloth Cupboard
Box 2263
Boise, ID 83701
(208) 345-5567
Offers a wide variety of exciting fabrics, including designer fabrics.

The Cotton Shoppe
Box 3168
Key Largo, FL 33037
Offers designer fabrics by Hoffman, Mary Ellen Hopkins, RJR, and others.

International Fabric Collection
3445 West Lake Road
Erie, PA 16505
(814) 838-0740
Offers unusual fabrics from around the world.

Kasuri Dyeworks
1915 Shattuck Avenue
Berkeley, CA 94704
Offers yukata and other Japanese fabrics, as well as sashiko supplies.

Quilts & Other Comforts
P.O. Box 394-1
Wheatridge, CO 80034-0394

Skydyes
83 Richmond Lane
West Hartford, CT 06117
Offers one-of-a-kind hand-painted fabrics.

Tabitha Quilts
10 Francine
Acton, MA 01720
or
827 Gull
Kalamazoo, MI 49001
Offers custom-made contemporary patchwork clothing and retail sale of unusual fabrics.

Textile Reproductions
c/o Kathleen B. Smith
Box 48

West Chesterfield, MA 01084
Offers materials and kits for eighteenth-century needlework, vegetable dyeing, and other historical textile work.

True Colors
R.D. 3, Box 91
Wood Road
Pittstown, NJ 08867
Offers landscape-style hand-dyed fabrics, hand-marbled fabrics (all 100% cotton), marbling kits, and fiber-reactive dye kits.

KITS, NOTIONS, PATTERNS, AND SEWING TOOLS

Cabin Fever Calicoes
Box 550106
Atlanta, GA 30355
(800) 762-2246
Offers graduated fabric packs and notions for quilters.

The Cloth Cupboard
Box 2263
Boise, ID 83701
(208) 345-5567
Offers a variety of notions, including glass-head silk pins for piecing and appliqué.

Critter Pattern Works
c/o Debora Konchinsky
204 Independence Court
Blandon, PA 19510
(215) 926-6117
Offers custom-made patterns for realistic animal designs suitable for block quilts and decorating clothing.

Keepsake Quilting
44 Dover Street
Box 1459
Meredith, NH 03253
Offers notions, fabric packs, and books.

Log Cabin Quilts
9 Central Street
Woodstock, VT 05091
Offers notions, stencils, and muslin clothing for decorating with patchwork.

The Vermont Patchworks
Box 229
Shrewsbury, VT 05738
(800) 451-4044
Offers a wide variety of books and sewing tools.

AND MORE

Amish Goods
Box 6835
5718 25th Avenue, NW
Rochester, MN 55903
Offers expert hand-quilting of quilts and wall hangings at reasonable rates.

Hard-to-Find Needlework Books
c/o Bette S. Feinstein
96 Roundwood Road
Newton, MA 02164
(617) 969-0942
Offers out-of-print quilting and needlework books, as well as current titles.

Randy Miller
North Road
E. Alstead, NH 03602
Offers beautifully detailed pewter buttons for quilted and other clothing.

Norwood
Box 167
Fremont, MI 49412
(616) 924-3901
Offers quality hoops and frames.

Printworks, Ltd.
2096 Durham Road
Madison, CT 06443
Offers custom-made stencils for quilting and other sewing projects.

QUILTER'S ORGANIZATION

American Quilter's Society
Box 3290
Paducah, KY 42002-3290
(800) 626-5420
Offers *American Quilter,* an important quarterly magazine for quilters interested in design. Membership also includes free admission to the yearly AQS Quilt Show and discounts on popular quilting books.

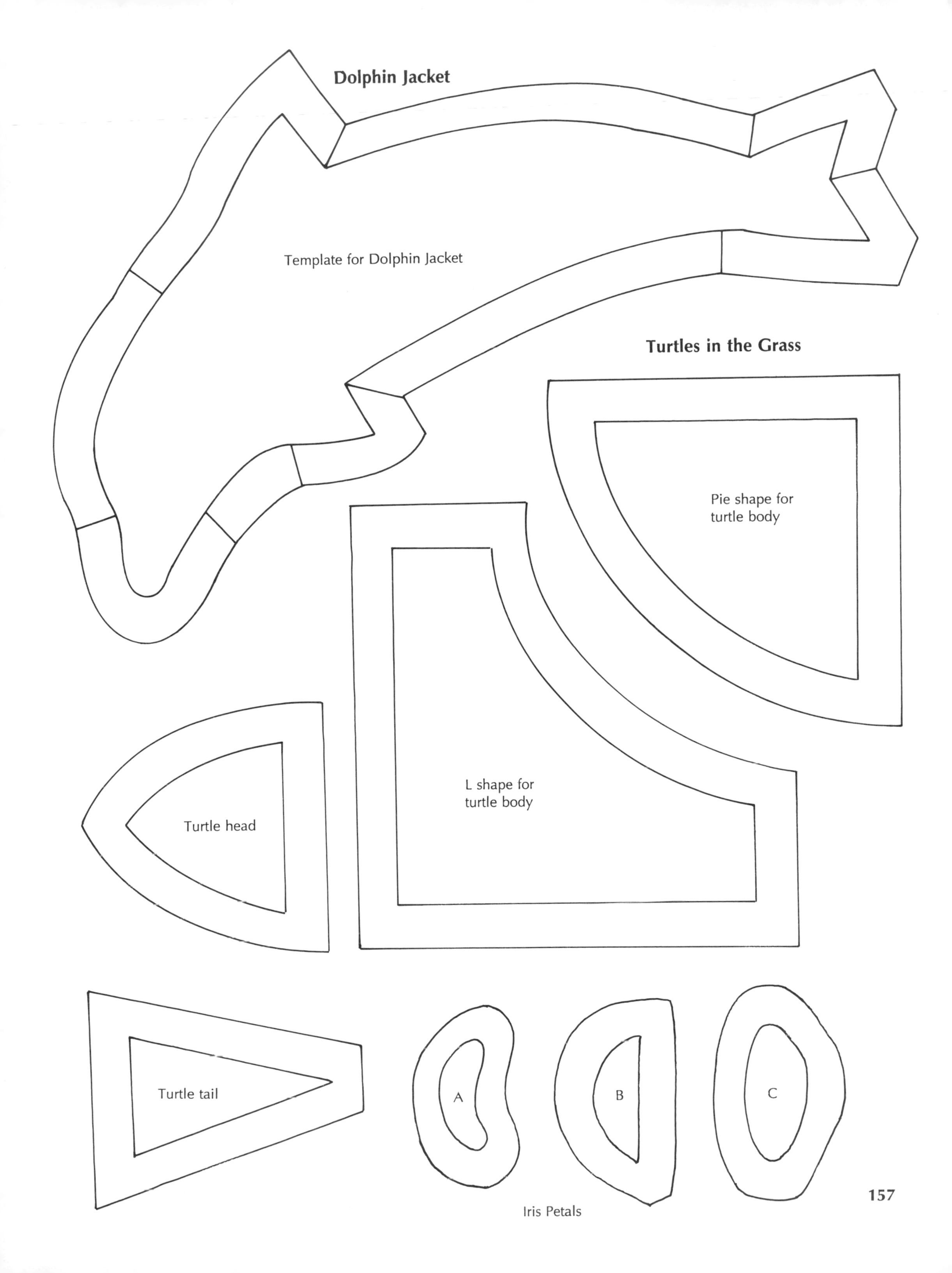
Dolphin Jacket
Template for Dolphin Jacket
Turtles in the Grass
Pie shape for
turtle body
L shape for
turtle body
Turtle head
Turtle tail
A
B
C
Iris Petals

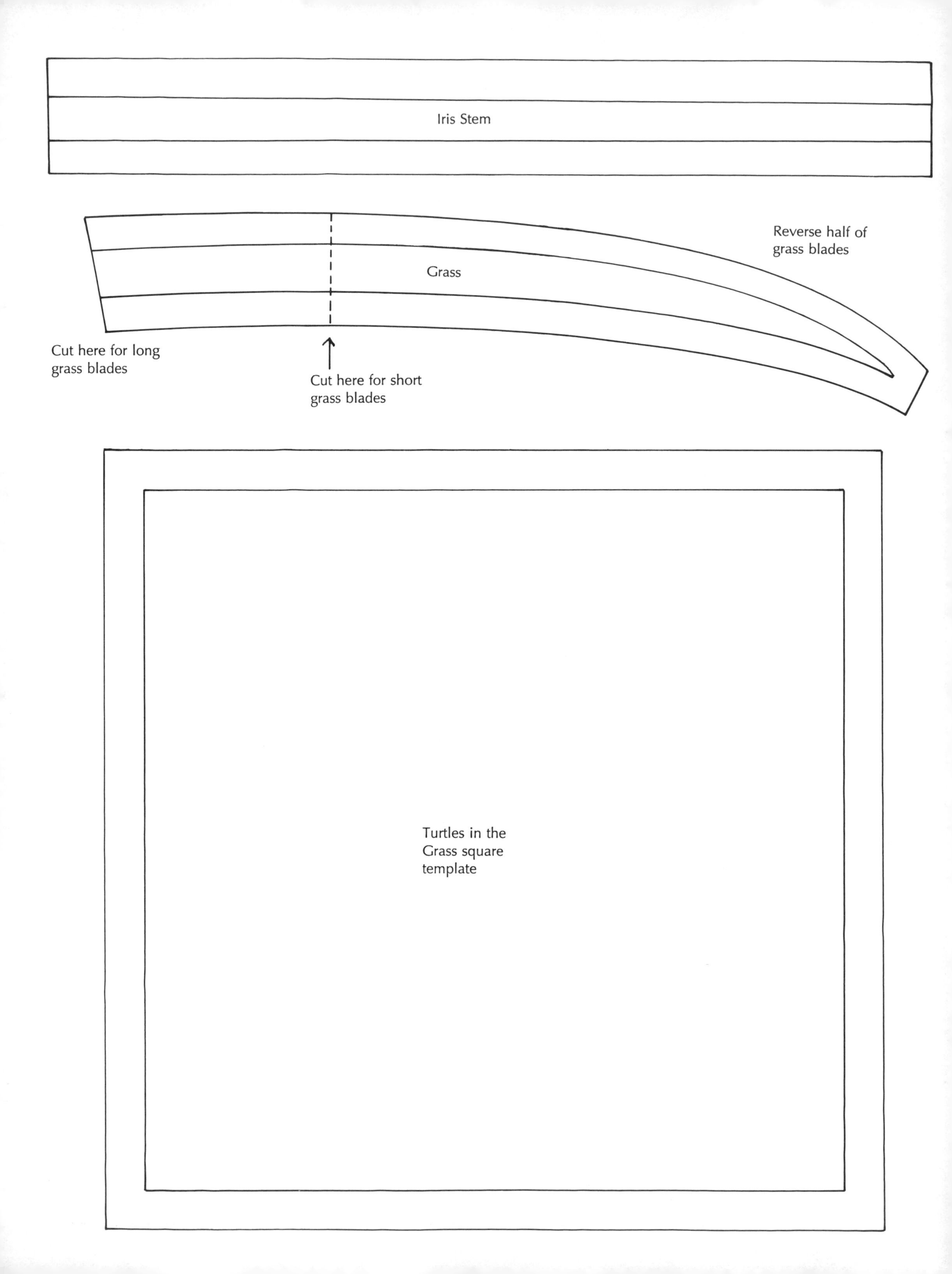
Iris Stem
Reverse half of grass blades
Grass
Cut here for long grass blades
Cut here for short grass blades
Turtles in the Grass square template

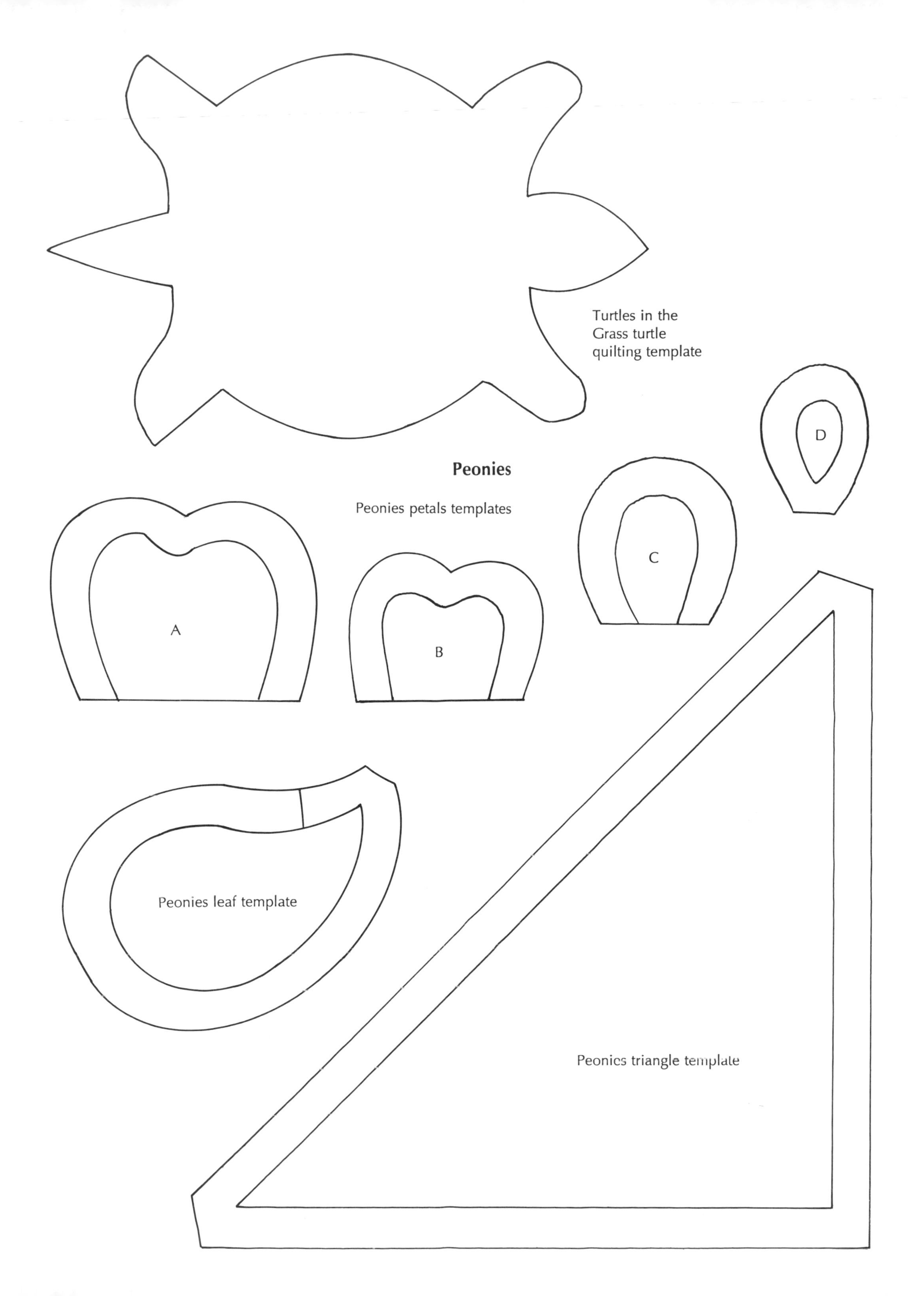
Turtles in the
Grass turtle
quilting template
Peonies
Peonies petals templates
A
B
C
D
Peonies leaf template
Peonics triangle template

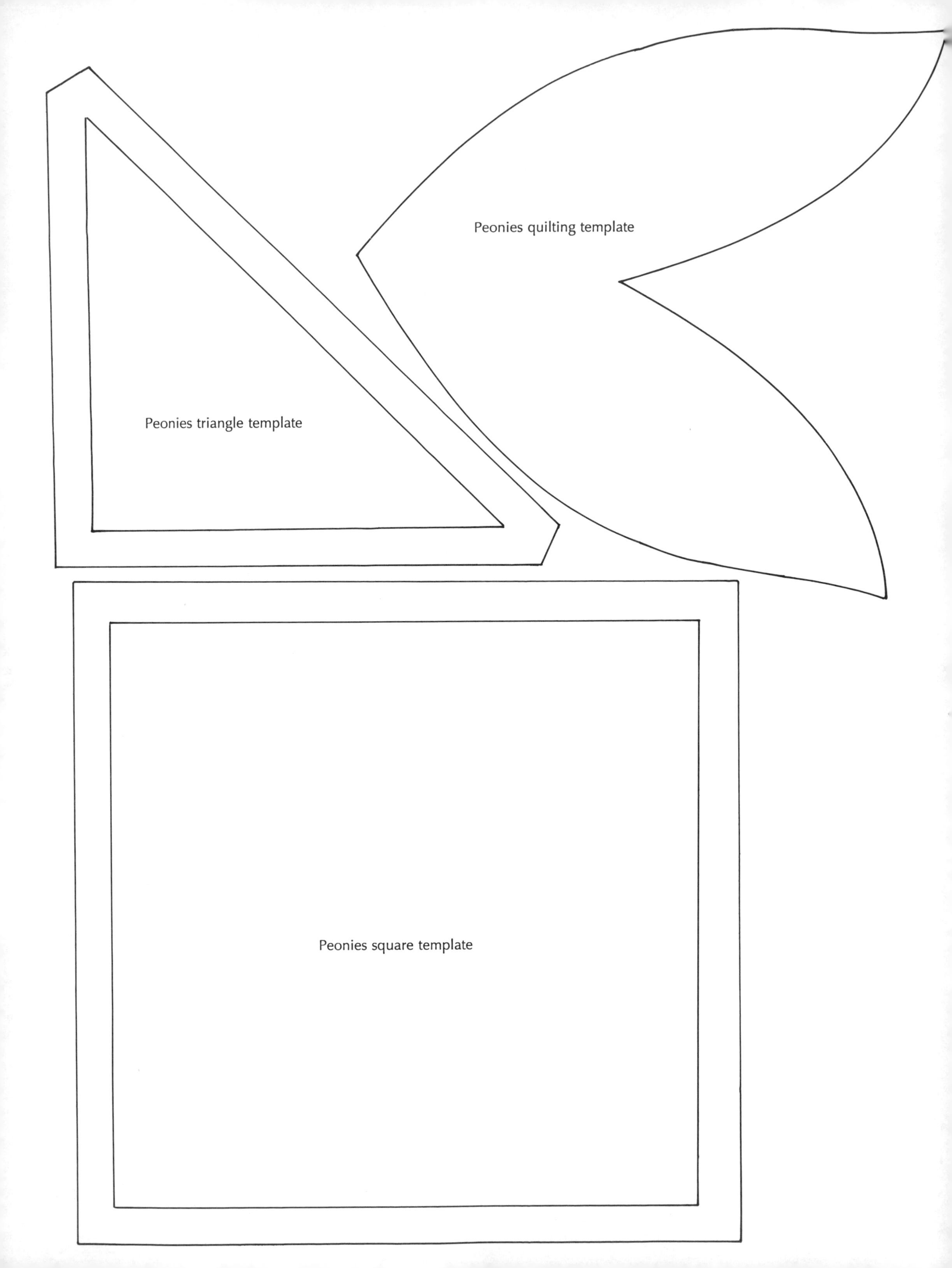
Peonies quilting template
Peonies triangle template
Peonies square template

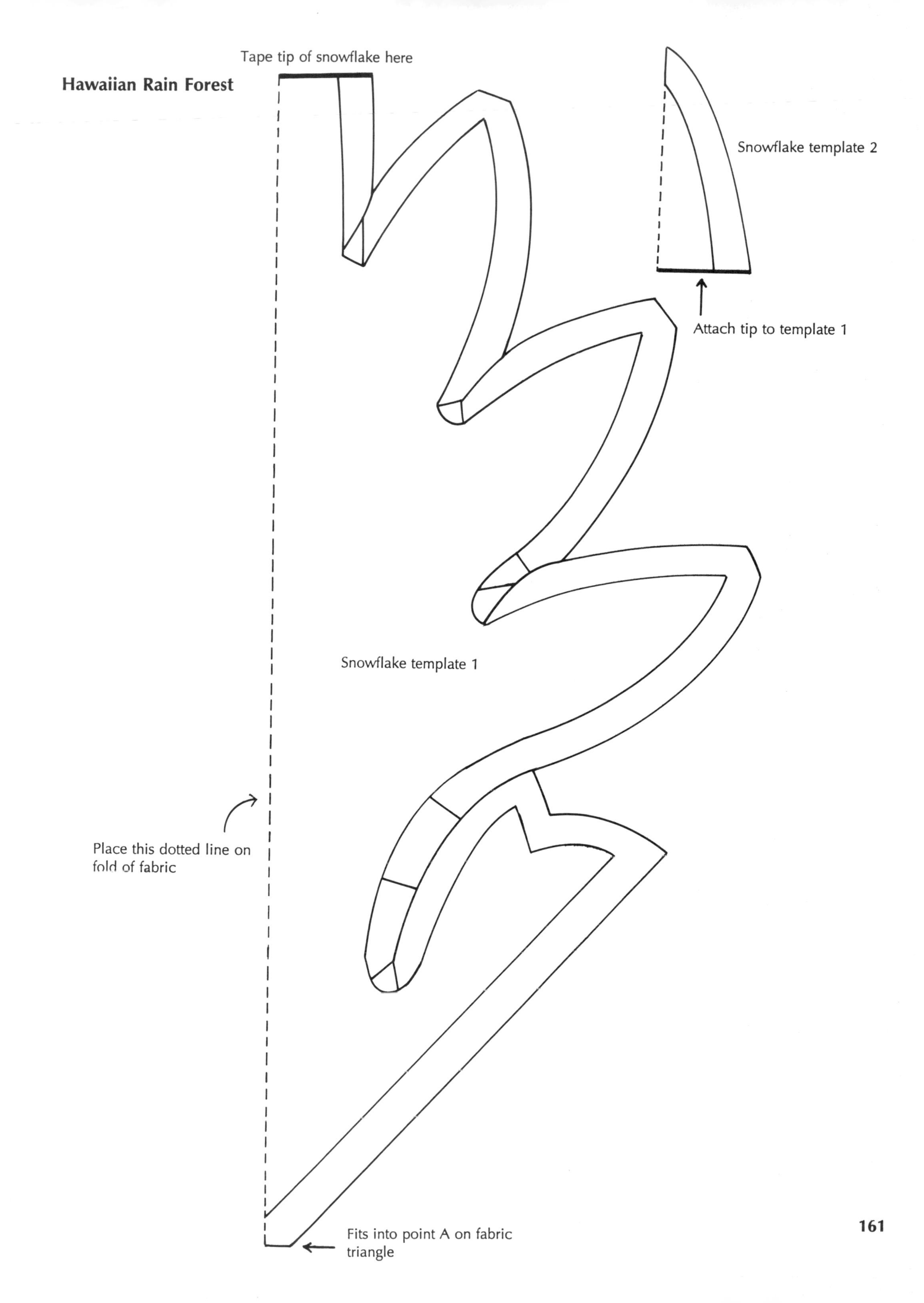
Hawaiian Rain Forest
Tape tip of snowflake here
Snowflake template 2
Attach tip to template 1
Snowflake template 1
Place this dotted line on fold of fabric
Fits into point A on fabric triangle

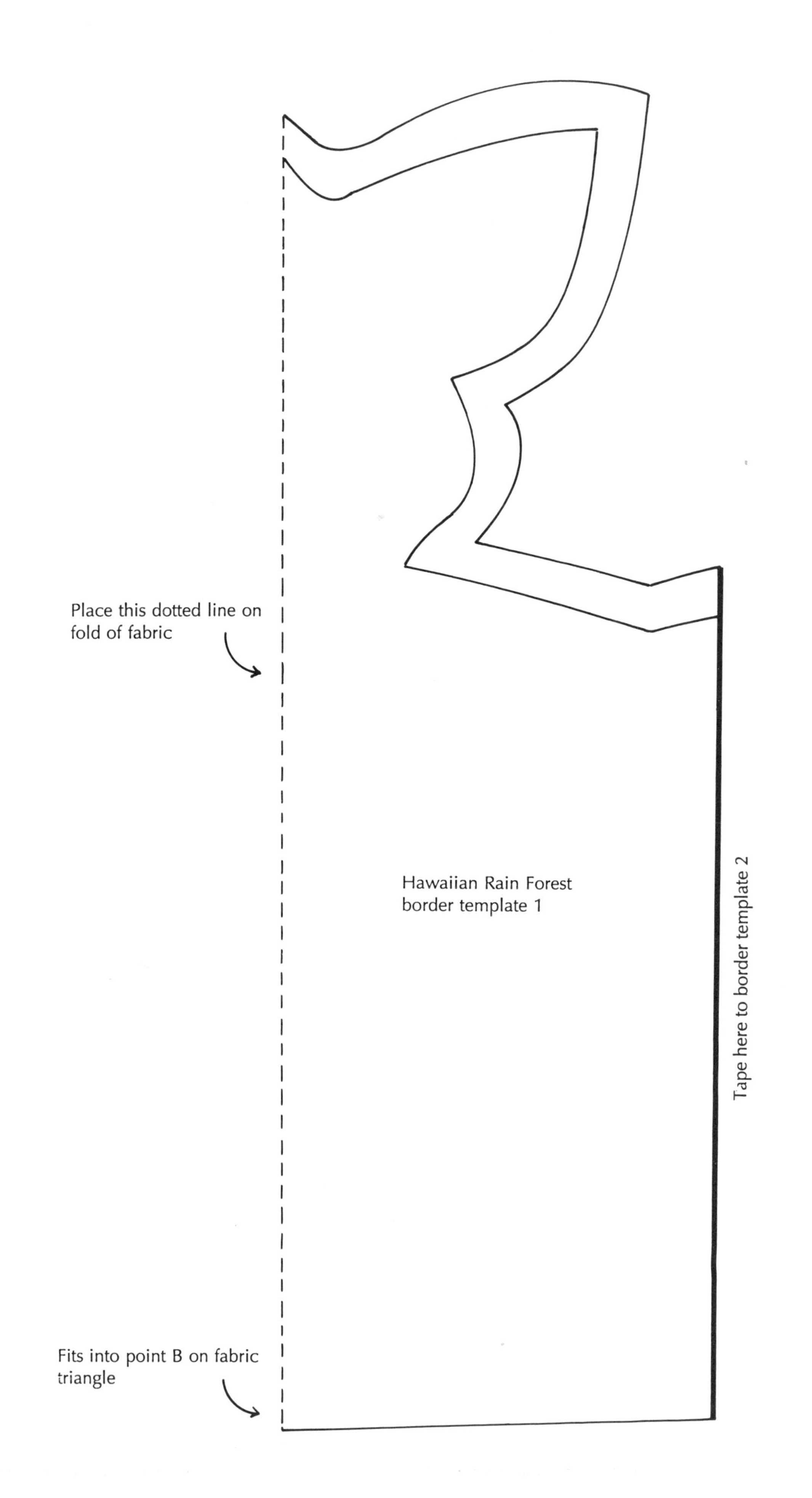
Place this dotted line on fold of fabric
Hawaiian Rain Forest border template 1
Tape here to border template 2
Fits into point B on fabric triangle

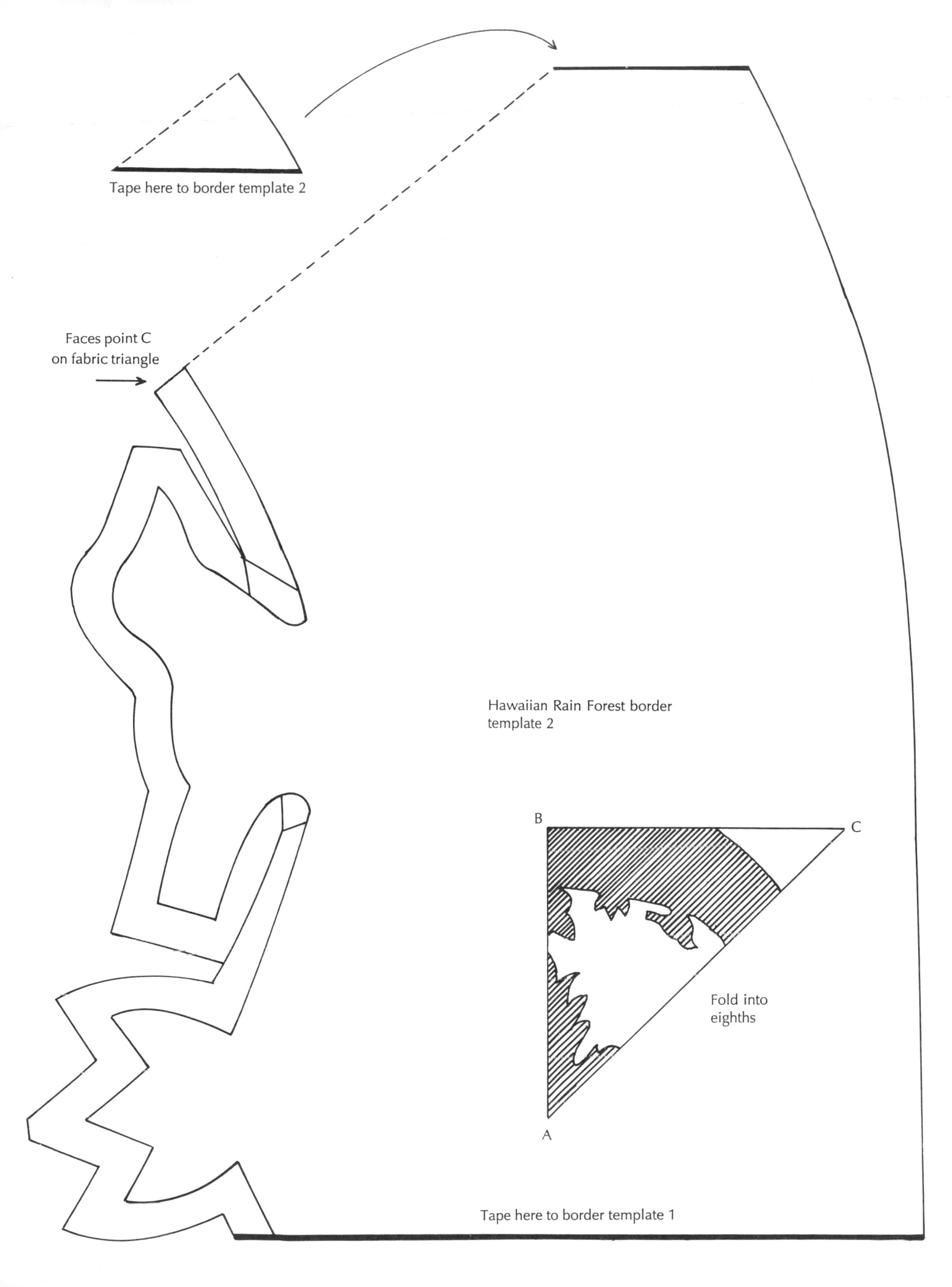
Tape here to border template 2
Faces point C
on fabric triangle
Hawaiian Rain Forest border
template 2
B
C
Fold into
eighths
A
Tape here to border template 1

Across the Lake

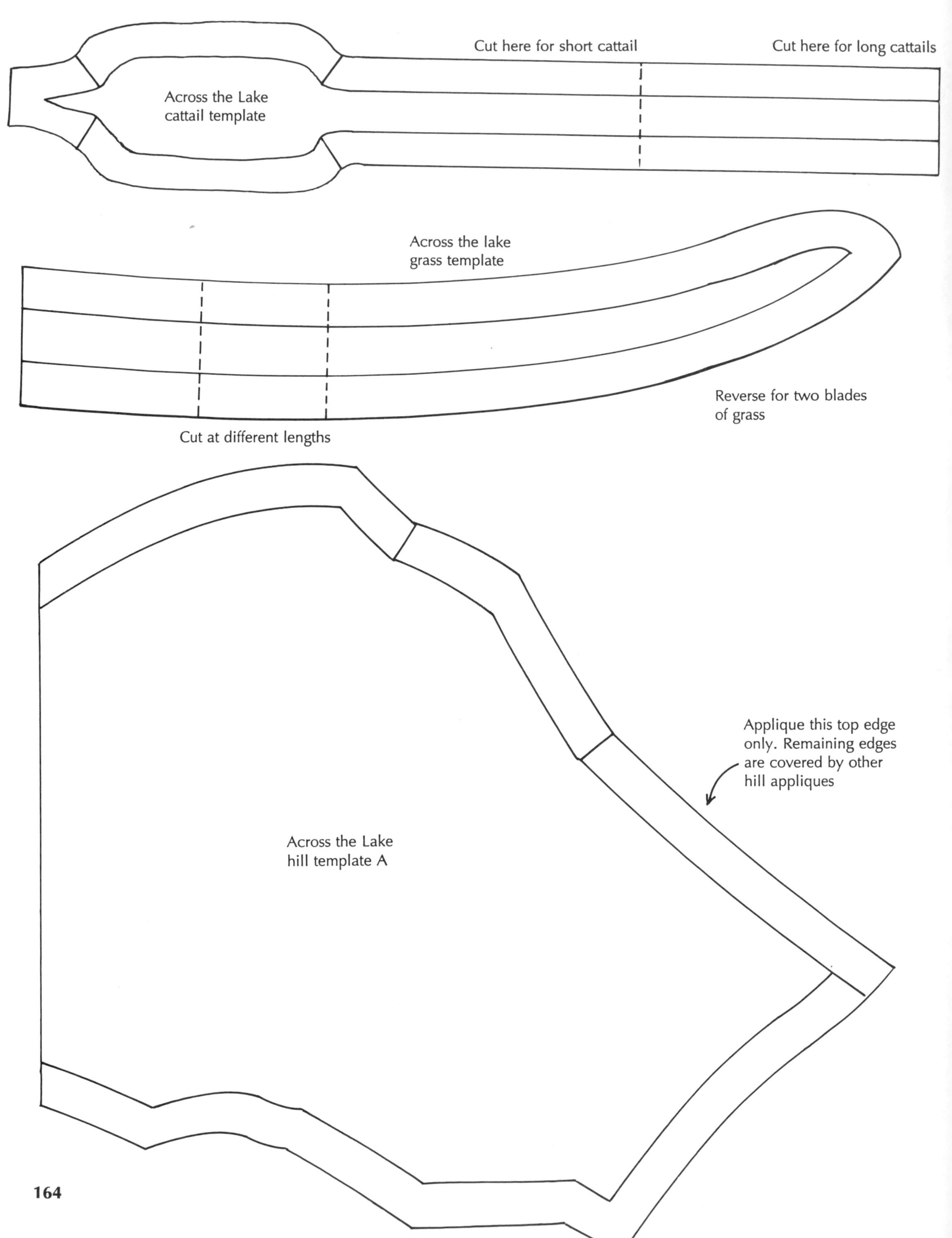

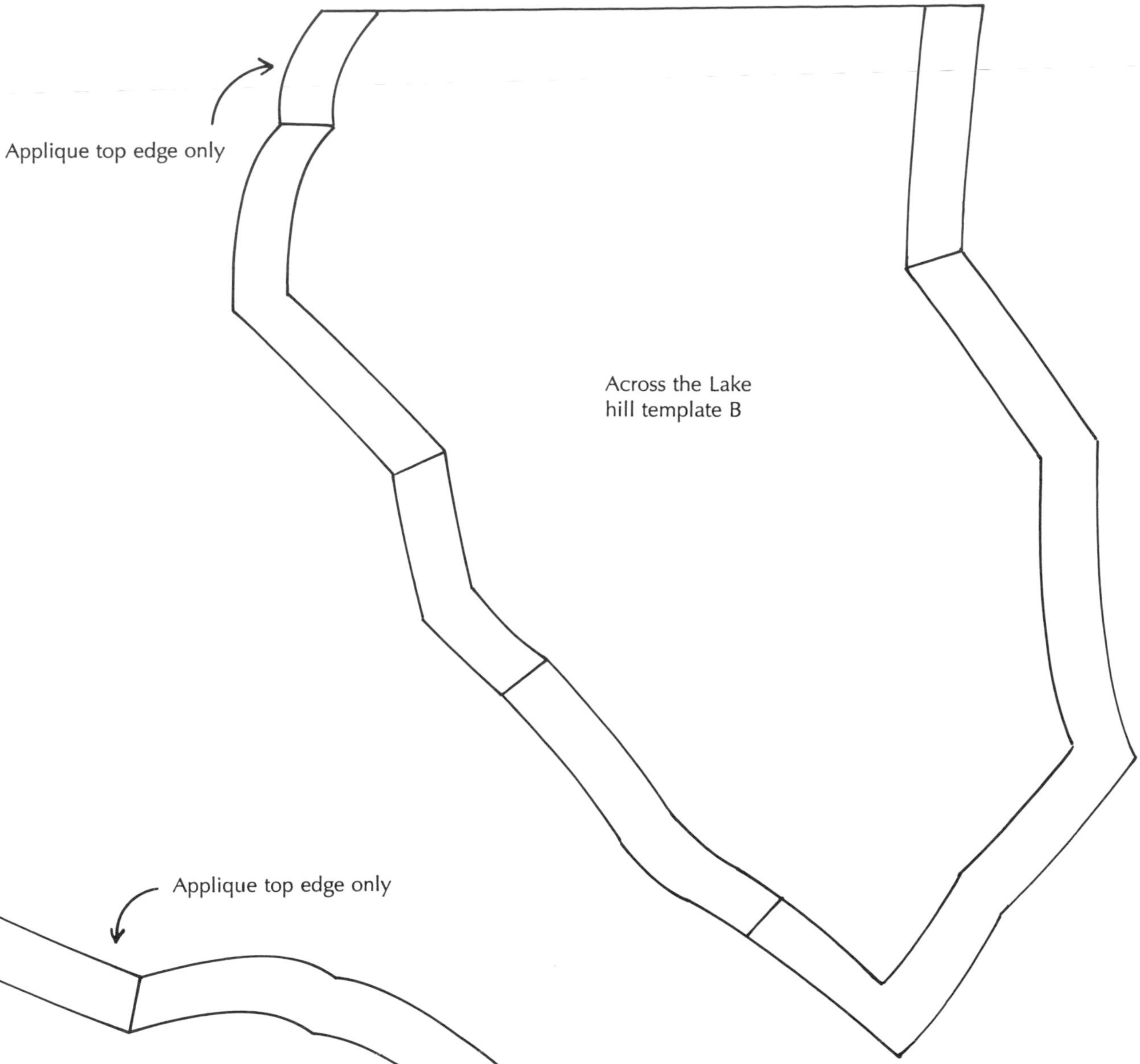

Applique top edge only

Across the Lake
hill template B

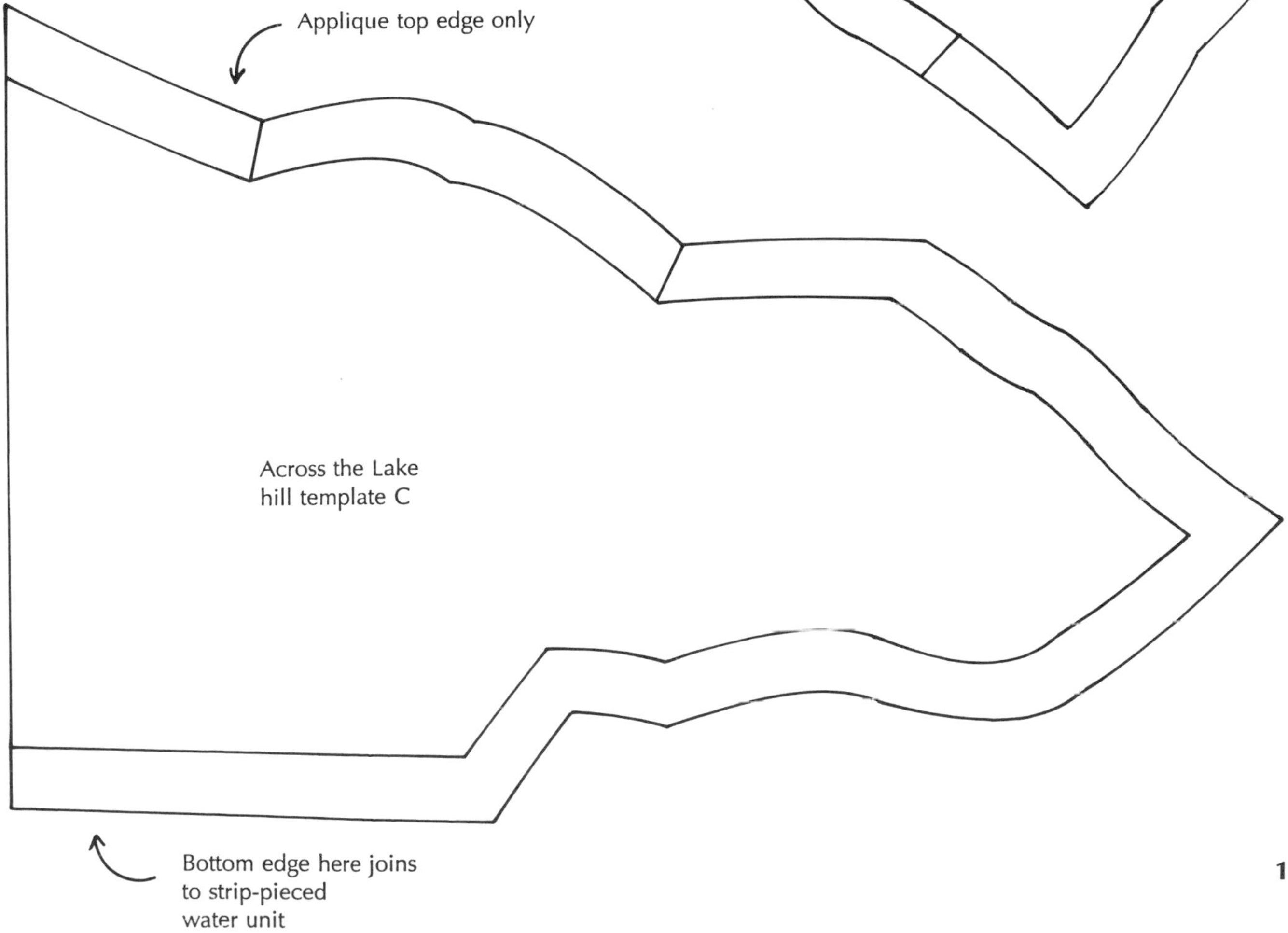

Applique top edge only

Across the Lake
hill template C

Bottom edge here joins
to strip-pieced
water unit

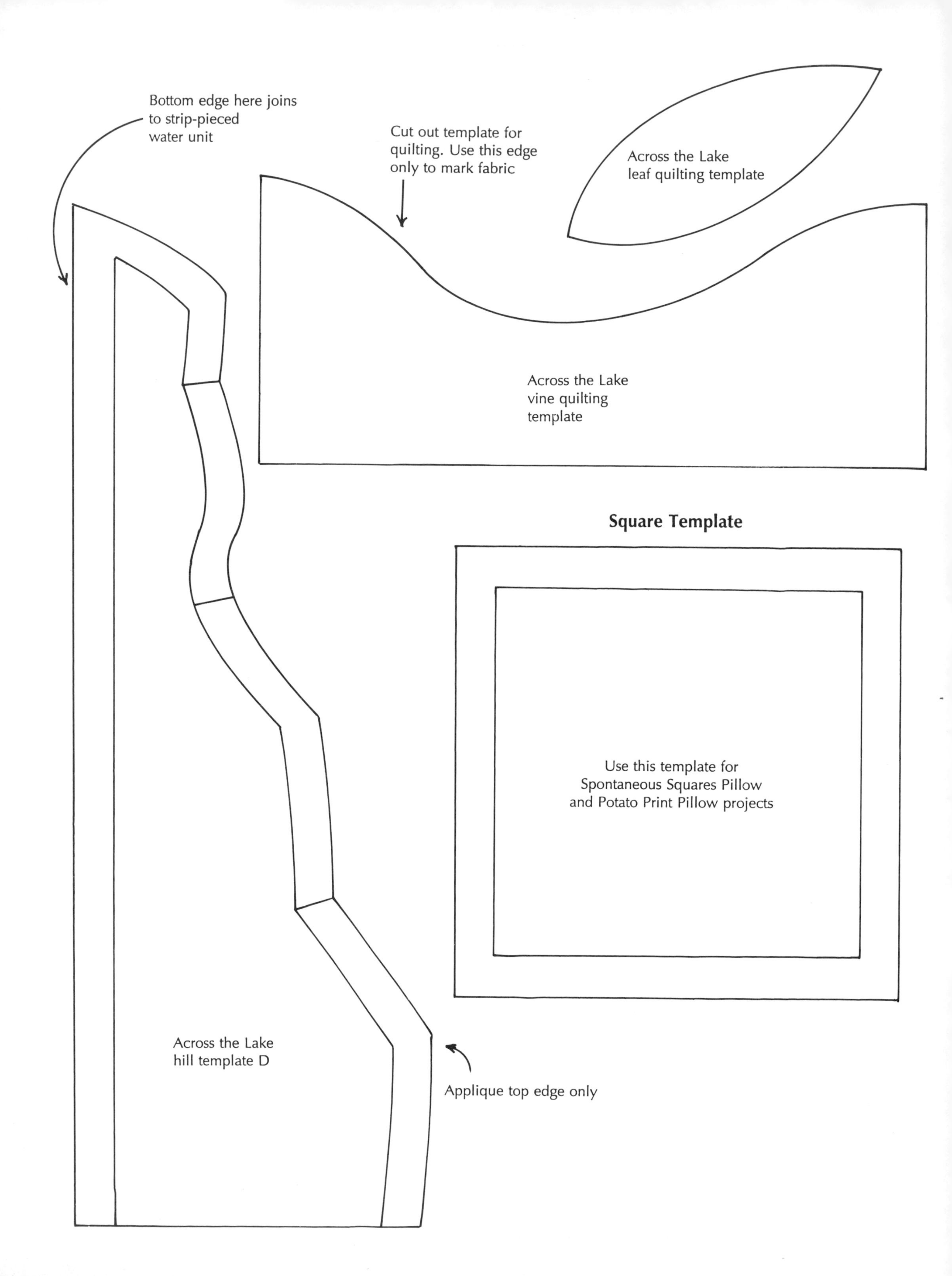

Bottom edge here joins
to strip-pieced
water unit
Cut out template for
quilting. Use this edge
only to mark fabric
Across the Lake
leaf quilting template
Across the Lake
vine quilting
template
Square Template
Use this template for
Spontaneous Squares Pillow
and Potato Print Pillow projects
Across the Lake
hill template D
Applique top edge only

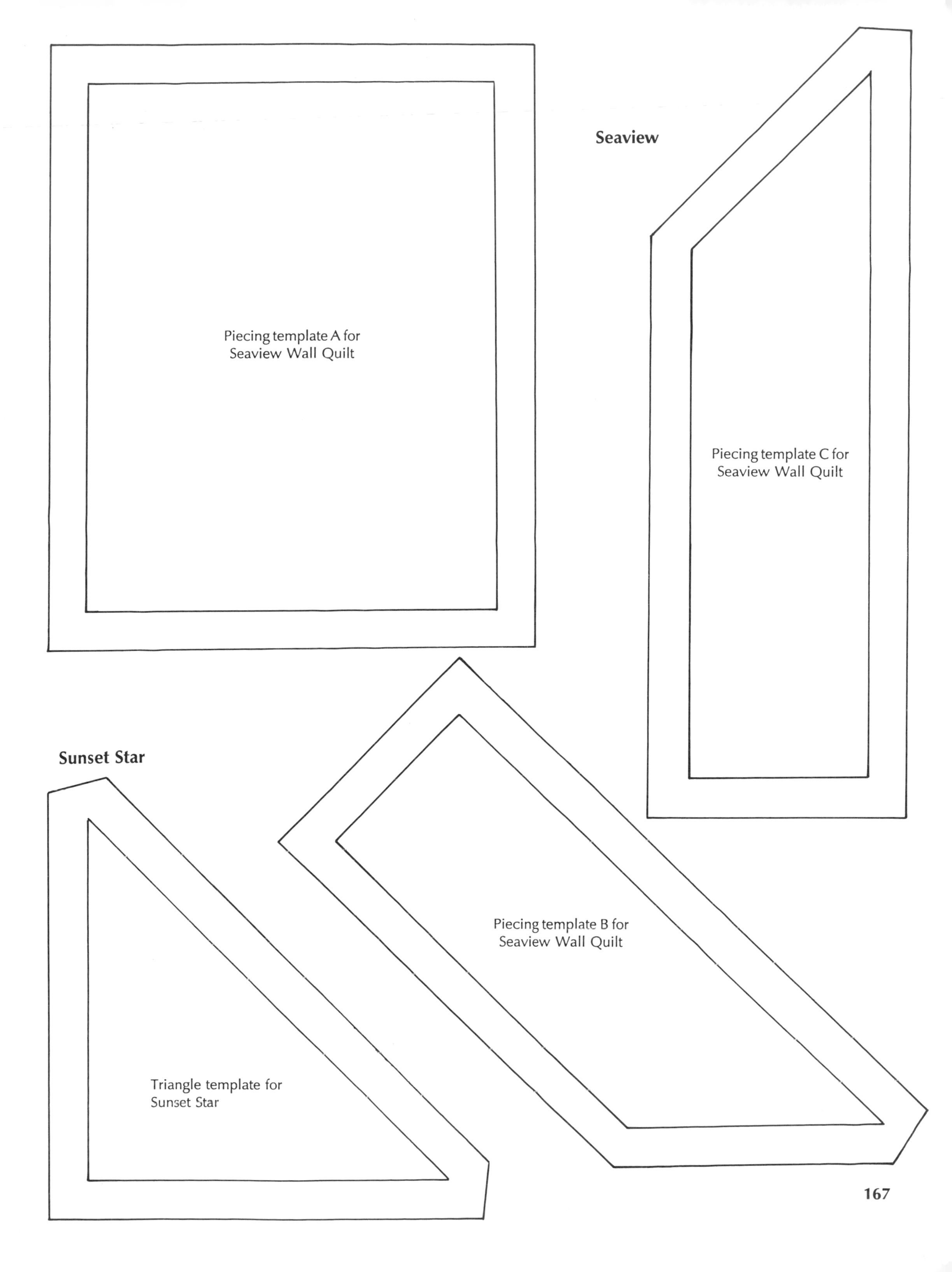
Seaview
Piecing template A for
Seaview Wall Quilt
Piecing template C for
Seaview Wall Quilt
Sunset Star
Piecing template B for
Seaview Wall Quilt
Triangle template for
Sunset Star

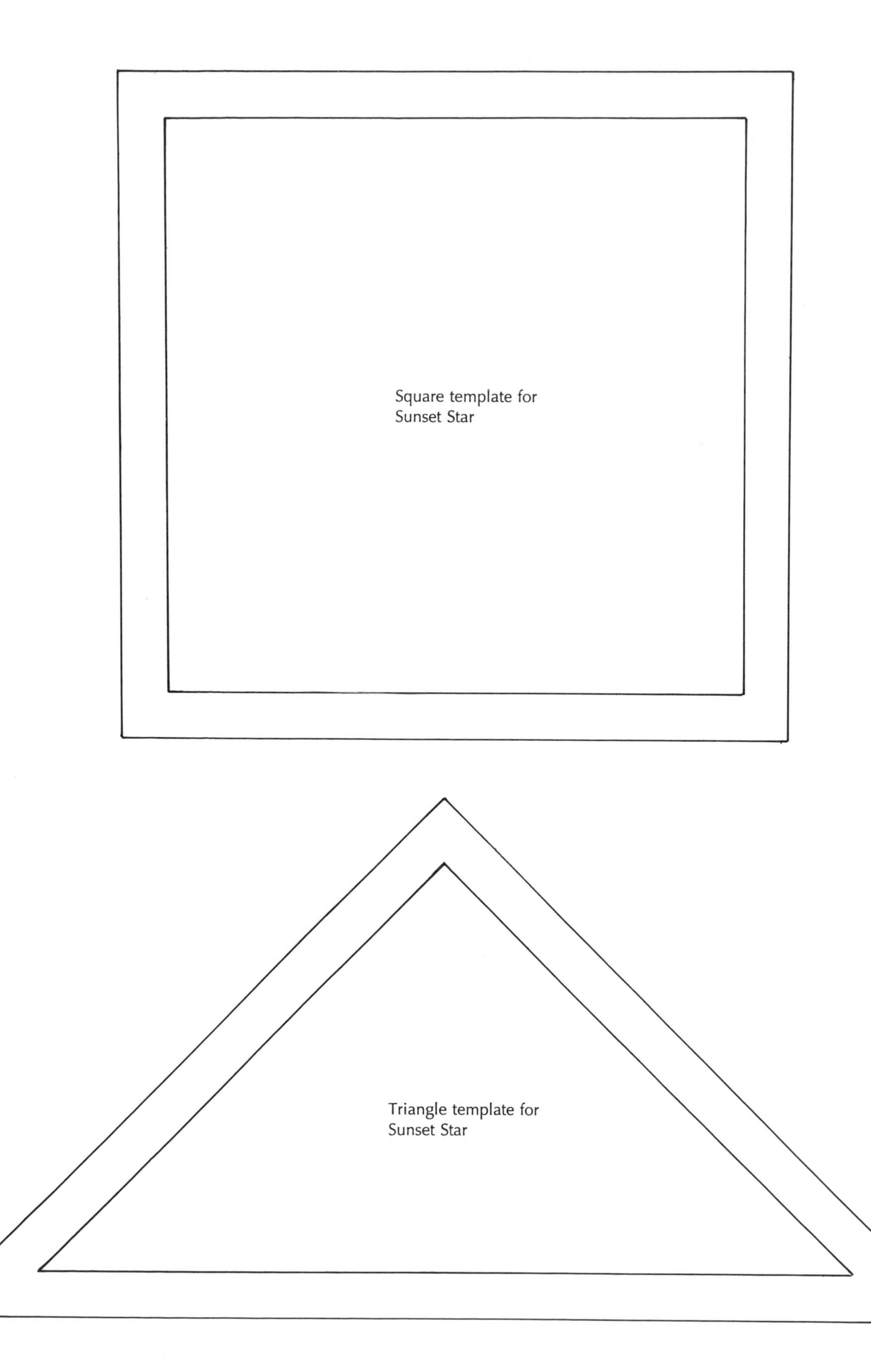
Square template for
Sunset Star
Triangle template for
Sunset Star

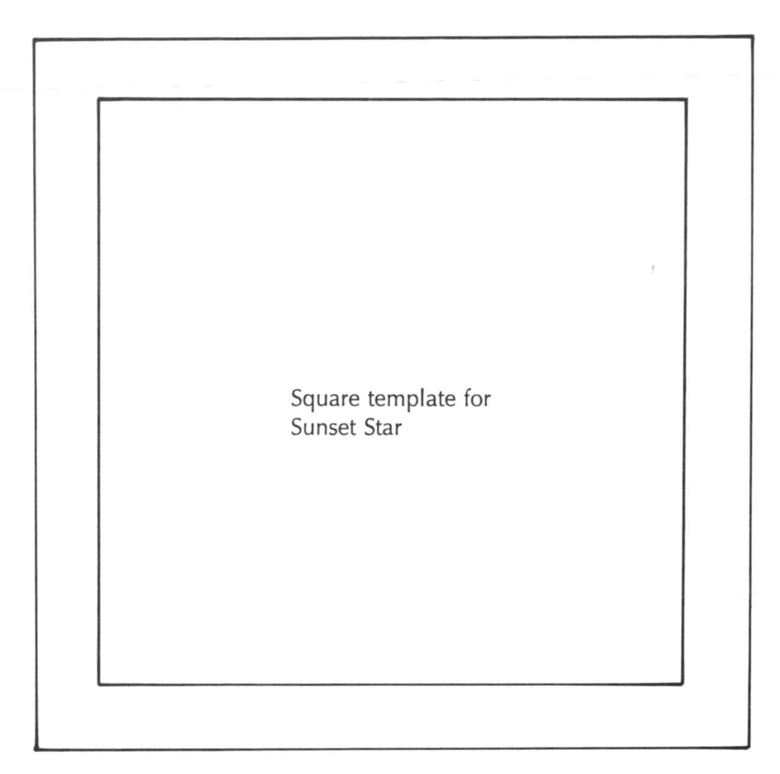

Snow in the Mountains

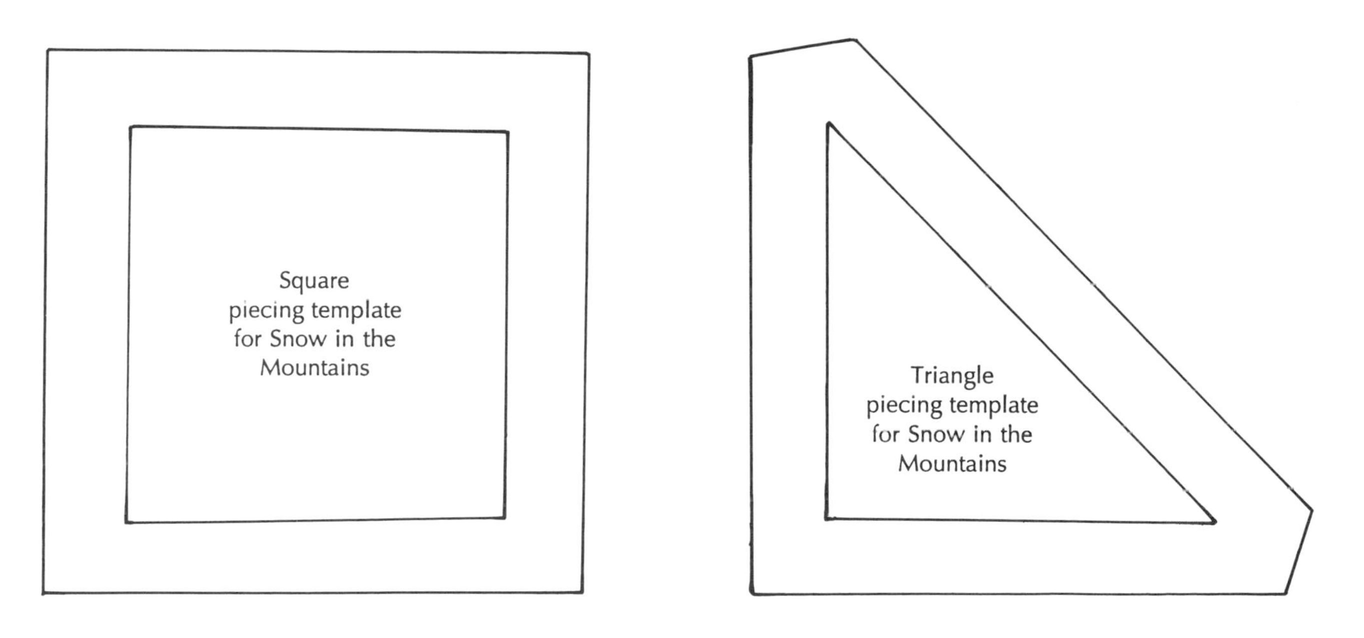

Index

Italic page numbers indicate information in illustrations.